John Algernon Owens

Sword And Pen

Ventures And Adventures Of Willard Glazier

John Algernon Owens

Sword And Pen
Ventures And Adventures Of Willard Glazier

ISBN/EAN: 9783741118012

Manufactured in Europe, USA, Canada, Australia, Japa

Cover: Foto ©Andreas Hilbeck / pixelio.de

Manufactured and distributed by brebook publishing software (www.brebook.com)

John Algernon Owens

Sword And Pen

Sword and Pen;

OR,

Ventures and Adventures

OF

WILLARD GLAZIER,
(The Soldier-Author,)

IN

WAR AND LITERATURE,

COMPRISING

INCIDENTS AND REMINISCENCES OF HIS CHILDHOOD; HIS CHEQUERED LIFE AS A STUDENT AND TEACHER; AND HIS REMARKABLE CAREER AS A SOLDIER AND AUTHOR: EMBRACING ALSO THE STORY OF HIS UNPRECEDENTED JOURNEY FROM OCEAN TO OCEAN ON HORSEBACK.

BY

JOHN ALGERNON OWENS.

Illustrated.

PHILADELPHIA:
P. W. ZIEGLER & COMPANY, PUBLISHERS,
915 ARCH STREET.
1881.

Entered according to Act of Congress, in the year 1880, by
JOHN ALGERNON OWENS,
In the Office of the Librarian of Congress, at Washington, D. C.

TO

ULYSSES SIMPSON GRANT,
WHOSE SWORD,
AND TO
HENRY WADSWORTH LONGFELLOW,
WHOSE PEN,

Have so Nobly Illustrated the Genius and Valor of their Country,

THE AUTHOR,

IN A SPIRIT OF PROFOUND ADMIRATION FOR
THE RENOWNED SOLDIER,

AND OF MEASURELESS GRATITUDE TO
THE IMMORTAL WRITER,

Dedicates This Book.

PREFACE.

No apology will be required from the author for presenting to the public some episodes in the useful career of a self-made man; and while the spirit of patriotism continues to animate the sturdy sons of America, the story of one of them who has exemplified this national trait in a conspicuous measure, will be deemed not unworthy of record. The lessons it teaches, more especially to the young, are those of uncompromising *duty* in every relation of life—self-denial, perseverance and "pluck;" while the successive stages of a course which led ultimately to a brilliant success, may be studied with some advantage by those just entering upon the business of life. As a soldier, Willard Glazier was "without fear and without reproach." As an author, it is sufficient to say, he is appreciated by his *contemporaries*—than which, on a literary man, no higher encomium can be passed. The sale of nearly half a million copies of one of his productions is no slight testimony to its value.

Biography, to be interesting, must be a transcript of an eventful, as well as a remarkable career; and to be instructive, its subject should be exemplary in his aims, and in his mode of attaining them. The hero of this story comes fully up to the standard thus indicated. His career has been a romance. Born of parents of small means, but of excellent character and repute; and bred and nurtured in the midst of some of the wildest and grandest scenery in the rugged county of St. Lawrence, close by the "Thousand Isles," where New York best proves her right to be called the Empire State through the stamp of royalty on her hills and streams—under the shadow of such surroundings as these, my subject attained maturity, with no opportunities for culture except those he made for himself. Yet he became possessed of an education eminently useful, essentially practical and calculated to establish just such habits of self-reliance and decision as afterwards proved chiefly instrumental in his success. Glazier had a fixed ambition to rise. He felt that the task would be difficult of accomplishment—that he must be not only the architect, but the builder of his own fortunes; and as the statue grows beneath the sculptor's hand to perfect contour from the unshapely block of marble, so prosperity came to Captain Glazier only after he had cut and chiseled away at the hard surface of inexorable circumstance, and moulded therefrom the statue of his destiny.

J. A. O.

PHILADELPHIA, *June 14th,* 1880.

CONTENTS.

CHAPTER I.

ORIGIN OF THE GLAZIER FAMILY.

Lineage of Willard Glazier.—A good stock.—Oliver Glazier at the Battle of Bunker Hill.—The home of honest industry.—The Coronet of Pembroke.—The "Homestead Farm."—Mehitable Bolton.—Her New England home.—Her marriage to Ward Glazier.—The wild "North Woods."—The mother of the soldier-author 21

CHAPTER II.

BIRTH AND CHILDHOOD OF WILLARD GLAZIER.

The infant stranger.—A mother's prayers.—"Be just before you are generous."—Careful training.—Willard Glazier's first battle.—A narrow escape.—Facing the foe.—The "happy days of childhood."—"The boy is father to the man" . . 27

CHAPTER III.

EARLY LIFE AND HABITS.

Scotch-Irish Presbyterianism of twenty-five years ago.—The "little deacon."—First days at school.—Choosing a wife.—A youthful gallant.—A close scholar but a wild lad.—A mother's influence.—Ward Glazier a Grahamite.—Young Willard's practical jokes.—Anecdote of Crystal Spring.—"That is something like water" 34

CHAPTER IV.

WILLARD GLAZIER AT SCHOOL.

School-days continued.—Boys will be boys.—Cornelius Carter, the teacher.—Young Willard's rebellion against injustice.—Gum-chewing.—Laughable race through the snow.—The tumble into a snow-bank, and what came of it.—The runaway caught.—Explanation and reconciliation.—The new master, James Nichols.—"Spare the rod and spoil the child."—The age of chivalry not gone.—Magnanimity of a school-boy.—Friendship between Willard and Henry Abbott.—Good-bye to the "little deacon" 42

CHAPTER V.

ECCENTRICITIES OF HENRY GLAZIER.

Henry Glazier.—A singular character.—"Kaw-shaw-gan-ce" and "Quaw-taw-pee-ah."—Tom Lolar and Henry Glazier.—Attractive show-bills.—Billy Muldoon and his trombone.—Behind the scenes.—"Sound your G!"—The mysterious musician.—What happened to Billy.—"May the divil fly away wid ye!" . 50

CHAPTER VI.

VISIONS OF THE FUTURE.

The big uncle and the little nephew.—Exchange of ideas between the eccentric Henry Glazier and young Willard.—Inseparable companions.—Willard's early reading.—Favorite authors.—Hero-worship of the first Napoleon and Charles XII. of Sweden.—The genius of good and of evil.—Allen Wight.—A born teacher.—Reverses of fortune.—The shadow on the home.—Willard's resolve to seek his fortune and what came of it.—The sleep under the trees.—The prodigal's return.—"All's well that ends well" 58

CHAPTER VII.

WILLARD GLAZIER AT HOME.

Out of boyhood.—Days of adolescence.—True family pride.—Schemes for the future.—Willard as a temperance advocate.—Watering his grandfather's whiskey.—The pump behind the hill.—The sleigh-ride by night.—The "shakedown" at Edward's.—Intoxicated by tobacco fumes.—The return ride.—Landed in a snow-bank.—Good-bye horses and sleigh!—Plodding through the snow 68

CHAPTER VIII.

ADVENTURES—EQUINE AND BOVINE.

Ward Glazier moves to the Davis Place.—"Far in the lane a lonely house he found."—Who was Davis?—Description of the place.—A wild spot for a home.—Willard at work.—Adventure with an ox-team.—The road, the bridge and the stream.—"As an ox thirsteth for the water."—Dashed from a precipice!—Willard as a horse-tamer.—"Chestnut Bess," the blooded mare.—The start for home.—"Bess" on the rampage.—A lightning dash.—The stooping arch.—Bruised and unconscious . . 75

CHAPTER IX.

THE YOUNG TRAPPER.

A plan of life.—Determination to procure an education.—A substitute at the plow.—His father acquiesces in his determination to become a trapper.—Life in the wild woods along the Oswegatchie.—The six "dead falls."—First success.—A fallacious calculation.—The goal attained.—Seventy-five dollars in hard cash!—Four terms of academic life.—The youthful rivals.—Lessons in elocution.—A fight with hair-brushes and chairs!—"The walking ghost of a kitchen fire."—Renewed friendship.—Teaching to obtain means for an education 87

CHAPTER X.

THE SOLDIER SCHOOL-MASTER.

From boy to man.—The Lyceum debate.—Willard speaks for the slave. — Entrance to the State Normal School. — Reverses. —Fighting the world again.—Assistance from fair hands. —Willard meets Allen Barringer.—John Brown, and what Willard thought of him.—Principles above bribe.—Examination.—A sleepless night.—Haunted by the "ghost of possible defeat." — "Here is your certificate." — The school at Schodack Centre. — At the "Normal" again. — The Edwards School.—Thirty pupils at two dollars each.—The "soldier school-master."—Teachers at East Schodack.—The runaway ride.—Good-by, mittens, robes and whip!—Close of school at East Schodack 102

CHAPTER XI.

INTRODUCTION TO MILITARY LIFE.

The mutterings of war.—Enlistment.—At Camp Howe.—First experience as a soldier.—"One step to the front!"—Beyond Washington.—On guard.— Promotion.—Recruiting service.— The deserted home on Arlington Heights.—"How shall I behave in the coming battle?"—The brave Bayard.—On the march. — The stratagem at Falmouth Heights.—A brilliant charge.—After the battle 118

CHAPTER XII.

FIRST BATTLE OF BRANDY STATION.

The sentinel's lonely round.—General Pope in command of the army.—Is gunboat service effective?—First cavalry battle of Brandy Station.—Under a rain of bullets.—Flipper's orchard.— "Bring on the brigade, boys!"—Capture of Confederate prisoners.—Story of a revolver.—Cedar Mountain.—Burial of the dead rebel.—Retreat from the Rapidan.—The riderless horse.—Death of Captain Walters 128

CHAPTER XIII.

MANASSAS AND FREDERICKSBURG.

Manassas.—The flying troops.—The unknown hero.—Desperate at-

tempt to stop the retreat.—Recruiting the decimated ranks.—
Fredericksburg.—Bravery of Meagher's brigade.—The impregnable heights.—The cost of battles.—Death of Bayard.—Outline of his life 135

CHAPTER XIV.

UNWRITTEN HISTORY.

"What boots a weapon in a withered hand?"—A thunderbolt wasted.—War upon hen-roosts.—A bit of unpublished history.—A fierce fight with Hampton's cavalry.—In one red burial blent.—From camp to home.—Troubles never come singly.—The combat.— The capture.—A superfluity of Confederate politeness. —Lights and shadows 144

CHAPTER XV.

THE CAPTURE.

A situation to try the stoutest hearts.—Hail Columbia!—Every man a hero.—Kilpatrick's ingenuity.—A pen-picture from "Soldiers of the Saddle."—Glazier thanked by his general.—Cessation of hostilities.—A black day.—Fitzhugh Lee proposes to crush Kilpatrick.—Kil's audacity.—Capture of Lieutenant Glazier.—Petty tyranny.—"Here, Yank, hand me that thar hat, and overcoat, and boots" 155

CHAPTER XVI.

LIBBY PRISON.

"All ye who enter here abandon hope."—Auld lang syne.—Major Turner.—Hope deferred maketh the heart sick.—Stoicism.—Glazier enters the prison-hospital—A charnel-house.—Rebel surgeons.—Prison correspondence.—Specimen of a regulation letter.—The tailor's joke.—A Roland for an Oliver.—News of death.—Schemes for escape.—The freemasonry of misfortune.—Plot and counter-plot.—The pursuit of pleasure under difficulties 166

CHAPTER XVII.

PRISON LIFE.

Mournful news.—How a brave man dies.—New Year's day.—Jolly under unfavorable circumstances.—Major Turner pays his respects.—Punishment for singing "villainous Yankee songs."—Confederate General John Morgan.—Plans for escape.—Digging their way to freedom.—"Post No. 1, All's well."—Yankee ingenuity.—The tunnel ready.—Muscle the trump card.—No respect to rank.—*Sauve qui peut!*—A strategic movement.—"Guards! guards!"—Absentees from muster.— Disappointed hopes. — Savage treatment of prisoners. — Was the prison mined? 179

CHAPTER XVIII.

DANVILLE.—MACON.—SAVANNAH.

Belle Boyd, the Confederate spy.—National characteristics.—Colonel Mosby.—Richmond to Danville.—Sleeping spoon-fashion.—Glazier's "corrective point" suffers.—Saltatory entrance to a railroad car.—Colonel Joselyn.—Sympathy of North Carolinians.—Ingenious efforts to escape.—Augusta.—Macon.—Turner again!—"Carelessness" with firearms.—Tunneling.—Religious revival.—Order from Confederate War Department.—Murder!—Fourth of July.—Macon to Savannah.—Camp Davidson.—More tunneling 194

CHAPTER XIX.

UNDER FIRE AT CHARLESTON.

Under siege.—Charleston Jail.—The Stars and Stripes.—Federal compliments.—Under the guns.—Roper Hospital.—Yellow Jack.—Sisters of Charity.—Rebel Christianity.—A Byronic stanza.—Charleston to Columbia.—"Camp Sorghum."—Nemesis.—Another dash for liberty.—Murder of Lieutenants Young and Parker.—Studying topography.—A vaticination.—Back to reality . 206

CHAPTER XX.

THE ESCAPE FROM COLUMBIA.

Mysterious voices.—"I reckon dey's Yankees."—"Who comes there?"—The Lady of the Manor.—A weird spectacle.—The struggle through the swamp.—A reflection on Southern swamps in general.—Tired nature's sweet restorer . . . 221

CHAPTER XXI.

LOYALTY OF THE NEGROES.

Startled by hounds.—An unpleasant predicament.—A Christian gentlewoman.—Appeal to Mrs. Colonel Taylor.—"She did all she could."—A meal fit for the gods.—Aunt Katy.—"Lor' bress ye, marsters!"—Uncle Zeb's prayer.—Hoe-cake and pinders.—Woodcraft *versus* astronomy.—Canine foes.—Characteristics of the slave.—Meeting escaped prisoners.—Danger.—Retreat and concealment 223

CHAPTER XXII.

PROGRESS OF THE FUGITIVES.

Parting company.—Thirst and no water.—Hoping for the end.—The boy and the chicken.—Conversation of ladies overheard.—The fugitives pursued.—The sleeping village.—Captain Bryant.—The alba sus.—Justifiable murder, and a delicious meal.—Darkies and their prayers.—Man proposes; God disposes.—An adventure. —A *ruse de guerre*.—Across the Savannah . . . 238

CHAPTER XXIII.

THE PERILS OF AN ESCAPE.

Alligators.—A detachment of Southern chivalry.—A scare.—Repairs neatly executed.—Misery and despair.—Virtue its own reward.—Hunger and desperation.—Audacity.—A Confederate officer.—"A good Union man."—"Two sights and a jambye."—A narrow escape 249

CHAPTER XXIV.

TRIED AS A SPY.

Fugitive slaves.—A rebel planter.—The big Ebenezer.—A sound of oars.—A *ruse de guerre*.—Burial of a dead soldier.—A free ride.— Groping in the dark.—"Who goes there!"—Recaptured.—*Nil desperandum*.—James Brooks.—Contraband of war.—Confederate murders.—In the saddle again.—A dash for freedom.—Again captured.—Tried as a spy 261

CHAPTER XXV.

FINAL ESCAPE FROM CAPTIVITY.

In jail.—White trash.—Yankees.—Off to Waynesboro.—No rations. —Calling the roll.—Sylvania.—Plan for escape.—Lieutenant John W. Wright.—A desperate project.—Escaped!—Giving chase.— The pursuers baffled.—Old Richard.—"Pooty hard case, massa." —Rebel deserters.—The sound of cannon.—Personating a rebel officer.—Mrs. Keyton.—Renewed hope.—A Confederate outpost. —Bloodhounds.—Uncle Philip.—March Dasher.—Suspicion disarmed.—"Now I'ze ready, gemmen."—Stars and stripes.—Glorious freedom.—Home 274

CHAPTER XXVI.

GLAZIER RE-ENTERS THE SERVICE.

Glazier's determination to re-enter the army.—Letter to Colonel Harhaus.—Testimonial from Colonel Clarence Buel.—Letter from Hon. Martin I. Townsend to governor of New York.—Letter from General Davies.—Letter from General Kilpatrick.—Application for new commission successful.—Home.—The mother fails to recognize her son.—Supposed to be dead.—Recognized by his sister Marjorie.—Filial and fraternal love.—Reports himself to his commanding officer for duty.—Close of the war and of Glazier's military career.—Seeks a new object in life.—An idea occurs to him.—Becomes an author, and finds a publisher 295

CHAPTER XXVII.

CAREER AS AN AUTHOR.

Glazier in search of a publisher for "Capture, Prison-Pen and Escape."—Spends his last dollar.—Lieutenant Richardson a friend in need.—Joel Munsell, of Albany, consents to publish.—The author solicits subscriptions for his work before publication.—Succeeds.—Captain Hampton.—R. H. Ferguson.—Captain F. C. Lord.—Publication and sale of first edition.—Great success.—Pays his publisher in full.—Still greater successes.—Finally attains an enormous sale.—Style of the work.—Extracts.—Opinions of the press 304

CHAPTER XXVIII.

"THREE YEARS IN THE FEDERAL CAVALRY."

Another work by Captain Glazier.—"Three Years in the Federal Cavalry."—Daring deeds of the Light Dragoons.—Extracts from the work.—Night attack on Falmouth Heights.—Kilpatrick's stratagem.—Flight of the enemy.—Capture of Falmouth.—Burial of Lieutenant Decker.—Incidents at "Brandy Station."—"Harris Light" and "Tenth New York."—"Men of Maine, you must save the day!"—Position won.—Some press reviews of the work 313

CHAPTER XXIX.

"BATTLES FOR THE UNION."

"Battles for the Union."—Extracts.—Bull Run.—Brandy Station.—Manassas.—Gettysburg.—Pittsburg Landing.—Surrender of General Lee.—Opinions of the press.—Philadelphia "North American."—Pittsburg "Commercial."—Chicago "Inter-Ocean."—Scranton "Republican."—Wilkes-Barre "Record of the Times."—Reading "Eagle."—Albany "Evening Journal" 322

CHAPTER XXX.

"HEROES OF THREE WARS."

Literary zeal.—"Heroes of Three Wars."—Extract from preface.—Sale of the work.—Extracts: Washington.—Winfield Scott.—Zachary Taylor.—Grant.—Sheridan.—Kilpatrick.—Press reviews, a few out of many: Boston "Transcript."—Chicago "Inter-Ocean."—Baltimore "Sun."—Philadelphia "Times."—Cincinnati "Enquirer."—Worcester "Spy."—Pittsburg "Gazette" 341

CHAPTER XXXI.

OCEAN TO OCEAN ON HORSEBACK.

From Boston to San Francisco.—An unparalleled ride.—Object of

xvi CONTENTS.

the journey.—Novel lecture tour.—Captain Frank M. Clark.—
"Echoes from the Revolution."—Lecture at Tremont Temple.—
Captain Theodore L. Kelly.—A success.—Proceeds of lecture.—
Edward F. Rollins.—Extracts from first lecture.—Press notices 364

CHAPTER XXXII.

FROM OCEAN TO OCEAN.

In the saddle.—Bunker Hill.—Arrives in Albany.—Reminiscences.
—The Soldiers' Home.—Contributions for erecting Soldiers'
Home.—Reception at Rochester.—Buffalo.—Dunkirk.—Swanville.—Cleveland.—Massacre of General Custer.—Monroe.—
Lectures for Custer Monument.—Father of General Custer.—
Detroit.—Kalamazoo.—An adventure.—Gives "Paul Revere"
a rest.—Decatur.—Niles.—Michigan City.—Chicago . 376

CHAPTER XXXIII.

OCEAN TO OCEAN ON HORSEBACK.

Returns to Michigan City.—Joliet.—Thomas Babcock.—Herbert
Glazier.—Ottawa.—La Salle.—Colonel Stevens.—Press Notice.—
Taken for a highwayman.—Milan.—Davenport.—Press Notice.
—Iowa City.—Des Moines.—Press Notice.—Attacked by prairie
wolves.—Council Bluffs.—Omaha 401

CHAPTER XXXIV.

OCEAN TO OCEAN ON HORSEBACK.

Captain Glazier as a horseman.—Cheyenne.—Two herders.—Captured by Indians.—Torture and death of a herder.—Escape.—
Ogden.—Letter to Major Hessler.—Kelton.—Terrace.—Wells.—
Halleck.—Elko.—Palisade.—Argenta.—Battle Mountain.—Golconda.—Humboldt.—"The majesty of the law."—Lovelock's.—
White Plains.—Desert.—Wadsworth.—Truckee.—Summit.—Sacramento.—Brighton.—Stockton.—SAN FRANCISCO . . 410

CHAPTER XXXV.

RETURN FROM CALIFORNIA.

Returns to the East by the "Iron Horse."—Boston *Transcript* on
the journey on horseback.—Resumes literary work.—"Peculiarities of American Cities."—Preface to book.—A domestic incident.
—A worthy son.—Claims of parents.—Purchases the Old Homestead, and presents it to his father and mother.—Letter to his
parents.—The end 431

ILLUSTRATIONS.

	PAGE
PORTRAIT OF THE SOLDIER-AUTHOR......*Frontispiece*	
BIRTHPLACE OF WILLARD GLAZIER	26
THE FIRST BATTLE	32
RACE WITH THE SCHOOLMASTER	44
TRAGIC EXPERIENCE WITH AN OX-TEAM	80
THE YOUNG TRAPPER OF THE OSWEGATCHIE	90
A CAVALRY COLUMN ON THE MARCH	118
NIGHT ATTACK ON FALMOUTH HEIGHTS	126
ILLICIT TRADING ON THE RAPPAHANNOCK	130
BURIAL OF CAPTAIN WALTERS AT MID-NIGHT	134
SERGEANT GLAZIER AT ALDIE	146
LIEUTENANT GLAZIER AT BRANDY STATION	156
CAVALRY FIGHT AT NEW BALTIMORE—LIEUTENANT GLAZIER TAKEN PRISONER	160
LIBBY PRISON	166
THE HOLE IN THE FLOOR	192
TUNNELING—THE NARROW PATH TO FREEDOM	198
CHARLESTON JAIL—CHARLESTON, SOUTH CAROLINA	206
THE ESCAPE FROM COLUMBIA—CROSSING THE DEAD-LINE	216
THE ESCAPE—FED BY NEGROES IN A SWAMP	220
THE PURSUIT OF KNOWLEDGE UNDER DIFFICULTIES	224
UNCLE ZEB'S PRAYER	232
THE ESCAPE—CROSSING THE SAVANNAH AT MIDNIGHT	246
A MUTUAL SURPRISE	258
RECAPTURED BY A CONFEDERATE OUTPOST	266
THE ESCAPE AND PURSUIT	270
THE ESCAPE FROM SYLVANIA, GEORGIA	276
INTERVIEW WITH JOEL MUNSELL	306
CAVALRY FORAGING-PARTY RETURNING TO CAMP	312
A CAVALRY BIVOUAC	320
BATTLE OF GETTYSBURG	332
CAPTAIN GLAZIER AT TREMONT TEMPLE—BOSTON	364
BOSTON TO BRIGHTON—FIRST DAY OF THE JOURNEY	376
A NIGHT AMONG WOLVES	400
CAPTURED BY INDIANS, NEAR SKULL ROCKS, WYOMING	412
PURSUED BY THE ARRAPAHOES	418
THE LAST SHOT	422
RIDING INTO THE PACIFIC, NEAR CLIFF HOUSE—SAN FRANCISCO	428

SWORD AND PEN.

CHAPTER I.

ORIGIN OF THE GLAZIER FAMILY.

Lineage of Willard Glazier.—A good stock.—Oliver Glazier at the Battle of Bunker Hill.—The home of honest industry.—The Coronet of Pembroke.—The "Homestead Farm."—Mehitable Bolton.—Her New England home.—Her marriage to Ward Glazier.—The wild "North Woods."—The mother of the soldier-author.

WILLARD GLAZIER comes of the mixed blood of Saxon and of Celt. We first hear of his ancestors upon this side of the Atlantic at that period of our nation's history which intervened between the speck of war at Lexington and the cloud of war at Bunker Hill.

Massachusetts and the town of Boston had become marked objects of the displeasure of the British Parliament. Later, in 1775, Ethan Allen had startled Captain Delaplace by presenting his lank figure at the captain's bedside and demanding the surrender of Ticonderoga in the name of the "Great Jehovah and the Continental Congress." In the language of Daniel Webster, "A spirit pervaded all ranks, not transient, not boisterous, but deep, solemn, determined."

War on their own soil and at their own doors was indeed a strange work to the yeomanry of New England; but their consciences were convinced of its necessity, and when their country called them to her defense they did not withhold themselves from the perilous responsibility.

The statement of Quincy seemed to pervade all hearts. Said that distinguished son of genius and patriotism, "Blandishments will not fascinate us, nor will threats of a halter intimidate; for, under God, we are determined that wheresoever, whensoever, and howsoever we shall be called to make our exit, we will die free men."

At such a time, and among such men, we find enrolled in the ranks of the patriot army Oliver Glazier, the great-grandfather of the subject of the present work.

Oliver's father was John Glazier, a Massachusetts Lancastrian, born in 1739. John Glazier was the son of William Glazier, born about the year 1700, his ancestry being respectively of English and of Scotch extraction. Oliver himself, however, was born in the town of Lancaster, in the province or colony of Massachusetts, May twenty-third, 1763.

Hence the blood of Norman, of Saxon and of Celt, that had forgotten the animosities of race and mingled quietly in the veins of his ancestors, had become purely American in Oliver, and though but little over fourteen years of age, we find him doing yeoman service upon the ramparts of Bunker Hill.

That he performed well his part in the struggle for liberty, is evident from the fact that he appears upon the rolls as a pensioner, from the close of that memorable contest until the time of his death.

Mr. Frank Renehan, in a sketch contributed by him

to an elaborate work which was published by the New York and Hartford Publishing Company in 1871, comments as follows upon the coincidence of Oliver Glazier in 1775 and Willard Glazier in 1861—both being at the time of entering service comparatively boys in age, enlisting for the defense of their country: "The former, though then but fourteen years of age, participated with the patriots in the battle of Bunker Hill, and to the last contributed his young enthusiasm and willing services to the cause he had espoused; thus giving early testimony of his devotion to the land of his adoption and of fealty to the principles of popular government involved in the struggle for American independence. So remarkable an instance of ancestral fidelity to the interests of civil liberty could not but exercise a marked influence upon those of the same blood to whom the tradition was handed down, and here we find our subject, a scion of the third generation, assisting in 1861 on the battlefields of the South, in maintenance of the liberty his progenitor had contributed to achieve in 1775 on the battlefields of the North! This is not mentioned as a singular fact—history is replete with just such coincidences, but merely for the purpose of suggesting the moral that in matters of patriotism the son is only consistent when he imitates the example and emulates the virtues of his sires."

In this eloquent passage occurs an error of fact. Oliver Glazier while in the patriot army was *not* fighting for the "land of his adoption." As we have seen, he was native here and "to the manor born." Indeed, in the light of historic proof and with the example of men descended from Washington and Light Horse Harry Lee before us, we are rather inclined to admire the paragraph as a fine specimen of rhetorical composition than to admit its accuracy as a deduction in philosophy.

Subsequent to his term of military service—an experience through which he had safely passed—Oliver Glazier became a resident of West Boylston, Massachusetts, where he married a Miss Hastings.

The name of Glazier, Lower tells us, is purely English, and is derived from the title given to the trade. However that may be, those who have borne it have always expressed a pride in having sprung from the great mass—the people—and have held with the philosopher of Sunnyside, that whether " hereditary rank be an illusion or not, hereditary virtue gives a patent of nobility beyond all the blazonry of the herald's college." The name of Hastings takes its rise from a nobler source; for Mrs. Oliver Glazier brought into the family as blue blood as any in all England. The great family which bears that name in Great Britain can show quarterings of an earlier date than the battle which gave a kingdom to William of Normandy. Macaulay says that one branch of their line, in the fourteenth century, " wore the coronet of Pembroke; that from another sprang the renowned Lord Chamberlain, the faithful adherent of the White Rose, whose fate has furnished so striking a theme both to the poet and historian," and while it is probable that this wife of an American patriot was many degrees removed from the powerful leaders whose name she bore, the same blood undoubtedly flowed in her veins that coursed through theirs.

Oliver, during the many years of a happy married life which terminated in his death at the ripe age of ninety-three, became the father of eight children. Jabez, his son, left Boylston at an early age, and after considerable "prospecting" finally married a Miss Sarah Tucker and settled in the township of Fowler, St. Lawrence County, New York. Out of their union sprang George, Ward, and Henry Glazier, the second of whom, during a visit he made to his "down East" relations, married a young lady by the name of Mehitable Bolton, of West Boylston, Mass.

This young lady was a true representative of the New England woman, who believes that work is the handmaid of religion. She entered a cotton factory at Worcester when only seventeen years of age, and worked perseveringly through long years of labor, often walking from her home in West Boylston to the factory at Worcester, a distance of seven miles. At the time of her marriage—which occurred when she was twenty-five—she had accumulated the snug little sum of five hundred dollars, besides possessing a handsome wardrobe, all of which was the fruit of her own untiring industry.

If it be true that the mothers of men of mark are always women of strong and noble characters, then we are not surprised to find in the mother of Willard Glazier those sterling qualities which made her young life successful.

The early married life of Ward Glazier was passed upon the farm first cleared and cultivated by his father, and which has since become known to the neighborhood as the "Old Glazier Homestead." This farm is situated in the township of Fowler, midway between the small villages of Little York and Fullersville.

The township is a tract of rugged land, containing only the little village of Hailesborough, besides those already named. Along its borders rushes and tumbles a turbulent stream which still retains its original Indian appellation—the Oswegatchie; a name no doubt conveying to the ear of its aboriginal sponsors some poetical conceit, just as another stream in far off Virginia is named the Shenandoah, or "Daughter of the Stars."

Those who are at all familiar with the scenery that prevails in what in other sections of the country are called the great North Woods, and in their own neighborhood the great South Woods, can readily imagine what were the geological and scenic peculiarities of Fowler township. Bare, sterile, famished-looking, as far as horticultural and herbaceous crops are concerned, yet rich in pasture and abounding in herds—with vast rocks crested and plumed with rich growths of black balsam, maple, and spruce timber, and with huge boulders scattered carelessly over its surface and margining its streams, St. Lawrence County presents to-day features of savage grandeur as wild and imposing as it did ere the foot of a trapper had profaned its primeval forests.

Yet its farms and its dwellings are numerous, its villages and towns possess all the accompaniments of modern civilization, the spires of its churches indicate that the gentle influences of religion are not forgotten, and there, as elsewhere, the indomitable will of man has won from the wilderness a living and a home.

BIRTH-PLACE OF WILLARD GLAZIER.

CHAPTER II.

BIRTH AND CHILDHOOD OF WILLARD GLAZIER.

The infant stranger.—A mother's prayers.—"Be just before you are generous."—Careful training.—Willard Glazier's first battle.—A narrow escape.—Facing the foe.—The "happy days of childhood."—" The boy is father to the man."

THE Glazier Homestead, as we have said, is upon the main road leading from Little York to Fullersville. It is a substantial and comfortable farmhouse, with no pretension to architectural beauty, but, nevertheless, is a sightly object in a pleasant landscape. Standing back two hundred feet from the road, in a grove of gigantic elms, with a limpid brook of spring water a short distance to the right, and rich fields of herd grass stretching off rearwards towards the waters of the Oswegatchie, which hurry along on their journey of forty miles to the St. Lawrence River, the old house is sure to attract the attention of the traveller, and to be long remembered as a picture of solid and substantial comfort.

In this old house, upon the morning of August twenty-second, 1841, to Ward Glazier and Mehitable, his wife, a son was born who was subsequently named Willard. The father and mother were by no means sentimental people—they were certainly not given to seeing the poetical side of life; they were plain, earnest people, rough hewn out of the coarse fibre of Puritanism, but the advent of this little child brought a joy to their hearts that had its softening influence upon the home in which he was to be reared.

The thoroughness of Ward Glazier's nature, that conscientiousness in excess which made him radical in all things, was of the *heart* as well as of the head, and though not a demonstrative man, the intensity of his paternal love cropped out in many ways. As to his wife, hers was truly "mother's love." And what notes are there attuned to sacred music, in all the broad vocabulary of the English tongue, which gives any idea of the sentiment that links a woman to her babe, except the three simple syllables, "mother's love!" Brooding over the tiny stranger, ready to laugh or cry; exultant with hope and pride, despondent with fear, quivering with anguish if the "wind of heaven doth visit its cheek too roughly," and singing hosannas of joy when it lisps the simpler syllables that she so patiently has taught, covering it with the broad wing of her measureless affection, and lavishing upon it such "sighs as perfect joy perplexed for utterance, steals from her sister sorrow," there is nothing except God's own illimitable affection for his creatures, that can rival in depth and strength and comprehensiveness, a mother's love.

The heart of Ward Glazier's wife, at this time, blossomed in absolutely rank luxuriance with this feeling, and ran riot in the joy of its possession; but she determined within herself that it should be no blind or foolish worship. It grew, therefore, into a sober, careful, provident affection.

Quiet and unobtrusive in manner, her face always wore a look of gravity befitting one who felt that God had entrusted to her charge a fresh human soul to mould for good or evil. She fully realized the fact that her son would grow up with honor or sink down into ignominy just as she should guide or spoil him in his youth. She quite comprehended the stubborn truth, that while the father to some extent may shape the outward career of his son, the mother is responsible for the coloring of his inner life: and that

> "All we learn of good is learned in youth,
> When passion's heat is pure, when love is truth."

Though of Puritan stock, though reared in the austere faith of John Knox, there was nothing hard or harsh in this mother's character, and still less was there anything of the materialist about her. She would have utterly scouted the doctrine of Cabanis and his school, which held that the physical was the whole structure of man; that all instincts, passions, thoughts, emanated from the body; that sensibility is an effect of the nervous system, that passion is an emanation of the viscera, that intellect is nothing more than a cerebral secretion, and "self-consciousness but a general faculty of living matter." She had drunk inspiration of a different kind from her infancy. In her New England home the very atmosphere was charged with religious influences. She was taught, or rather she had learned without a teacher, not only to see God in the flowers and in the stars, but to recognize his immediate agency in all things terrestrial.

Night after night, listening to the tremulous tones of her father as he read a lesson from the sacred page, not only to those of his own blood, but to his "manservant, his maid-servant, and the stranger within his gates," she had felt the presence of a tangible God, and when, at last, she followed the fortunes of the chosen one of her heart far into the great North Woods, nature spoke to her from the forest and the cataract, deepening each early impression and intensifying each early belief, until she realized as a living fact that the "Lord was ever in his holy temple" and that his temple was the universe.

To a woman like this every act of life became a matter of conscience, and the training of her child of course became such to Mrs. Glazier. She had watched the pitfalls which the "world, the flesh and the devil"—that trinity of evil—provide for the feet of the unwary, and she determined that young Willard's steps, if she could prevent it, should never stray that way.

Her husband took life and its duties much more easily. He was less rigid in his sense of parental responsibility. While a man of great rectitude of purpose, he was good-natured to a fault—somewhat improvident, careless of money, ever ready to extend aid to the needy, and especially disinclined to the exercise of harshness in his home, even when the stern element of authority was needed. In short, he was one of those big-hearted men who are so brimful of the "milk of human kindness" that the greatest pain they ever feel is the pain they see others suffer. His plan therefore was, spare the rod even if you *do* spoil the child.

But—perhaps fortunately for young Willard—Mrs. Glazier held different views. From his very infancy she endeavored to instil into his nature habits of truthfulness, industry and thrift. "Never waste and never lie" was her pet injunction. Her aim was not to make her son a generous, but a *just* man. "One hour of justice is worth an eternity of prayer," says the Arabian proverb, but Mrs. Glazier, while she exalted justice as the greatest of the virtues, also believed that in order to make man's heart its temple, prayer was an absolutely necessary pre-requisite. She likewise endeavored from the first to habituate the boy's mind to reflect upon the value of money and the uses of economy. She would have "coined her blood for drachms" if that would have benefited her husband or her son. Her savings were not spent upon herself, but in the hard school of a bitter experience she had learned that money means much more than dollars and cents—that its possession involves the ability to live a life of honor, untempted by the sordid solicitations that clamor round the poor man's door and wring the poor man's heart.

The result was that as soon as he began to comprehend her words, young Willard had impressed upon his memory maxims eulogizing all who practise habits of sobriety, industry and frugality, and denunciatory of all who fail to do so.

His mother never wearied of teaching him such sayings of Dr. Franklin as these: "Time is money," "Credit is money," "Money begets money," "The good paymaster is lord of another man's purse," and "The sound of a man's hammer heard by his creditor at six o'clock in the morning makes him easy six months longer, while the sound of his voice heard in a tavern, induces him to send for his money the next day;" "Trifling items aggregate into large totals," while the text that ruled the house was that of the Scripture, "If any would not work neither should he eat."

The effect of the constant teaching of such lessons was not however perceptible in the lad's habits in very early life. He was no model little boy, no monster of perfection—he was like the boys that we see around us every day—not one of the marvels we read about. But the seed was sown in his soul which was destined to quicken into fruit in after life.

At the early age of four years his mother began to teach him to read and write, and under her loving tuition he acquired a knowledge of these two branches of culture quite rapidly.

Just about this time an incident occurred which came near finishing young Willard's career in a manner as sudden as it would have been singular.

The "Homestead Farm" was at that time pretty well stocked for a place only containing one hundred and forty acres, and among the cattle was a sturdy Alderney bull whose reputation for peace and quietness was unusually good.

On a certain morning, however, early in the spring of the year 1845, young Master Willard happened to overhear a conversation between two of the farm hands, in the course of which one of them declared that "old Blackface was tarin' round mighty lively." This statement interested the lad to such an extent that he concluded to go and see how this "tarin' round" was done.

Accordingly, taking advantage of a moment when his mother's attention was occupied, he started for the barnyard, into which Mr. Bull had been turned only a few moments before. Now as young Willard was somewhat smaller than the visitors our bovine friend was in the habit of receiving, such an unwarrantable

THE FIRST BATTLE.
"When I'm a big man I'll toss you in the air."

intrusion was not to be tolerated for a moment. Accordingly, no sooner had Willard set his little feet within the enclosure of the barn-yard than the bull gave a roar of rage, and catching the boy on the tips of his horns, which fortunately were buttoned, sent him twenty feet up in the air, preparing to trample him out of existence when he should come down. Luckily some of the men were attracted to the scene, who secured his bullship and rescued the child. Willard was not seriously hurt, and the instant he regained his feet, he turned round, shook his tiny fist at the now retreating animal and shouted out in a shrill treble, "When I get to be a big man I'll toss you in the air!"

Having thus taken the bull by the horns in a literal as well as figurative sense, the lad began gradually to develop into that terrible embodiment of unrest—a boy. He exhibited no very marked peculiarities up to this time to distinguish him from other youths; but just grew into the conglomerate mass of good, bad and indifferent qualities which go to make up the ordinary flesh-and-blood boy—brimful of mischief and impatient of restraint.

3

CHAPTER III.

EARLY LIFE AND HABITS.

Scotch-Irish Presbyterianism of twenty-five years ago.—The "little deacon."—First days at school.—Choosing a wife.—A youthful gallant.—A close scholar but a wild lad.—A mother's influence.—Ward Glazier a Grahamite.—Young Willard's practical jokes.—Anecdote of Crystal Spring.—"That is something like water."

IT must not be supposed that young Willard's home was gloomy and joyless, because it was presided over by a religious woman. The Presbyterians of that day and that race were by no means a lugubrious people. They did not necessarily view their lives as a mere vale of tears, nor did they think the "night side of nature" the most sacred one. The Rev. Mr. Morrison, one of their divines, tells us that "the thoughtless, the grave, the old and the young, alike enjoyed every species of wit," and though they were "thoughtful, serious men, yet they never lost an occasion that might promise sport," and he very pertinently asks, "what other race ever equaled them in getting up corn-huskings, log-rollings and quiltings?—and what hosts of queer stories are connected with them!" Fond of fun, there was a grotesque humor about them, which in its way has, perhaps, never been equaled.

"It was the sternness of the Scotch Covenanter softened by a century's residence abroad, amid persecution and trial, united to the comic humor and pathos of the Irish, and then grown wild in the woods among their own New England mountains."

Such was the Scotch-Irish Presbyterianism of that period.

Other cheerful influences were also at work in the two villages that comprised the town of Fowler. The only house of worship in the town proper was a Universalist church, and the people were compelled for the most part, notwithstanding their individual creeds, to worship in a common temple where the asperities of sectarian difference had no existence.

Ward Glazier, at that time, was an adherent of Universalism, while his wife held different views. But he was ever ready to ride with his wife and son to the church of her choice at Gouverneur, a distance of six miles, and returning, chat with them pleasantly of the sermon, the crops, the markets and the gossip of the town.

In truth, young Willard's early home was a good and pleasant one, and having learned, under his mother's careful training, to read exceedingly well, for a boy of his age, by the time he reached his fourth year he became noted for his inquiring disposition, his quiet manner, and a quaint habit of making some practical application of the "wise saws" with which his mother had stored his juvenile mind.

The result was that up to this period of his existence he was an old-fashioned little fellow, and somehow had acquired the sobriquet of the "little deacon."

At about five years of age, however, a change took place in the boy.

The bird that flutters and twitters in the parent nest is a very different thing from the emancipated fledgeling, feeling its newly acquired power of flight, and soaring far up and out into the woods and over the fields; and the boy whose experience of life is confined to the household of his parents, is not less different from the lad who has gone beyond it into the bustle and turmoil of that epitomized world,—a public school.

Little Willard, like other youths, was thrown into this new sphere of action suddenly, and without any adequate idea of what was there expected of him. The first day passed as all first days at school pass, not in study, but in looking on and becoming accustomed to the surroundings, himself in turn being the subject of scrutiny by his school-mates, as the "new boy." The day did not end, however, without its incident.

Young Willard as soon as he had made his bow to his new teacher, was placed upon a bench in close proximity to a pretty little girl of about his own age. Instead of wasting his time therefore, by studying the less attractive lineaments of his male companions, he made a careful comparison between this young lady and the other girls present, the result of which was that the moment he was permitted to go out during the customary recess, he bounded off home at the top of his speed, and with all the exuberance natural to his years announced to his astonished mother, "Mother! mother! I've picked out my wife!"

Susceptibility to the influence of beauty seems, at this period of Willard's life, to have been one of his prominent characteristics, for in addition to exhibiting itself in the manner described, upon another occasion not long afterwards it broke out as follows:

Every school-boy is aware that there is nothing so humiliating to a male pupil at a public school as to be called a "girl-boy." Hence, for trivial offences a boy is often punished by being sandwiched between two girls, and compelled to remain there until the offence committed has been sufficiently atoned for. Now young Willard was frequently guilty of talking during study hours, and his teacher determined to try this species of punishment upon him with a view of correcting the offensive habit. As soon, therefore, as he caught him indulging in the prohibited practice, he was ordered to take his place between two very young ladies of six and eight summers respectively. To the amazement of his teacher, young Willard sustained the infliction smilingly, and believing that this was an indication that the culprit recognized the justice of the punishment and was practising a commendable patience, he very soon called him up to his own desk, reasoned with him upon the necessity of observing the rules of school, and released him with an admonition to be careful for the future, as a repetition of his offence would certainly be followed by a repetition of the punishment.

Willard said nothing, but went to his desk, and for the space of five minutes, perhaps, there was complete silence in the school-room. Then Mr. —— was startled to hear a distinct, clear, unmistakable whisper break in upon his meditations, and became as suddenly struck with the conviction that it was uttered by Master Willard Glazier.

The countenance of the pedagogue grew dark and stern. Fire shot from his usually calm eyes, and his expression betokened the fact that this flagrant act of disobedience was more than he could bear. Indignation however soon gave place to astonishment, for the little fellow, without waiting for a single word from his teacher's lips, quietly arose to his feet, and with the placid expression of an individual performing a meritorious action, marched across the school-room and deliberately seated himself in the place he had before occupied between the two little girls.

"Willard Glazier!" thundered the master, "come here, sir, immediately!"

The boy of course instantly obeyed.

"What do you mean, sir!" exclaimed the teacher, "how dare you conduct yourself in this disgraceful manner, sir!"

Young Willard looked astonished.

"Why, Mr. ——," said he, "didn't you say that if I whispered to Myron Sprague again, I should go back and sit between Lizzie and Annie?"

"Yes, sir, I did, and how dare you disobey me in this way?"

"Why, sir," said Willard, "I whispered again to him, because, sir,—because—I like to sit there, sir."

A light dawned upon the mind of the master, and thereafter he adopted a less attractive mode of punishing Willard's offences. To some of my readers such incidents may seem too trivial for record, and no doubt such days as these *are* foolish days, but are they not in our memories, among our very happiest too? As David Copperfield said of such, so say we, that "of all my time that Time has in his grip, there's none at which I smile so much, or think of half so kindly."

The usual surroundings of a public school made a great change in the existence of Willard Glazier, and it is necessary to note its influence, for in writing the

PRACTICAL JOKES. 39

life of a man in its private as well as its public relations, the chief point to be considered is that which men call *character*, and how it was formed and fashioned.

If the truth must be told, the " little deacon " had not been a month in attendance at school before he was up to every imaginable species of mischief that the fertile brain of a school-boy could conceive—provided its execution did not involve unequivocal untruth or palpable dishonesty.

No human being, save one, was exempt from his practical jokes. That one was his mother. In his wildest moods, a glance of reproach from her would check him. His father, however, enjoyed no such immunity, and in a kindly way, he delighted in tormenting the good man whenever the opportunity offered.

For instance, that worthy gentleman, among other idiosyncracies, was a follower of the so-called Dr. Sylvester Graham, an ex-Presbyterian clergyman who, in 1832, inaugurated, by a familiar course of lectures, a new system of dietetics.

The Grahamites, as they were called, held that health is the necessary result of obeying certain physical laws, and disease the equally certain result of disobeying them; that all stimulants are pernicious to the human body, and should be rejected, except in those rare cases where it becomes necessary to administer one known poison as an antidote to another equally deadly, in order to neutralize its effects or expel it from the system. Dr. Graham condemned the use of tea, coffee and spices, tobacco, opium, and not only alcoholic drinks but even beer and cider, declaring that all were equally poisonous, and that they only differed in the degree in which their evil qualities were concentrated or expanded.

Ward Glazier held this theory to be the result of a profound philosophy, and considered the observance of the course of diet he prescribed to be the only way in which a human being could secure for himself a sound mind in a sound body. In medicine, Mr. Glazier was an equally rigid hydropathist. He held that the system of water cure was the only rational system of healing. One of his individual fancies was to drink only water obtained from a particular spring. This spring was beautifully clear and cold, and was situated at the distance of about sixty rods from the house. It was Willard's allotted duty each day to fill a large pitcher from its crystal treasures for use at meals. In order to do this, the brooklet being extremely shallow, and running over masses of pebbles, he was compelled to kneel and dip it up with a cup, —an operation requiring both time and patience. Now within a few yards of this place flowed a small stream or creek considerably deeper and of larger volume, fed by a number of rills, and as the boy had conceived the impression that his father only fancied a distinction where there was really no difference, between the waters of the rival streams, it occurred to him that he might just as well plunge his pitcher in the latter, fill it with a single effort, and thus save himself what he especially disliked,—useless labor. This he did with the following result:

Ward Glazier was just about sitting down to dinner as Willard entered, and observing that his son came from the immediate vicinity of the creek, poured out and tasted a little of the water with evident dissatisfaction.

"Willard," said he, "you didn't get this from the spring; this is creek water. Now go right back and get a pitcherful from the spring."

Off started Master Willard to do as he was bidden, but on his way, the originator of all mischief suggested to his fertile brain the idea of playing a trick upon his father; so instead of going to the spring, he simply loitered for a few moments out of sight of such of the family as might be at the windows,

"Under an elm whose antique roots peep out
Upon the brook, that brawls along the wood."

He then quietly sauntered back, with the identical pitcher of water with which he had come forth.

"There," said he, emphatically, as if he had fulfilled his mission, at the same time placing the pitcher near his father's plate upon the table. The good man took it up, examined the contents with a critical eye, poured out a glassful of the sparkling liquid and drained it to the last drop.

"Ah," said he, with a sigh expressive of great satisfaction, "*that* is something like water! *that* does a man good!"

This evidence of parental fallibility Master Willard enjoyed hugely, but it was many years before he ventured to give his father an opportunity to join in the laugh at his own expense, by telling him of the occurrence.

CHAPTER IV.

WILLARD GLAZIER AT SCHOOL.

School-days continued.—Boys will be boys.—Cornelius Carter, the teacher.—Young Willard's rebellion against injustice.—Gum-chewing.—Laughable race through the snow.—The tumble into a snow-bank, and what came of it.—The runaway caught.—Explanation and reconciliation.—The new master, James Nichols. —"Spare the rod and spoil the child."—The age of chivalry not gone.—Magnanimity of a school-boy.—Friendship between Willard and Henry Abbott.—Good-bye to the "little deacon."

WILLARD GLAZIER was, by no means, what is termed a bad boy, at school.

It is true he was full of mischief; was the last in for study and the first out for recreation, but he was neither disobedient nor inattentive to his lessons. One scholarly element, however, he lacked. The bump which phrenologists term reverence had small development in him at this period of his existence. His record always stood high in the matter of lessons, but low in the matter of conduct. Instances of insubordination occurred whenever he thought he was treated unfairly, while no boy was ever more ready to submit to authority when wisely and justly administered. The following incident is an illustration in point:

One of his teachers bore the name of Cornelius Carter. We have been unable to ascertain this gentleman's nationality, nor would his history, if known to us, be pertinent to this work, but we have reason to believe that he was of Scottish descent, if not actually a native of that

> "Land of brown heath and shaggy wood,
> Land of the mountain and the flood."

At all events he possessed all the sterling qualities of that clear-headed people.

A man of fine parts and scholarly attainments, earnestly bent upon doing his whole duty, vigorous, energetic and thorough in everything, Carter was just the man to conduct a school with mathematical precision, but at the same time, his natural irritability was such that the whirlwind was less fierce than his wrath, when the latter was aroused. About the time of his advent among the pupils at the Little York public school, gum-chewing had become an accomplishment among the boys, and though it was a species of amusement positively forbidden, was carried on surreptitiously throughout the school.

One dark winter morning just after a heavy fall of snow, it happened that our friend Willard, though placed upon a bench in the middle of a row of these gum-chewing juveniles, was himself not chewing, for the simple reason that he had no gum to chew, and his next neighbors were niggardly enough to refuse to give him any.

Suddenly the hawk eye of Carter swept down upon the offending group; and quite assured that if mischief was in progress, young Glazier was in it, came forward and stretching out his long arms, placed his palms upon the outermost cheek of each "end boy," and brought the heads of the entire line together with a shock that made them ring again. Then, without a word, he caught each urchin in turn by the collar of his coat, and with one vigorous jerk swung him into the middle of the floor and in his sternest tones bade them stand there until further orders.

Willard did not at the moment venture to say anything, but stood with the rest, nursing his wrath. Had he really been at fault he would have thought nothing of it, but first to have been deprived by circumstances of the opportunity to break the rules, and then to be punished for a breach of them, was too much.

He waited, without a word, until the group of delinquents, after listening to a scathing lecture, were dismissed to their seats. He then deliberately proceeded to put his books under his arm, preparatory to making a start for home.

One of the monitors, a large boy, observing this movement, informed Mr. Carter that Willard Glazier was going to "cut for home," in other words, to leave school without permission.

The master, upon receiving this intelligence, started down the aisle towards young Willard; but that restive youth perceiving the movement, made rapid time for the door, and dashed down-stairs closely pursued by the now furious pedagogue.

Having some rods the advantage at the start, the boy reached the exterior of the building first, and struck out in a straight line for home.

The storms which prevailed throughout the entire winter in St. Lawrence County, had piled up their accumulated snows over the space of ground that separated the school-house from Willard Glazier's home. Over this single expanse of deep snow many feet had trodden a hard path, which alternate melting and freezing had formed into a solid, slippery, back-bone

looking ridge, altogether unsafe for fast travel. Over this ridge young Willard was now running at the top of his speed. In view of the probable flogging behind, he took no heed of the perils of the path before him.

> "So like an arrow, swift he flew
> Shot by an archer strong,
> So did he fly, which brings me to
> The middle of my song."

As for Carter, not a whit daunted by the icy path and the fact that he was hatless, in slippers, and clad only in a long, loose summer coat worn in the heated school-room, he gave chase in gallant style, and while Willard possessed the advantage of an earlier start, the teacher's long legs compensated for the time gained by his pupil, and made a pretty even race of it.

On he went therefore, his coat-tails standing out straight like the forks of a boot-jack, and a red bandanna handkerchief streaming in the wind from his pocket behind like some fierce piratic flag! On, too, went Master Willard Glazier, until both—one now nearly upon the heels of the other—reached a troublesome miniature glacier, when each missed his footing.

Down went the boy's head and up went the master's heels, and the pair lay together, panting for breath, in the drifts of a contiguous snow-bank.

"Ah, ha!" said Carter, when he had recovered sufficiently to speak, "so you were going home, were you?"

"Yes," said young Willard, as his head emerged from the drift, looking like an animated snow-ball, "and I would have reached there, too, if I hadn't slipped."

This was all that was said, at the time, but as Mr. Carter led his prisoner back, an explanation took place, in which the lad so strongly insisted that his escapade arose from a sense of the gross injustice done him, that Carter's own sense of right was touched, and after admonishing the boy to take a different mode of redressing his grievances in the future, he agreed to forego the flogging and let Master Willard finish the balance of the session in the customary way.

After this occurrence, Willard got along very well under the tuition of Mr. Carter, and it was not until some years later, when a gentleman by the name of Nichols took charge of the school, that anything transpired worthy of note.

James Nichols was a devout believer in Solomon's maxim that to spare the rod is to spoil the child. The whip was his arbiter in all differences which arose between his pupils and himself. He never paused, as Mr. Montieth has lately done, to consider that at least two-thirds of the offences for which children are flogged at school are "crimes for which they are in nowise responsible," and "when stripped of the color given to them by senseless and unmeaning rules, they are simply the crimes of being a boy and being a girl," and are "incited by bad air, cold feet, overwork and long confinement; crimes which the parents of these same children are accustomed to excuse in themselves, when they sit in church, by the dulness of the sermon, or other circumstances that offend against nature and which they sometimes soothe with fennel or hartshorn, or change of position, and not unseldom with sleep." In school discipline Mr. Nichols was a pure materialist. He never realized Cayley's profound lesson that

BREACH OF DISCIPLINE. 47

"education is not the mere storing a youthful memory with a bundle of facts which it neither digests nor assimilates," but that it is the formation and training of a *mind*. Under his *regime* the rod ruled everything. Even the offence of whispering was punished by the lash.

Upon one occasion, when young Willard was seated between two brothers—Henry and Brayton Abbott by name—engaged in solving Algebraic problems, a whispered inquiry, regarding the lesson, passed from one to the other.

Mr. Nichols at the moment happened to glance towards them, and conjectured, by the movement of Willard's lips, that he was violating the rule against whispering.

"Willard Glazier!" said he, angrily, "come out here, sir!"

The boy obeyed.

"Now then, Willard," said Mr. Nichols, "I presume you understand the rules of this school?"

"I think I do, sir."

"Very well, then you know that whispering during the hours of study is a breach of its discipline, and that I must punish you."

Willard said nothing.

"Have you a knife, sir?" pursued the teacher.

"No, sir," replied the boy, not quite certain whether the knife was wanted for the purpose of scalping him, or merely with a view of amputating the unruly member which had been the instrument of offence. "Well, take this one," said Nichols, handing him a five-bladed pocket-knife, with the large blade open, "go out and cut me a good stout stick."

The boy by no means relished the prospect this mission suggested, but seeing no means of escape, he went to a grove in the neighborhood and cut a stick whose dimensions resembled a young tree—shrewdly suspecting that Nichols would never venture to use a club of such size.

With this stick he stalked majestically back to the school-room. As he entered, he saw Henry Abbott standing up in front of the teacher's desk, and heard him utter these words:

"It is not fair, Mr. Nichols, to flog Willard alone. It was my fault, sir. I beckoned to Brayton and whispered first. That is what started it. You should whip me, too, sir."

The master, as we have said, was stern and uncompromising, but his nature was not entirely devoid of feeling, and as he heard the brave admission, his eye lighted up with sudden softness.

"Go back to your seats, boys," said he, "I will not flog either of you to-day. Lads that are brave enough to face the punishment of one offence as you have done, can, I hope, be trusted not to soon commit another."

The incident was one that raised the tone of the whole school, and it gave rise to a warm feeling of admiration in Willard Glazier's breast for Henry Abbott which did Willard good, and made the two youths firm friends.

Thus the years sped on—dotted with little incidents that seem too trivial to relate, and yet each one of which had *some* effect upon the future life and character of young Willard. He had become a pretty wild boy by this time, and the cognomen of the "little deacon" was dropped without ceremony.

Although he was marked high for scholarly attainment, he received many a bad mark for violating the rules of school.

This state of affairs existed until the boy had reached the age of eleven years, when he was brought into contact with two diametrically opposite influences, one of which was calculated to *make* and the other to *mar* his future character and fortunes.

CHAPTER V.

ECCENTRICITIES OF HENRY GLAZIER.

Henry Glazier.—A singular character.—"Kaw-shaw-gan-ce" and "Quaw-taw-pee-ah."—Tom Lolar and Henry Glazier.—Attractive show-bills.—Billy Muldoon and his trombone.—Behind the scenes.—"Sound your G!"—The mysterious musician.—What happened to Billy.—" May the divil fly away wid ye!"

AT this time there resided in the paternal homestead a younger brother of Ward Glazier named Henry, who was Willard's senior by about eleven years, and, physically speaking, was a splendid specimen of masculine development. Like his brothers Ward and George, he stood six feet in his stockings, and literally looked down on his fellows.

He had conceived a great liking for his nephew Willard, and on many a hunting excursion in the "Great North Woods," the boy was his only companion. This affection, however, was not unmingled with some contempt for the lad's diminutive stature.

Upon one occasion, during a visit to West Boylston, he made it his business to search out the relatives of Willard's mother, in order to ascertain what sort of stock she came from. On returning home, this son of Anak exclaimed, with a dejected air:

"Mother, I'll be hanged if I ain't discouraged! Our Willard will always be a little runt. His mother's folks ain't bigger'n a pinch of snuff!"

How far the prediction has been verified any one who has seen the compact, sinewy form of the young soldier will understand.

Henry Glazier reveled in everything sensational. His ideal of heaven was a succession of tableaux in which he was to play the principal part.

At one time he joined another eccentric character named Tom Lolar, an Indian of the Seneca tribe, whose lands in the long ago of Indian history bordered the blue waters of Lake Seneca in central New York. This peculiar pair proceeded to electrify certain rural communities in their immediate neighborhood with huge posters, announcing that on a given night:

KAW-SHAW-GAN-CE,

OR

THE RED WILD CAT,

THE

Great Chief of the Walaitipu Indians,

Now traveling for the benefit of his tribe, proposes to exhibit to an enlightened public the

TROPHIES WON BY HIS BRAVES,

In their battles with other Ferocious Tribes beyond the Rocky Mountains, and the Great Chief will likewise give an exhibition of the

WAR DANCES OF HIS NATION.

Accordingly upon the night in question Tom Lolar as "*Kaw-shaw-gan-ce,*" and Henry Glazier as ticket agent, reaped such an excellent harvest that the latter concluded to start a "live Indian" upon his own account.

This he accordingly did, dubbing the prodigy of his creation "Quaw-taw-pee-ah," or the "Red Wild Cat."

Whether this venture was successful or not we have failed to learn, but there is one story connected with it which is too good to be lost, though it lacks satisfactory evidence of authenticity.

The legend runs that our enterprising manager went three miles away and hunted up a genuine old native of Erin who had deserted from the British army, where he held some position in one of the military bands attached to a regiment stationed in Canada. With true Irish instinct this exile of Erin had brought his trombone across the border, and "the enterprising manager"—to use the language of the bills—"secured in him the services of an eminent musician, lately of her Majesty's Royal Band," to discourse sweet music during the entire performance. This and other attractive announcements drew a goodly crowd of lads and lasses from far and near to the place appointed, and when the doors—otherwise tent-flaps—were open, the assemblage marched in to the entrancing strains of the trombone, as played by "Professor Muldoonati" *alias* Billy Muldoon.

Everything passed off well. "Quaw-taw-pee-ah" presented to the *elite* of the locality a type of the aboriginal American, which at least possessed the merit of originality. If the audience expected to be astonished they were not disappointed; for such an Indian as they then beheld no living eye had ever looked upon before.

Mr. Catlin would have admitted that this noble red man was alien to any of his tribes, and even Cooper's

Leather-Stocking would have conceded that his was a new revelation of savage humanity. It is barely possible that Buffalo Bill may have dreamed of something like him, and it is not impossible that the late Edwin Forrest may have actually been on speaking terms with his brother, but outside of these two gentlemen, we do not believe that human imagination ever conceived a child of the forest in any respect resembling "Quaw-taw-pee-ah" on his opening night.

It did seem a little singular to combine the convivial music of "St. Patrick's day in the morning" with such diabolical grimaces and gestures as those which the Great Chief used in the pantomimic expression of his sentiments. But the people were prepared for originality, and they had it. At any rate the performance received their loud applause. At last, however, it was over: the successive scenes of the programme had come and gone—the war dances were finished, the curtain had fallen on the last act, and Billy Muldoon's trombone had subsided into silence. But if the performance within was wild, it was nothing to the wild night without. It was the seventeenth of March, and the snow had been steadily falling since morning, shrouding the hills and all the surrounding country with a mantle as white and cold as a winding sheet.

The wind had increased since nightfall, and by the time "Quaw-taw-pee-ah" had washed his face of its red lead, and Mr. Muldoon had been paid his share of the proceeds, it was blowing "great guns," as the sailors say. Out into such a night as this the audience dispersed: but the lights of home shone through the blinding storm near at hand, and buffeting with the fierce gusts of whirling snow and wind was only brave sport for them. Not so, however, with Mr. Billy Muldoon. *His* home was three miles away, and though the prospect without was anything but pleasant, he prepared to face it like a man. His only precaution was to see that an old army canteen was filled afresh with the best whiskey the neighborhood afforded. Then he started on his homeward journey.

At first it was pretty hard work. The snow had drifted into heaps in some places, and rose almost to the little man's waist. Still he struggled bravely on, only stopping now and then to celebrate the anniversary of Ireland's Patron Saint by taking a long pull and a strong pull at the canteen.

For a half-hour or more he made but slow progress through the pitiless, pelting storm, and he heartily cursed his folly in attempting the task of coming home at all, on such a night as this. But a change came o'er the spirit of his dream. As the contents of the canteen had diminished, Billy's spirits had risen in exact proportion, his heart had grown strong and he began to despise the difficulties in his way. In fact he was as happy as a prince, and rather liked the idea of facing the snow drifts and fighting the wind. So on he went. What seemed strange to Billy was the fact that there seemed to be so much sameness in the surrounding features of the landscape—or so much of it as he could discover, during the momentary lulls of the storm. He therefore stopped short, steadied himself for a moment, and took another drink; which proceeding seemed to clear up his mind on the puzzled subject, for muttering that it was "all roight," he once more started forward.

Another half-hour passed and still another, and yet Billy found the road open before him, with no sign of his own humble little home. He began to grow very tired and considerably muddled, and paused at length to consider the situation.

In front of him he perceived something so like the lane that led to his own shanty that he joyfully proceeded, and at length reached what he believed to be a back door that he had directed his wife to leave "on the latch" for his return.

What surprised him was that he could see no light within. He was, however, sufficiently aware of the fact that he had taken more of "the crayther" than his good woman would approve of, so not caring to wake her up, he stole to the door and tried to lift the latch. It was fastened. Everything within was dark as Erebus, and not a sound could be heard except the low breathing of what he supposed to be his sleeping children. This rather excited Billy's wrath. He had been particular in his injunction to leave the door unbolted, and it was hard to be kept out in the storm on such a night as this. He called out—at first in a whisper, then louder and louder—to Kathleen to let him in. There was no response. Yet he certainly heard the movement of feet within. What could it mean? The little man finally swore a big oath and fiercely demanded admittance; but still there came no reply. He then essayed to force the door, and to his utter amazement the upper part of it gave way, opening out like a window-shutter, while the lower part remained firm. The musician therefore climbed up, and seating himself on the edge of the door, peered in. He could see nothing but a black void. To use his own figure of speech, "yez might as well hunt for Giueral Washington's will down a black dog's throat, as attimpt to see the nose on yer face in there!"

He was nearly paralyzed with astonishment. Suddenly a bright thought struck him. He raised his trombone to his lips, and in spite of the mingled emotions that agitated his breast, blew upon it a blast loud enough to have waked the dead.

Imagine therefore how his previous astonishment was deepened into almost idiotic wonder when he heard a reply from what appeared to be a trombone of more gigantic power than his own. "Bur-r-r!" went Mr. Muldoon's instrument.

"Boo-o-o!" replied the invisible respondent.

Billy was amazed. Billy was awe-stricken. But the instinct of the musician rose above all other emotions.

"Sound your G!" said Billy.

"Boo-o-o!" was the answer in a deeper base than before.

"Yer out o' tune, ye domned old fool!" says Billy.

"Boo-o-o!" came the response once more.

"Sound yer G, and take that, ye murtherin spalpeen!" said the now thoroughly exasperated musician, dashing his own instrument in the direction of his invisible rival.

Just then poor Billy saw a ferocious-looking pair of eyes glaring at him, and before he had time to add another word, some huge object rushed towards him, struck him a determined blow, and lifting him off his perch sent him into the middle of the road.

The fact is, Billy had wandered very much out of his way, and had mistaken Ward Glazier's barn for his own dwelling. The supposed rival musician was our old acquaintance, "Black-face," the Bull.

Billy picked himself up from the snow, and, regardless of his bruised body and aching bones, steadied himself for a last shot at the enemy. The little man looked in the direction where he thought his adversary ought to be, and though he could see nothing through the darkness and storm, he shouted out, in accents of blended dignity and contempt:

"May the divil fly away wid ye! Ye may be the sthronger of the two, but, be jabers, yer no museecian!"

How he eventually got home and what were his sentiments regarding the adventure with which he had met, are facts that do not concern this history; but it is quite probable that he wondered as we have often done, that St. Patrick, while engaged in the laudable task of expelling snakes from the soil of the Emerald Isle, did not also provide that such reptiles should keep out of the boots of her sons.

CHAPTER VI.

VISIONS OF THE FUTURE.

The big uncle and the little nephew.—Exchange of ideas between the eccentric Henry Glazier and young Willard.—Inseparable companions. — Willard's early reading. — Favorite authors. —Hero-worship of the first Napoleon and Charles XII. of Sweden.—The genius of good and of evil.—Allen Wight.—A born teacher.—Reverses of fortune.—The shadow on the home. —Willard's resolve to seek his fortune and what came of it.—The sleep under the trees.—The prodigal's return.—"All's well that ends well."

BETWEEN Henry Glazier and young Willard a singular friendship had sprung up. The great, six-foot uncle and the quaint, old-fashioned boy were much together.

In the woods and fields, at junketings and corn-huskings, the pair were often seen in grave converse, and while Willard was ever eager to hear the stories of his uncle's mad adventures and queer scrapes, Henry Glazier, in turn, would listen with a species of reverent wonder to the child's recital of striking passages of history or of fiction which he had picked up in the course of a varied and desultory reading—a taste for which was developed even at that early age. The volumes to which he had access were few in number, but he had read their pages again and again, and the subjects of which they treated were, for the most part, of just such a character as were calculated to attract the attention of a man of action rather than of thought.

Among them were "Rollin's Ancient History," "Robinson Crusoe," "The Arabian Nights," "Life of Charles XII. of Sweden," "Kossuth and his Generals," and "Napoleon and his Marshals,"— everything relating to the career of the great Corsican being devoured with the greatest avidity.

He began, of course, by reading the descriptions of battles. All boys do so. But gradually his interest in such exciting events extended to the actors in them, and again to the causes that led to them, and at length the books were read from the preface to the end.

The conversations between the uncle and nephew were far from exercising a good influence over the boy. If Willard related some daring deed from the life of Charles XII. or of the great Napoleon—his own especial hero—his uncle Henry would match it with some equally striking, if less civilized adventure in the forest or upon the river, in which he or some of his whilom associates had played the principal part. All this was, to a certain extent, calculated to unsettle the lad's mind for the common, routine duties of a useful existence. Fortunately, however, at about the time that it began to produce that effect, another opposite and more powerful influence was brought to bear upon him which changed the current of his ambition, and turned his attention to matters less exciting in their character, but destined to exert a much greater influence over his future life. I allude to his association with his teacher, Allen Wight.

The small, plain brick school-house at Little York stands there, we believe, to-day as it did then in all its native and naked ugliness. Such a structure, looking at it æsthetically, is not a cheerful sight to the lover of learning, but at that period it was under the mastership of a mind of no ordinary calibre. From all that we can learn of him, Allen Wight was that remarkable character—a born educator. He did not believe his duty was performed by merely drilling his pupils, parrot-like, to repeat other men's sentiments. He knew that the minds of mortals, particularly if young and fresh, are as diverse in their springs of action as the laws of the universe, and he conceived it to be his duty to study the individual characteristics of each scholar under his charge, as he would have familiarized himself with the notes of a piece of music before he attempted to play it. His method was that of the Jesuit, carried out in a Protestant fashion. In young Glazier he took especial interest. He liked the sturdy little fellow who, though full of youthful vim, could yet sit down and discuss the difference between a Macedonian phalanx as described by Rollin and a *corps d'armée* as manœuvred by Soult, and he determined if possible—to use his own phraseology—"to make a man of him."

His first step was to lead the boy's mind up to a habit of reasoning upon the present and the past, and upon the every day world of practical realities with which he had to do. When this habit had become sufficiently matured in him, the wise teacher told him the story of his own life, with its struggles, its disappointments and its triumphs, thinking thus to stimulate his favorite pupil to greater efforts and better achievements in the path of knowledge. He talked to young Willard as he would have talked to a man, yet with all the gentleness of manner he would have used in addressing a woman. Every incentive which he could place before the boy, every appeal to both heart and brain which he could make, Allen Wight used—as the mechanic would use the lever—to bring out all that was noblest and best in him—to develop all the sleeping possibilities of his young nature.

Ward Glazier had not been as prosperous in his worldly affairs as his patriotism and honesty deserved, and things at the old "Homestead" looked rather gloomy. Poverty is a fearful darkener of child-life, and while its shadow rarely fell on Willard, who was always at school or roving the woods and fields with his uncle Henry, to his sisters and brothers it frequently presented its dark face and whispered unpleasant prophesies of the future.

Of course it was not that abject kind of poverty which stints the supply of food and fire in a house. It did not still the prattle of the children, or banish childish mirth from the dwelling. It was not the wolf at the door, but the wolf in the dim possible distance when the poor father, bent with age, would perhaps be unable to keep his little flock together. But the boy had never thought of such a possible time. *His* visions of the future were of sights to be seen in the great world—of a time when he would be large enough and free enough to accompany his uncle Henry upon some of his wild adventures among civilized or savage races, and of the delights of unlimited books to be read upon subjects most congenial to his mind. He therefore made no allowance for his father's gloomy face and short words, and often thought him stern when he was only sad.

A slight incident, however, changed all this and compelled him to face life not as a dream but as a reality. One evening Willard's father came home very tired and somewhat dispirited by some adverse circumstances, such as occur in every man's business life at times, and of course he was not in the most pleasant frame of mind to encounter the petty annoyances of a household. Something that Willard said or did, capped the climax of his irritability and he called the boy a fool. It was a very unusual thing for Ward Glazier to speak with even apparent harshness to his children, and the lad felt it, therefore, all the more keenly. He became very thoughtful and silent, and crept off to bed earlier than usual only to lay awake most of the night brooding over the insult, and debating within himself what to do in order to vindicate his outraged dignity. The conclusion at which he finally arrived was that when the morning came, he would run away from home and seek his fortune in the great world. The fact is he had been reading Robinson Crusoe but a day or two previous, and that charming story had made a great impression on his mind. Under its weird influence his vivid imagination conjured up possible scenes of adventure in which he was to emulate the courage and sagacity of that celebrated truant, and eventually come home, as Robinson did, a man full of knowledge with which to astonish the family, and with wealth to lavish on brothers and sisters, and make comfortable the declining years of his parents. "*Then* his father would not think him a fool," said this youthful logician to himself. His active little brain was too highly stimulated by his great resolve to permit much sleep that night, and his bosom swelled proudly as he thought how bravely he would encounter misfortune and face danger for the sake of the glorious future he saw in the distance. His boyish heart thrilled strangely within him as he pictured to himself how full of amazement his brothers and sisters would be, when they found he had gone forth all alone to seek his fortune. Even the little sleep, therefore, that he obtained, was but a dreamy repetition of his waking thoughts, and when the first gray streak of dawn told of the coming day, the boy arose and quietly dressing himself for his journey, emerged from the house, passed down the avenue under the broad elms and struck the highway. He shivered a little as the chill air of morning touched his cheek, and his ambitious dream did not look quite so glowing and glorious as it had done when snugly ensconced in his comfortable bed, but still he had a consciousness that he was doing something very manly, and he walked on with a firm step and determined heart.

It is true he had no very definite idea of *where* he was going,—he only thought of doing great things and seeing strange sights. His whole plan of travel was comprehended in the one idea of *going out into the world*. That was all. Accordingly the youth trudged on for miles without weariness,—for his head was still thronged with thick coming fancies of the possible future that lay before him, and for some time the exulting sense of freedom that ever accompanies disenthralment of any kind, thrilled his whole being with a firm resolution to accomplish great things.

At the expiration of a few hours, however, the fatigue involved in so unusual a tramp before breakfast, began to tell upon him, and as he mechanically slackened his pace, his reflections assumed a less jubilant and less satisfactory character. He had walked nearly fourteen miles and was already footsore. "Going out into the world," began to seem not quite so enchanting a proceeding as it had appeared to be at starting. For the first time since the idea of "seeking his fortune" had entered his mind, he asked himself *where* he was to seek it.

The reply to this inquiry was not easy. Meanwhile the sun had mounted high up in the heavens and was shining brightly, the birds were singing their matin songs, and in the roadside pastures the cattle were quietly grazing. It was a peaceful, pastoral scene, but its peace did not enter the heart of the wanderer. Somehow the world did not appear half so attractive in his eyes as it had looked when he stole forth from his father's gate in the cold gray of the morning twilight. His step, therefore, was less elastic and his bearing less assured now than then, and at length he sat down under a large beech-tree by the roadside, to reflect upon the situation. He began to feel very weary, and the sudden transition from action to repose induced a drowsiness that in a few minutes overcame his waking sense and launched him into the sea of forgetfulness. The young head sank lower and lower on his breast, and finally, sleep . . . "that knits up the ravelled sleeve of care," . . . "sore labor's bath, balm of hurt minds, great Nature's second course," came to him unawares, and for some hours he was totally oblivious of all surroundings.

It was a dreamless sleep, and noon had come when he awoke. For a few moments he was unable to recall where he was or how he had come there, but in a very short time the recollection of everything that had happened to him since the evening before swept over his mind like a flood. Every circumstance now, however, was viewed in a far different light. Somehow, the provocation which had sent him into the wide world to seek his fortune did not seem half so great as it had seemed only the night before. The example of De Foe's hero was not so completely alluring, and a portion of that history which the evening previous he had not deemed worthy of a thought, now rose vividly before him. He seemed to read again these words:

"My father, a grave, wise man, gave me serious and excellent counsel against what he saw was my design. He told me it was for men of desperate fortunes on the one hand, or of aspiring superior fortunes on the other, who went abroad upon adventures, to rise by enterprise and make themselves famous in undertakings of a nature out of the common road: that these things were all either too far above me, or too far below me: that mine was the middle state or what might be called the upper station of humble life, which he had found by long experience was the best state in the world, the most suited to human happiness. The wise man gave his testimony to this when he prayed to have 'neither poverty nor riches.'" And then came the thought that all that Robinson ever gained in fame or fortune, failed to still the quiet but terrible whisper of his conscience whenever he thought of those he had abandoned for a roving life. So intently did he think upon these things, he seemed actually to behold the wanderer upon his sea-girt island with lawless Will Atkins and the gentle French priest beside him, while the words of the

repentant mutineer seemed to be hissed into his ear:—
"No, sir, I did not cut his throat, but I cut the throat
of all his comforts. I shortened his days and I broke
his heart by the most ungrateful, unnatural return, for
the most tender and affectionate treatment that father
ever gave or child could receive." Young Willard
could not but remember that *his* parents had been
most kind and tender, that *his* father had lavished
upon him during all the years of his childhood a most
prodigal wealth of affection : and the one harsh epithet
he had received seemed as nothing among the multitude
of kind and loving words that had never been withheld
from him. His heart told him that something deeper
than any ordinary woe would darken his mother's
quiet face when she beheld his empty chair and realized
that he had gone, perhaps never to return, without one
farewell word to her. Such reflections as these, that
he wondered had not occurred to him before, now took
possession of his mind and, impelled by their influence,
he arose and slowly started back towards home. As
he came within sight of the old place he saw his
father in the distance reaping, and the sight filled him
with gladness.

> "From the top of the road, through the gap was seen
>   Down a zigzag road cut up by rills,
>   The velvet valley cradled between
>   Dark double ridges of 'elm' clad hills;
>   And just beyond, on the sunniest slope,
>   With its windows aglint in the sunset warm,
>   In the spot where he first knew life and hope,
>   Was the dear old house of the 'Homestead' farm."

But he was not just then in a frame of mind to
meet the parental eye, and he therefore skirted round
a piece of woods which concealed him from his father's

view and reaching the door unobserved, crept into the house.

Though his absence had been discovered, and its cause, if not known, at least shrewdly suspected, his father and mother in their reception of him very wisely ignored all knowledge of his truancy and treated the young prodigal with such unusual marks of kindness and indulgence, that he was completely melted, and felt, with keen remorse, that he had been upon the eve of becoming a most wretched ingrate. The lesson of the experiment was not lost upon him, and he never again tried the foolish venture.

CHAPTER VII.

WILLARD GLAZIER AT HOME.

Out of boyhood.—Days of adolescence.—True family pride.—Schemes for the future.—Willard as a temperance advocate.—Watering his grandfather's whiskey.—The pump behind the hill. The sleigh-ride by night.—The "shakedown" at Edwards.—
—Intoxicated by tobacco fumes.—The return ride.—Landed in a snow-bank.—Good-bye horses and sleigh!—Plodding through the snow.

WARD GLAZIER—putting his theories to the test of practice—believed it best to allow the error of his son to work out its own punishment, without adding a word to indicate that he knew it had been committed. The wisdom of such reticence is not often recognized by parents placed in similar circumstances, but it would perhaps be better for the children if it were. At the same time the father thought it expedient to apprise Allen Wight of the matter. That gentleman readily acquiescing in his plans, saw in the recoil which would probably succeed such an escapade in the mind of a sensitive and generous boy, the opportunity he sought to arouse him to a sense of the duties that lay before him in his future career, in living a useful and worthy life.

One afternoon, therefore, when they were enjoying a quiet chat after school hours, he managed—without the slightest allusion to the runaway freak—to turn the conversation to the subject of "self-made men."

Not, be it understood, that species of fungi who only love their maker, because being

"*Self*-made, *self*-trained, *self*-satisfied,"

they are

"Themselves their only daily boast and pride."

Not the Randall Leslies, or the Peter Firkins of the world or that other

"Score of Peter Funks,
Of the mock-mining stamp, who deal in chunks
Of confidence, ores and metals as examples
And sell the bowels of the earth by samples;"

but that higher race who have achieved noble things despite all the drawbacks of poverty and friendlessness.

He spoke of Clive, the Shropshire farmer's son, who, according to the greatest of modern historians, equalled Lucullus in war and Tergot in peace; that reformer who out of the discordant elements of an Indian ochlocracy consolidated and perfected an empire, one of the most splendid the world contains.

He spoke, too, of that other Indian ruler who as he lay dreaming a boy's day-dream one holiday, upon the bank of a stream that flowed through Daylesford Manor—the manor which one ancestor's sword had won and another ancestor's folly had lost—the boy formed a scheme of life that culminated in the extension of the same empire beyond all previous expectation, and in linking his own name so inseparably with the story of his country, that no man can write the history of England without writing the life of Hastings.

Other examples of great ends achieved with little means, by men in our own land, were talked over.

Franklin the *boy*, walking up Market street, Philadelphia, a penny-roll under each arm and munching a third, under the laughing observation of Miss Read, his future wife—and Franklin the sage and Minister, representing his government at the most elegant court in Europe, were contrasted for his edification. Various modern instances were added, Mr. Wight keeping in view Pope's axiom that

"Men must be taught as if you taught them not,
And things unknown proposed as things forgot."

When the boy's mind had been sufficiently awakened he followed the advice of the old adage to "strike while the iron is hot," and impressed upon him the fact that being the eldest son he was naturally the prop of his house; nor did he ignore the truth, unpalatable as it might be, that Willard could hope for no material aid from the hands of his parents. He must carve his own way. He must build even the ladder up which he was to climb. Others had done so—why not he? And then he told him that the way to do it successfully was to acquire knowledge and cultivate wisdom; for

"Knowledge and wisdom, far from being one,
Have, oft times, no connection.
Knowledge dwells in the thoughts of other men,
Wisdom in minds attentive to their own."

Working upon what he rightly conjectured to be the boy's newly awakened sense of the kindness of his father, he spoke of that good man's pecuniary reverses, and professed his faith in Willard as the future regenerator of the fallen fortunes of Ward Glazier's family.

The boy's generous enthusiasm was awakened at once. His ordinary school tasks and home duties no longer looked commonplace, and were no longer distasteful to him. They were but incidents in a general plan of usefulness, and he performed them with an air of cheerfulness that pleased his teacher and delighted his parents. He volunteered to help his father in the fields, and while but a boy in years, he yet performed the work of a man. In fact, he had discovered that every duty of life has its heroic side, and needs only the impulse of high and noble motives to be invested with dignity and interest.

Meanwhile, he did not neglect his studies. The idea of intellectual culture was no longer a mere abstraction. Books were not only what they always had been—reservoirs of knowledge, alluring to his imagination, and fascinating to his mind—but they were now looked upon as levers, with which he was to move the world. Knowledge *now* meant the means whereby, in the days to come, he was to acquire the power to make his father and mother comfortable for the balance of their lives: and to surround his sisters with those luxuries which go far towards making existence a thing of grace and refinement. When, therefore, he worked during the warm days of summer, aiding his father in the care of the farm, the summer evenings found him poring earnestly over his books—practical and useful ones now—and the harvest once gathered, he was back again in his old place at school, where he studied steadily and hard. His teacher, Allen Wight, looked on and was satisfied. And yet Willard was a wild boy—as wild as any in the school. His relish for fun and frolic was as keen as ever, but it was now subordinated to his judgment. His practical jokes were fewer, and the peculiarities of his father no longer furnished him with a subject for their perpetration. Now and then, however, the old exuberance of mischief *would* break out, and upon one occasion his grandfather became its victim.

As that mosaic styled "character" is nothing more than an aggregate of just such trivial things, we trust our readers will pardon us if we relate the incident in point.

When Willard was over nine years of age, his father moved from the Old Homestead Farm and purchased a place named the Goodrich Farm, where he opened a country store. The venture proved to be an unfortunate one, and, after a series of pecuniary vicissitudes, he left the place, and, at the period to which we refer, was the occupant of a farm known in that section as the Davis Place.

This place and the Glazier Homestead occupied positions upon opposite sides of the same public road—the former being one mile nearer the town of Fullersville.

Meantime, the Homestead was occupied and cultivated by Jabez Glazier, the grandfather of Willard, and upon certain occasions the boy was sent over to stay for a few days at that place, to help the old gentleman in many little ways connected with its cultivation.

At that time and in that locality it was customary during the haying season to deal out to the men employed stated rations of whiskey every day. A bottle was filled for each one, and, being placed by the recipient in a swathe of the newly-cut grass, frequent visits were made to the spot and frequent libations indulged in. Ward Glazier and his wife being determinedly opposed to the use of ardent spirits under any circumstances whatever, the custom was dispensed with at the Davis Place; but at the Old Homestead, under the rule of Jabez Glazier, the time-honored usage was staunchly maintained. Young Willard had been so deeply inoculated with his parents' opinions on this subject, that he had delivered an address before the society of "Sons of Temperance" at Fullersville even at that early age, and his disgust may be imagined when he found himself selected by his grandfather to go to the village store for the necessary quantity of "Old Rye." He asked that some other messenger might be sent, but the old gentleman was inflexible. Nobody but Willard would satisfy his whim—perhaps because he felt that, in the custody of his grandson, the "fire-water" would not be tampered with on its return to the farm. Willard did not openly rebel against his grandfather's commands—since it was the fashion in those days for children to be obedient—but turned his attention to gaining his object by means of a little strategy. Not far from the house on the road leading to the store stood an old pump, concealed from view by an intervening building and a rising hill. Here this youthful disciple of Father Mathew made it a practice regularly to stop, and pouring out half the contents of the jug he carried, refilled it with the crystal liquid from the pump.

At first this *improvement* in their potations seemed hardly to attract the attention of the individuals interested; but, as each day the proportion of water increased, the dilution at last forced itself upon their attention, and every one agreed that the store-keeper was cheating old Jabez in the "Rye" business. The result of it all was the withdrawal of Jabez Glazier's custom from the establishment in question, and the future purchase of "spiritual" goods by Mr. Jabez himself in person.

Thus Willard's object was attained, and the cold-water people were no longer vexed by the inconsistent spectacle of a son of temperance playing Ganymede to a set of drinking, though by no means drunken, hay-makers.

Not often, now, did young Willard figure as chief in any mad scrape or wild boyish adventure. Those times were left behind. Once, indeed, his uncle Henry, the patron of the great chief "*Kaw-shaw-gan-ee*," swooped down upon the household, and, in an enormous four-horse sleigh of his own construction, took him, together with a gay and festive party of lads and lasses, off to Edwards, a village nine miles away. Here the rustic party had a "shake-down," and young Willard got fearfully sick in a dense atmosphere of tobacco smoke. The feast over, he was tightly packed in the sleigh with the buxom country girls and their muscular attendants, while Henry Glazier drove across country through a blinding snow-storm and over measureless drifts. The party was stranded at last on a rail fence under the snow, and the living freight flung bodily forth and buried in the deep drifts. They emerged from their snowy baptism with many a laugh and scream and shout, and tramped the remainder of the distance home. The horses having made good their escape, Willard was carried forward on his uncle Henry's back.

CHAPTER VIII.

ADVENTURES—EQUINE AND BOVINE.

Ward Glazier moves to the Davis Place.—"Far in the lane a lonely house he found."—Who was Davis?—Description of the place.—A wild spot for a home.—Willard at work.—Adventure with an ox-team.—The road, the bridge and the stream.—"As an ox thirsteth for the water."—Dashed from a precipice!—Willard as a horse-tamer.—"Chestnut Bess," the blooded mare.—The start for home.—"Bess" on the rampage.—A lightning dash.—The stooping arch.—Bruised and unconscious.

IT will be remembered that when Ward Glazier left the Homestead, he removed to a neighboring farm known as the Goodrich Place,—a fine, comfortable, well-stocked and well-tilled farm, presenting an appearance of prosperity to the eye of the observer and calculated to make the impression that its owner must be well-to-do in the world. As we have heretofore hinted, however, Ward Glazier failed to prosper there. Why this was the case it is hard to tell. A late writer has suggested that "not only the higher intellectual gifts but even the finer moral emotions are an incumbrance to the fortune-hunter." That "a gentle disposition and extreme frankness and generosity have been the ruin in a worldly sense of many a noble spirit;" and he adds that "there is a degree of cautiousness and distrust and a certain insensibility and sternness that seem essential to a man who has to bustle through the world and engineer his own affairs,"

—and if he be right, the matter may be easily understood.

However that may be, he failed to prosper, and as business misfortunes began to fall thick and fast upon his head, he gave up the farm to his creditors, together with all his other effects, and took up his abode at the Davis Place.

Who the particular Davis was whose name clung to the place we have been unable to ascertain, but when Ward Glazier moved there, the house seemed fairly to scowl upon the passer-by—so utterly unprepossessing was its appearance. A rude, capacious wooden structure, it stood fronting the highway, and was a place where the beautiful had no existence. The very soil looked black and rough—the vegetation ragged. Every inclosure was of stone or knotted timber, and even a dove-cot which in its fresher days some hand had placed upon the lawn, was now roofless and shattered, and lay prone upon the ground, a shapeless mass of collapsed boards. The lawn—if such it could be named—resembled a bleak shore, blackened with stranded wrecks of ships whose passengers had long years before gone down at sea. The broken windows in the dormitories were festooned with cobwebs that had housed long lines of ancestral spiders, and where a pane or two of glass remained among the many empty frames, one fancied a gibbering spectre might look out from the gloomy depths behind.

The back-ground against which this bleak and sombre place was thrown was no less grim and stern. Huge rocks in tiers, like stone coffins, rose in fierce ranges one above another up and up—back and farther back until they reached a point from whence a miniature forest of dwarf beech and maples, that appeared to crown the topmost bastion of them all, nodded in the swaying wind like funeral plumes upon a Titan's hearse.

In fact, the only gleam of light upon the place—and it was a crazy, fitful gleam at that—came from a rushing stream that took its source high up among the hills. This brook first seen off to the extreme left of the house, came dashing down the rocks until it reached a level. Then, swinging round with sudden swirl it engirdled the place, and after many a curious twist and turn got straight again and went onward far off among the neighboring fields and lost itself at last in the Oswegatchie. The interior of the house was just as wild and dreary as the exterior. The rooms, for the most part, were too large for comfort. When one spoke, a dozen ghostly echoes answered, and at twilight the smaller children huddled around the kitchen fire and seldom went beyond that cheerful room until bed time. Often, in the dead of night, the creaking of timber and the voices of the wind startled the little ones from sleep, and a sense of something unreal and mysterious overshadowed their young minds.

It was, take it all in all, a grim, gaunt, strange place in which to fix a home. It was there, however, in the midst of such sterile surroundings, that the next five years of Willard's life were mainly passed. There were no external influences brought to bear upon this portion of his existence that were not harsh and wild and stern. His father, honest even to the verge of fanaticism, was letting his heart corrode to bitterness under the sense of hopeless indebtedness. The churlish fields attached to the place offered but a grudging reward for the hardest labor. There was no hope of his acquiring a profession or even an education beyond the scant opportunity of Allen Wight's school, unless he himself could earn the means to pay for it. Still he was neither discouraged nor without hope. Instead of sinking under this accumulation of difficulties, his moral fibre was rendered more robust, and with it his physical strength and usefulness developed daily.

Thus a year sped on, and at the end of that time his father, as one means of adding something to his scanty resources, obtained the job of hauling a quantity of iron ore from the ore beds near Little York to a forge and furnace at Fullersville. Willard with an ox-team and his uncle Henry with a span of fine horses, were employed for the most part to do the actual hauling.

By this time Willard was quite familiar with the management of horses, and he had also learned to drive oxen, so that at the age of thirteen he worked with his ox-team as regularly and almost as efficiently as any of his grown-up uncles or even his father. The management of an ox-team, by the way, is quite different from that of horses, and at times it becomes very troublesome business, requiring for its successful accomplishment the very nicest admixture of courage, coolness and discretion. Willard, however, with the self-reliance that always characterizes a boy of his age, never for a moment doubted that he was adequate to the task, and as he had been placed in charge of a very fine yoke of oxen, took much pride in driving them in the same manner as he would have driven a span of horses, seated on the top of his load upon the wagon instead of being on foot and close by their heads, as prudence would have taught an older driver to do. The truth is, that if there was any human being before whom the boy delighted to exhibit himself as doing a manly part in his little circle of existence, that being was Henry Glazier.

Consequently, when his uncle's team was on the road, Master Willard took a position upon his own load with as important an air as if he were on the box of a coach-and-four, and guided his cattle as if they were animals of the most docile disposition, to halt at his whisper or proceed at his word. As the principal part of the work was performed at midsummer under the rays of a scorching sun, the cattle were, of course, irritable and restive to a degree that in colder weather would have seemed inconsistent with the phlegmatic characteristics of their race.

The road from Little York to Fullersville is a winding, narrow road, somewhat hilly in places, and neither very smooth nor level at any point. Midway between the two villages a brawling stream crosses the road, and making a turn empties itself, at the distance of about thirty yards, into the waters of the Oswegatchie. This stream is spanned by a rustic bridge at a very considerable elevation above the water. The banks are high and abrupt, and, as the traveler approaches them, he cannot fail to be attracted by the silvery sparkle of the waters far below. The view from the bridge takes in the white farm-houses with their emerald setting of rich grain-fields and meadow-lands, the distant forge with its belching smoke-stacks, the winding Oswegatchie, and the distant blue hills. If the month happens to be August, the traveler may hear the cheerful hum of busy industry, the swinging cradles of the harvesters or the steady roll of the reaper. Upon a day, late in this richest of summer months—August—in the year of our Lord 1854, Willard and his uncle Henry were slowly wending their way towards Fullersville—the former with his ox-team and the latter with a spanking span of horses. The beasts of burden by their drooping heads and slow pace evinced the fact that the loads of ore they were drawing were unusually heavy, and this, combined with the sultry atmosphere, was telling upon the strength of even such powerful beasts as they.

Willard, as usual, was seated upon the top of his load, and, as they neared the bridge, despite his familiarity with every detail of the scene, a sense of its exquisite beauty took possession of him, and, for a moment, he forgot that he was driving an ox-team. For a moment he was oblivious to the fact that it takes all a driver's care and skill to prevent mischief whenever a thirsty ox obtains a glimpse of water upon a summer's day. As they neared the bridge, the fevered eyes of the cattle caught sight of the limpid stream away down below, and, just as a cry of warning from his uncle recalled the boy to a sense of the deadly peril of his position, the cattle made an oblique plunge over the edge of the bank with two tons of iron-ore in lumps varying from five pounds to fifty, pouring a huge and deadly hail over their reckless heads. With rare presence of mind for a boy of his age, the instant he heard his uncle's warning cry, Willard realized the situation and jumped sideways from the wagon. As he did so, his hat fell off and rolled a short distance away. At the same moment a lump of ore, weighing not less than one-hundred pounds,

TRAGIC EXPERIENCE WITH AN OX-TEAM.

fell upon it and crushed it so deeply into the ground that it was completely hidden from view. Many months afterwards, some boys digging for fish-bait found the hat buried there, and returned to the village with a tale of some possible and unknown murder, committed when or by whom no one could tell.

As for the boy himself, he escaped with only a scratch or two and a few bruises, but that he escaped with his life or with sound limbs was almost a miracle; and, as his big-hearted uncle picked him up, he hugged the lad as one snatched from the very jaws of death. Willard was somewhat awed by the narrowness of his escape, and it was observed that his face wore an expression a shade graver than was its wont for several days after the occurrence.

The lesson, however, made no lasting impression. Scarce a week had gone by ere his life was once more imperilled, and this time the danger resulted from his own reckless over-confidence in himself.

It is a singular fact in the boy's history that every danger to which at this period of his life he was exposed, seems to have been twin-brother to some other hazard equally great, and which tripped upon its very heels.

As already stated, Willard was a good horseman for a boy of his age. He possessed considerable nerve, and, having been brought up among horses, knew a good deal about their ways. But his real knowledge upon the subject was nothing to that which he thought he possessed; and, though a stout little fellow, of course he lacked the muscle of steel that is required to master an enraged horse. But he had never hesitated to ride any steed in all that neighborhood, with the single exception of one of a pair of extremely beautiful but vicious mares, which on account of her color was named "Chestnut Bess."

This horse was as wild and untamed as the famous steed of Mazeppa, and even Henry Glazier, master-horseman though he was, seldom attempted to use this one, except in harness with her mate. The knowledge of this fact excited an overweening desire in Willard's breast to show them what *he* could do in the way of taming the hitherto untamed creature, and never having been unhorsed in his life, he determined, upon the first favorable opportunity, to try his powers upon the vicious animal. That opportunity was not long in coming. One summer morning it was arranged that Willard should go over to his grandfather's and aid in the cultivation of a large corn-field on the Homestead Farm. Willard made up his mind that, if he went, he would go in style on the back of "Chestnut Bess." He wanted to show his Uncle Henry and the others what the "little runt" was capable of accomplishing as an equestrian. Accordingly, he placed a good strong bridle upon the mare's head, gave an extra pull at the saddle-girth to assure himself there was no possibility of *that* failing him, and, taking a hoe, which he wished to use in his work on the farm, in his right hand, he led the mare quietly down the path, out through the gate, and into the road. Gathering the reins in his left hand, without giving her time to conjecture his object—for mounting her was no easy task—he jumped lightly into the saddle, and screwed his knees into her sides with all his might.

Now, this mare was not one of those ordinary

quadrupeds possessing a single vice, which the rider may learn and master. She was an animal of infinite resources. Her modes of attack were innumerable. It is true she rather preferred to settle matters upon the very threshold of the contest in a short, sharp way, by kicking her man before he could mount. But, if baffled in this design, she would vary the proceedings by dashing her head down between her knees, sending her heels up in the air, and, if possible, plunge the rider over her head to the ground; or, she would waltz round on her hind legs in such a way as to render the best balanced brain somewhat dizzy and uncertain; in the event of the failure of these coquettish pleasantries, she had not a single scruple against playing Shylock, and taking her pound of flesh out of his leg with her teeth. Thus, you see, it would not do to go to sleep upon her back; and Master Willard Glazier no sooner found himself firmly seated than he made up his mind that for the time, at least, he had his hands full of business. As the mare had been deprived of an opportunity to kick him, by the suddenness with which he sprang upon her back, she concluded to try her next favorite line of strategy and shake him off. So down went her head and up went her heels, and, had he been less on the alert, he must have gone to earth; but, with his knees dug into her sides as if they were the opposite jaws of a vice, for every jerk of her head *down* he gave one with the reins *up*, and at each jerk the hoe-handle gave her a rap over the ears, so that she began to find the fuu less agreeable than usual. Changing her tactics, with a bound she proceeded to execute a fine imitation of the "German," and spin round like a Fifth Avenue belle or a humming-top. But the boy's young, clear, temperate brain and well-disciplined nerves were proof even against this style of attack, and still firm in his seat, he belabored the brute with his hoe with such a perfect rain of blows that she gave up her prancing and dashed down the road at a break-neck pace. For perhaps five hundred yards the road led down hill, and then, crossing a stream, ascended again, the ascent being quite steep and by no means smooth.

While upon the descent, it was all Willard could do to hold on, for he was encumbered with the hoe, which at every jump of the mare struck the top of her head, until she absolutely flew. The few pedestrians upon the road that morning stopped in amazement to stare after the mad flight of horse and rider.

As soon as the bridge was crossed and they commenced the abrupt rise, "Chestnut Bess" began to slacken her pace, but the young gentleman, who by this time considered himself her master, would not agree to this. He proposed to give her a lesson, so he administered a good thrashing with his novel style of whip and compelled her to keep her pace all the way to the top of the hill, where horse and rider at length arrived in safety. From that point to the old Homestead the mare was perfectly willing to jog along quietly, and when they reached the farm you may be sure that the "spirit" of one "mortal" at least was "proud," as he related to his wondering kinsman how he had taken the mischief out of the chestnut mare.

The boy rose immeasurably in his uncle Henry's estimation by this feat, and all were delighted with his pluck, though Jabez Glazier, his grandfather, with his greater experience, warned him not to trust the beast too far, for, according to his belief, her eye had danger in it yet. When the day of work was ended, Willard once more mounted upon "Chestnut Bess" and rode towards home. For a short time the mare trotted quietly along, and the boy was more than ever convinced that he had broken her of her tricks.

This agreeable belief however was of short duration. The thought had hardly entered his head when she commenced her antics again. Her heels went skyward and her nose went down, and a repetition of the morning's performances succeeded.

There was quite as much vigor and pertinacity in her movements as if she were just starting out for the day. This time Willard had provided himself with a stout beech switch, and used its stinging persuasion with good effect. She danced, she pranced, she waltzed, she made sudden dashes and full stops. She would have rolled in the gravel if the boy's switch had ceased stinging her into motives for action, but she could not shake him off. He clung to her back like a little leech, and it began to look as if human will-power was going to conquer brute stubbornness, when suddenly a new idea seemed to enter the animal's head. Without a moment's warning, and utterly scorning the control of the bit which she had taken in her teeth, she swung round and at full gallop made straight for the Homestead farm from which she had so lately come. The farm-yard gate was wide open and she dashed in, making directly for the wagon-shed at the extreme end of the place, which was now empty. This shed, the top of which was supported by a cross-beam, was only just high enough to permit a wagon to be sheltered there, and if the horse got in, Willard saw at a glance that she would be obliged to lower her head to do so, and that in the course of her entry he must inevitably strike the beam and perhaps be instantly killed or swept off her back upon a pile of rocks that on either side walled the entrance to the shed.

His heart for once failed him, for there seemed no earthly hope of escape. There was no time to spring off, even if the speed at which he was going would have permitted him to do so, for in a shorter time than it has taken to describe the scene, the shed was reached, bang went the mare's head against the opposite end, and at the same instant Willard felt a dull thud against his person, realized the fact that he was being thrown into the air, and then came darkness and unconsciousness. He was dashed violently upon the stones, and when picked up his body was found to be much lacerated and bruised.

Fortunately, however, no bones were broken, though he was obliged to keep his bed for some days afterwards. No doubt while lying there during slow convalescence he mused upon the vicissitudes attendant upon the career of a horse-tamer. At all events from this time he became much steadier and more prudent, —the wild adventures of his earlier boyhood having entirely lost their attraction for him.

CHAPTER IX.

THE YOUNG TRAPPER.

A plan of life.—Determination to procure an education.—A substitute at the plow.—His father acquiesces in his determination to become a trapper.—Life in the wild woods along the Oswegatchie.—The six "dead falls."—First success.—A fallacious calculation.—The goal attained.—Seventy-five dollars in hard cash!—Four terms of academic life.—The youthful rivals.—Lessons in elocution.—A fight with hair-brushes and chairs!—"The walking ghost of a kitchen fire."—Renewed friendship.—Teaching to obtain means for an education.

AT this period of Willard's life, he is described by Mr. Rennehan as having acquired an appetite for the acquisition of knowledge which soon became the controlling passion of his nature, and, "thoroughly absorbed by this idea, he fixed upon the select school of his native town as the institution best adapted to initiate him in the course suited to the fulfilment of his laudable ambition."

But his determination to procure an education met with obstacles from the outset. How to defray the necessary expenses which such a course involved was the question which continually presented itself for his ingenuity to solve. His father's reverses placed it quite beyond the possibilities to hire help upon the farm, and Willard's services had therefore come to be looked upon as something of vital importance.

In dragging from the hard soil of the Davis place

the living which necessity compelled, he performed the work of a man, and the perfect trust which his father reposed in him gave his services additional value.

This fact increased the difficulty of his position; but though he made it a point to husband all his spare time for self-instruction, he was far from satisfied with the existing state of affairs, and pondered long and earnestly over the best means of securing the advantages of regular instruction.

At that time the streams tributary to the St. Lawrence were supplied with such fur-bearing animals as the mink, the musk-rat, the otter, and the more humble rabbit, the skins of all of which were more or less valuable and were hunted by professional trappers. These men found the business a reasonably lucrative one, and it commended itself especially to Willard, as health and strength were the only capital required. The grand difficulty was how to supply his place in the work of the farm. His father was a man who always listened with patience and sympathy. to any scheme that promised to benefit his children. His son, therefore, had no hesitation in laying the whole matter before him and seeking his advice upon the subject. He felt of course, that any proposition to withdraw his personal labor from the common stock of exertion by which the cultivation of the farm was rendered a possibility, was a direct pecuniary tax upon his father's resources; but he believed he could to a great extent neutralize the injury by supplying a substitute.

He also felt assured that although the step he proposed to take might be a present loss to the family it would prove an ultimate gain. He was thoroughly determined to make *his* life a success, and he was just as thoroughly determined that any success which might crown his efforts should be shared by his parents. It is true that the road looked long and the path rough, but he had a "heart for any fate," and his courage never failed. A substitute at the plow he knew he could obtain for a small sum, and the board of such a person would take the place of his own at the home table, and he never doubted that he could earn a sufficient surplus to pay the wages of such an assistant. At all events he made up his mind to try the experiment.

With young Willard, to think was to act, and this project was no sooner conceived than he proceeded to put it into execution. He laid his plans frankly before his father, who, to his great gratification, assented to his proposal. A man was hired for fifteen dollars a month to take Willard's place on the farm, and the latter made his first venture as a trapper.

His initial experiment was to set six traps of the pattern called a "dead fall" or "figure of four," and this resulted in the capture of two minks worth about eight dollars. With what an exultant heart he drew out his first mink and realized that by his own unaided exertions he had made some money, no boy or man need be told. He at once, however, entered into some rather fallacious calculations and built some extremely airy castles. It occurred to him that if out of six traps he could obtain two skins, out of one hundred he could obtain twenty-three, and so on, in proportion.

This, however, proved to be a miscalculation, it not

being so much the number of traps set, as the quantity of game in a given locality which regulates the amount of success for a trapper. Yet his efforts in this new business succeeded to a gratifying degree, and the fact of having exchanged the dull monotony of farm drudgery for the exhilarating excitement of a hunter's life, was in itself a sufficient reward for any amount of exertion. Indeed what mode of life could be happier or more free, for a healthy, strong-limbed youth of fifteen, than to live as he then did, almost entirely in the woods? Then too, his daily route lay in the midst of some of the finest scenery to be found anywhere in New York, even in that grand old county of St. Lawrence.

To a lover of nature nothing could be more alluring than the locality through which Willard, at that period of his life, trapped and hunted. To follow the winding waters of the Oswegatchie is to enjoy a perpetual feast. That river is one of a great family of rivers, among which may be enumerated the Rackett, the Grasse, the Indian, and the Black, all of which take their rise far up in the recesses of the great North Woods. Though not to any extent navigable, it is yet nearly as broad as the lovely and "blue Juniata" of "peaceful Pennsylvania."

At times turbulent and brawling, it is often vexed in its passage to the St. Lawrence by falls and cataracts varying in height and volume, but which in their infinite variety give a wild and romantic beauty to this poetical stream. At times it glides smoothly along through low meadow lands, and again it plunges into some dense thicket or brawls through some briery dell where the foliage is so thick that one can only see the

THE YOUNG TRAPPER OF THE OSWEGATCHIE.

glint and glisten of its waters at rare intervals, shining between the lapping leaves and tangled vines. Then again it sweeps onward through cleft rocks and jutting banks until, lost at last in the very heart of the primeval forest, its twilight waters reflect the images of giant trees which had their beginning on its banks a century ago.

Willard's life during that autumn passed in persevering work. Day by day he traveled his accustomed routes, while the leaves turned from green to red and from red to russet and brown, and at last fell from the naked branches of the forest trees with a little farewell rustle, to be trodden into the rich soil below.

By the time the first snow came he found himself much more robust physically, and with seventy-five dollars clear profit in his pocket. In addition to these advantages he also acquired the inestimable habit of self-reliance, so that when he entered upon a course of preparation for his academic life, it was with full faith in himself. For four terms, beginning August thirteenth, 1857, and ending the latter part of June, 1859, he remained at the excellent institution of learning which he had selected, and while there gained considerable credit as a hard student.

During the first of these terms a generous rivalry existed between himself and a youth by the name of Albert Burt, as to which should lead the class. As it turned out, however, they kept together and were both marked "perfect." The academy was under the management of the Rev. E. C. Bruce, M. A., Principal; and Andrew Roe, Professor of Mathematics. About a month or six weeks after he entered the school, he arranged to take lessons in elocution under a Professor

Bronson, that gentleman having organized a large class at the academy.

In a brief diary kept by him at the time, we find the remark that he was "greatly pleased with the Professor's method of teaching that important branch of study." Willard had advanced to the higher grade of Algebra and Grammar, had added Philosophy to the list of his studies, and having cultivated a natural turn for public speaking, he was elected on the eighteenth of December, 1857, a member of the Oratorical Society—an association connected with the institution. His boy experiences were very similar to those which happen to all lads in Academic life. He had his chums, among whom were Brayton Abbott and Ozias Johnson; he had his little flirtations with misses of his own age, and he had his fights, as all boys have.

Among the latter was one with Johnson, who was his room-mate, and who, being four years older than himself, undertook, for fun, to rub his face with a newly-purchased hair-brush. This kind of fun did not suit Willard, however, and he resented it by giving Johnson a "dig" in the ribs. Whereupon a fight ensued in earnest, and as Willard was too young and light to keep up the contest at close quarters, he dodged his adversary and covered his retreat by dropping chairs in front of Johnson's legs, which brought that young gentleman to the floor more than once, to his own intense disgust and Willard's great gratification. At length Johnson managed to corner his opponent, and then rubbed his face so thoroughly with the bristles that his comrades that morning thought he had caught the scarlet-fever, or as Dickens says, that he was the "walking ghost of a kitchen fire."

As generally happens, however, between two manly fellows, their combat inspired a feeling of mutual respect, and from being mere acquaintances they grew to be fast friends.

Study and sedentary habits at length so much impaired Willard's health that, in the latter part of the month of August, 1858, he was compelled to cease his attendance at school and go home. The thirtieth of September following, however, found him at the Teachers' Institute of St. Lawrence County, with the proceedings of which body he appears to have been highly gratified, for in the diary to which we have already referred he speaks of it in these words,—

"I am now attending the Teachers' Institute of this county, which is in session at Gouverneur, it having opened upon the twenty-seventh instant. The School Commissioners are Mr. C. C. Church and Allen Wight. I am highly pleased with the proceedings and the method of conducting the exercises of this apparently indispensable part of a Teacher's instruction,"—adding that it was his "intention to become a teacher the coming winter." Indeed, to be a teacher seems to have been his favorite scheme of life, and his highest ambition was ultimately to fill the chair of Mathematics in one of the great institutions of learning. That most exact of sciences was his favorite branch of study, and the intellectual stimulus which it imparts had for him a peculiar fascination.

In pursuance of his object, and in order, by teaching during one part of the year, to raise means to enable him to attend school during another portion, he set about procuring for himself a school. Fortunately for the accomplishment of his object, it was suggested to him to apply to the School Commissioner of his own Assembly district, and he did so. The examination which followed his application, owing to some local rivalry, was extremely rigid; but he passed through it with great credit and received the appointment he desired, being assigned forthwith to duty in the town of Edwards, St. Lawrence County. He commenced teaching in the bleak month of November, 1858, and was very earnest in fulfilling the duties of his position, taking every opportunity not only of instilling knowledge into the minds of his pupils, but also striving to imbue them with a love of self-culture. He labored hard in his efforts to earn means with which to support himself during the coming summer at the Gouverneur Wesleyan Seminary, and discovered while thus working that teaching was as much of a discipline for himself as for his pupils.

The time does not seem to have passed unpleasantly to him at this period of his career, for in an entry made in his diary on the twenty-eighth of November, 1858, he says:

"I am spending the evening with Mr. Hiram Harris and family, having come into the district this afternoon. My object here is to teach school for a term of three months in fulfilment of the contract existing between the trustees and myself. In compliance with a custom that prevails, I am expected to 'board around,' as it is styled, and Mr. Harris, being one of the Trustees, has invited me to spend my first week at his house.

"The School Commissioner of this Assembly district is Mr. C. C. Church, of Pottsdam, from whom I received a certificate based upon the recommendation of Commissioner Allen Wight of the first district. The School Trustees are E. L. Beardsley, Hiram Harris, and Jeptha Clark. The present term will be my first experience in the profession I have adopted. I do hope it will prove a useful one, for I am of opinion that a teacher's first experience is apt to give color to his whole future career." The day after this entry he adds that "only a small attendance greeted him upon opening his school," and after consoling himself with the reflection that this will leave him plenty of time for study, he adopted a single rule—"Do right;" and an additional motto, "A time and place for everything and everything in its time and place."

It will thus be seen that he had already acquired a clear idea of the importance of order in every pursuit, and knew that method gives to an ordinary mortal Briærean arms with which to accomplish whatever he may desire to do. How few attend to this knowledge until it is too late!

As a writer, whose words we think worthy of remembrance, has said:

"This is an era of doing things scientifically. People make scientific calculations of the weather, and the average number of murders for the next year. They measure the stars and they measure the affections, both scientifically. The only thing they fail to do scientifically is, to manage themselves. As a rule, they *drift*, and then find fault with fate and Providence because they don't drift into the right port. They drift *into* life with a multiplicity of vague dreams, which are somehow to be realized; but they have a very dim idea of ways and means. They drift through it, carelessly, with an inadequate knowledge of their own resources, and a still more inadequate notion of using them to the best advantage; they drift *out* of it with a melancholy sense of failure, both absolutely as to themselves and relatively as to the world. Of all their splendid possibilities, none are realized. Nothing is completed. They start wrong or they make one fatal step, and everything goes wrong all the way through. It seems as if most lives were only experiments. Now and then one is turned out which fits in its niche and is tolerably symmetrical. The rest are all awry, unfinished, misplaced, and merely faint suggestions of what might have been. Much of this is doubtless beyond mortal control, but a far greater portion is due to the lack of a nice direction of forces. The human mechanism is complicated, and a very slight flaw sets it all wrong. There may be too much steam or too much friction, or too little power or too little balance. But clearly the first step is to strengthen the weak points, to gauge its capabilities, to set it running smoothly, and to give it a definite aim. If existence were simply passive and the mission of man was to *be* instead of to *do*, he might perhaps be left to develop as the trees do, according to his own will or fancy or according to certain natural laws. But as it is the universal wish wherever one is, to be somewhere else, a little higher in the scale, it seems to be a part of wisdom, as well as humanity, to fit one for climbing. But many an aspirant finds his wings clipped in the beginning of his career, through the ignorance or carelessness of his friends, who never took the trouble of measuring his capabilities. He is treated as a receptacle into which a certain amount of ideas are to be poured, no matter whether they may answer to anything within him or not. He is turned out of an educational mill with five hundred others, and with plenty of loose knowledge, but without the remotest idea of what to do with it, or what nature intended him for, and with no especial fitness for any one thing. He can *think*, probably, if he has the requisite amount of brains, but how to establish a relation between thought and bread and butter is the problem. He has the requisite motive power, but it is not attached to anything. *He* does not know how to attach it, so he revolves in a circle, or makes a series of floundering experiments, that bear meagre fruit, perhaps when the better part of his life is gone. He knows *books*, but he does *not* know men. He is a master of theories, but cannot apply them. If he has a small amount of brains, his case is still more hopeless. To be sure, a proper amount of knowledge has been poured in, but it has all slipped through. He might have assimilated some other kind of knowledge, but that particular kind has left him with mental dyspepsia, and a vague feeling of hopelessness which is likely to prove fatal to all useful effort. Or perhaps he has talent, but is destitute of the requisite tact to make it tell upon the world. His success depends largely on his power to move others, but he has no lever and is forced to rely upon main strength, which involves a serious expenditure of vitality, with only doubtful results. He works all his life against perpetual friction, because no one had the foresight or insight to discern that this was the flaw in his machinery.

"Another fatal point is in the choice of a vocation. Having drifted through an education, he next drifts into his business or profession. He rarely stops to take an inventory of his capital, or, at best, he takes a very partial one. Chance or circumstance decides him. His grandfather sits on the judge's bench. He thinks the judge's bench a desirable place, so he takes to the law. He puts on his grandfather's coat without the slightest reference to whether it will fit or not. Perhaps he intends to grow to it, but a willow sapling cannot grow into an oak. It may grow into a very respectable willow, but if it aspires to the higher dignity, it will most likely get crushed or blown over. It may be that he has a grand vision of commercial splendor, and plunges into business life with a very good idea of Sophocles and Horace and no idea whatever of trade; with a very good talent for theories, but none whatever for facts; with some insight into metaphysics, but none at all into people. Instead of trying his strength in shallow waters, he starts to cross the Atlantic in a very small skiff. By the time he has reached mid-ocean he discovers his error, but it is too late to turn back; so he is buffeted about by winds and waves until he, too, goes down and counts among the failures.

"Another of the few points upon which life hinges is marriage, and people drift into that as they do into everything else. It is one of the things to be done in order to complete the circle of human experience. A man is caught by a pretty face and a winning smile. He takes no thought of the new element he is adding to his life, either with reference to his outward career or his inward needs. Caprice governs his choice, or perhaps a hard form of self-interest. Having committed one or two of the grand errors of life, he settles down to its serious business, and speedily discovers that he has a dead weight to carry. He has mistaken his vocation, whatever it may be.

"He is conscious now that it is too late to change; that he might have attained supreme excellence in some other calling. He toils with heavy heart and sinking spirit at the plodding pace of dull mediocrity. His work is drudgery and wearies him body and soul. Those who once smiled upon him pass him by. Men of far inferior capabilities distance him in the race. Perhaps too he has made another misstep, and has a wife who sympathizes neither with his tastes nor his trials: who has no comprehension of him whatever, save that he is a being whose business it is to love her and furnish her with spending money. The beauty which fascinated him has grown faded and insipid. The pretty coquetries that won him pall upon him; he is absolutely alone with the burden of life pressing heavily upon him. Is it strange that he is mastered in the battle and finally falls beneath the world's pitiless tread? This is a sad little picture, but it is an every-day one, and the world goes on its way as before.

"What matters it that a lonely, dissipated man has lain down in sorrow to rise no more! The world cannot stop to weep over the remains of the departed one it has trampled upon. Those whose business it is can take them on one side, lay them away under the green sod out of sight, shed a tear perhaps, and pass on until their turn comes to lay down wearily, go to sleep, and be laid away. The world chides, the world laughs, but it takes no cognizance of the grief—

"'That inward breaks and shows no cause without,
Why the man dies.'

"Yet there is but the difference of a point in the game between the victim and the hero. The cards are the same, or the victim, perhaps, *may* hold the best trumps, but he plays recklessly, loses his point, loses his game, loses all! On such slight things does human destiny hinge. The hero has all his resources at command—his game dimly outlined. He knows his winning cards, and he plays them skilfully.

"Every point tells. Nothing is left to chance that can be accomplished by foresight. He wins the game. He wins the prizes. He has the mastery of life. The world takes off its hat to him. Fortune and people smile upon him. Not that he is better than others—very likely he is not so good. But the world counts results. Becky Sharp is not a model, but Becky Sharp is a power. The world does not like her in the abstract, but it likes her dinners, it courts her smiles, it fawns upon her, it showers its good things upon her, all because *she has mastered it*. Becky Sharp is not a model. Her aims are unworthy, and her means unscrupulous; but she reads us a lesson in fact, in foresight, in energy, in the subtle art of making the most of limited resources. So long as life is a game, it is worth studying. The difference between playing it well and playing it ill, is the difference between light and darkness, between joy and desolation, between life and death."

Even at that early and immature time of his life, Willard Glazier had thought much upon this subject—examples of the disjointed successes of all unplanned and unmethodical careers having been brought too frequently into close proximity to his own door, not to have made an impression upon his inquiring mind.

Hence, at the very threshold of his life as a teacher, he resolved to have plan and purpose clearly defined in everything he did

CHAPTER X.

THE SOLDIER SCHOOL-MASTER.

From boy to man.—The Lyceum debate.—Willard speaks for the slave. — Entrance to the State Normal School. — Reverses. —Fighting the world again. — Assistance from fair hands. —Willard meets Allen Barringer.—John Brown, and what Willard thought of him.—Principles above bribe.—Examination.—A sleepless night.—Haunted by the "ghost of possible defeat." — "Here is your certificate." — The school at Schodack Centre.—At the "Normal" again. — The Edwards School.—Thirty pupils at two dollars each.—The "soldier school-master."—Teachers at East Schodack.—The runaway ride.—Good-by, mittens, robes and whip!—Close of school at East Schodack.

ALTHOUGH a very boy in years, young Glazier felt himself already stepping upon the boundary line of manhood, and, luckily for his future welfare, he comprehended the dangers and realized the responsibilities which attend that portion of human existence.

Upon the fifth of February, 1857, the dull routine of a teacher's duty was varied by a visit made to Edwards by Willard's uncle Joseph, and his sisters; and, after closing his school, the former went home with his visitors, and thence to a Lyceum which had been established in the Herrick School District, where a debate was in progress as to the relative importance, in a humanitarian point of view, of the bondage of the

African race in the Southern States, or the decadence of the Indian tribes under the encroachments of the Whites. The "question" assumed that the Aborigines were best worthy of sympathy; and young Glazier, being invited to participate in the discussion, accepted, and spoke upon the negative side of the question.

He little dreamed upon that winter's night, when, in the small arena of a village debating-club, he stood up as the champion of the slave, that the day was not far distant when he would ride rowel-deep in carnage upon battle-fields which war's sad havoc had made sickening, fighting for the same cause in whose behalf he now so eloquently spoke.

No prophetic vision of what fate held in store for him appeared to the ardent boy, speaking for those who could not rise from the darkness of their bondage to speak for themselves. No glimpse of weary months dragged out in Confederate prisons—of hair-breadth escapes from dangers dread and manifold—of hiding in newly-dug graves made to assist the flight of the living, not to entomb the dead—of lying in jungles and cypress-swamps while fierce men and baffled hounds were panting for his blood—of vicissitudes and perils more like the wild creations of some fevered dream than the plain and unvarnished reality: nothing of all this came before him to trouble his young hopes or cloud his bright anticipations of the future.

He spoke of freedom, and had never seen a slave. He pictured the cruelty of the lash used in a Christian land on Christian woman, be she black or white. He spoke of the deeper wrong of tearing the new-born babe from its mother's breast to sell it by the pound—

of dragging the woman herself from the father of her child and compelling her to mate with other men—of the fact that such wrongs were not alone the offspring of cruel hearts, nor of brutal owners, but arose from the mere operation of barbarous laws where masters, if left to themselves, would have been most kind. He spoke of such things as these, and yet he never dreamed that his words were but the precursors of deeds that would make mere words seem spiritless and tame.

Young Glazier spoke well. The little magnates of the place—the older men, after this, talked of him as of one likely to rise, to become a man of note, and their manner grew more respectful towards the young school-master. His occupations and amusements at this period of his existence, though simple in their character, were considerably varied.

Among other entries in his journal about this date, is one that so commends itself by its brevity and comprehensiveness that I quote it *verbatim*.

"Having," he says, "received an invitation upon the twenty-fourth of December, I attended a party at the residence of Jeptha Clark, whose excellent wife received me very kindly; upon Christmas day I visited T. L. Turnbull's school at Fullersville; upon Monday last called at Mr. Austin's school in the Herrick District; Tuesday, dropped down for a moment upon the students at Gouverneur; on Wednesday, returned home; and on Thursday, for the greater part of the day, assisted uncle Joseph in hauling wood from the swamps on the Davis Place."

Thus the time slipped rapidly by and his first term of teaching drew to a close. In the spring of 1859 he again became a member of the Gouverneur Wesleyan Seminary, and in May of that year, made the following characteristic entry in his diary:

"'Order is Heaven's first law.' A time and place for everything, and everything in its time and place, was the rule of conduct I adopted some time ago. In accordance with this determination I have laid out the following routine of occupation for each day. I intend to abide by it during the present term. I will retire at ten o'clock P. M., rise each morning at five o'clock, walk and exercise until six, then return to my room, breakfast and read history until eight, then take what the English call a 'constitutional,' viz.: another walk until prayers, devoting the time intervening between prayers and recitation, to Algebra. After recitation, I will study Geometry for three-quarters of an hour, Latin for half an hour, and be ready for recitation again at two o'clock. This will complete my regular course of study, and, by carrying out this routine, I can dine at noon, and also have a considerable amount of time for miscellaneous reading and writing, to say nothing of my Saturdays, upon which I can review the studies of the week."

To this plan young Glazier adhered conscientiously, and hence he made rapid progress and very soon found himself in a condition to take another forward step in the pathway of learning. That step was the entrance to the State Normal School at Albany. To go to West Point and receive the military training which our government Alma Mater bestows upon her sons at that place, had been his pet ambition for years—the scheme towards which all his energies were bent. But failing in this, his next choice was the Normal

School. Accordingly, on a certain September afternoon in 1859, he found himself in the capital city of the Empire State, knocking for admission at the doors of the State School. He was alone and among strangers in a great metropolis, with a purse containing the immense sum of eight dollars! For a course of seven or eight months instruction this was certainly a modest estimate of expenses! In fact, young Glazier had based his financial arrangements on a miscalculation of the amount furnished by the State. He did not then know that the only provision made by the body politic was for mileage, tuition and text-books. But on Monday morning, September seventeenth, 1859, he signed his name to the Normal pledge, and at the conclusion of the examination—which continued until September twenty-third—he was assigned to the Junior Class—there being at that time four classes: the Senior and sub-Senior, Junior and sub-Junior.

The next step was to find lodgings at a weekly or monthly price more suited to his means than those which he had temporarily taken at the Adams House on his arrival there the previous evening. Always frugal in regard to his personal expenditures, he knew that, in order to eke out the full term with his scanty resources, he must carry his habitual thrift to its fullest extent. He therefore scoured the town for apartments, aided by references from Professor Cochran, principal of the Normal, and finally obtained a room on Lydius street, almost within shadow of the Cathedral, and at the certainly reasonable rate of "six shillings per week." This room he shared with Alexander S. Hunter, from Schoharie County, and a member of the sub-Senior Class. For several weeks the young students boarded at this place, buying what food they required, which the landlady cooked for them free of charge. Seventy-five cents a week paid for their cooking and their rent!

But even this small outlay soon exhausted the meagre resources of young Glazier, and, at the end of the time mentioned, he went over into Rensselaer County, to look up a school, in order to replenish his well-nigh empty purse, and to enable him to proceed in his efforts to acquire an education. It was a bright clear morning in November when he left his boarding-place on Lydius street in quest of his self-appointed work, and, crossing the Hudson on a ferry-boat, walked all the way to Nassau by the Bloomingdale Road—a distance of sixteen miles. His object was to find Allen Barringer, School Commissioner for Rensselaer County, who, as he had been told, lived somewhere near Nassau. On the way to that village he passed two or three schools, concerning which he made inquiries, with a view to engaging some one of them on his return to Albany should he be so successful as to obtain a certificate from Mr. Barringer. At about two o'clock in the afternoon of this, to him, eventful day, young Glazier had arrived at the residence of Harmon Payne, near East Schodack, or "Scotts' Corners," as it was sometimes called. He had been referred to this gentleman as one likely to assist him in his endeavors to obtain a school. He had eaten nothing since morning, and, having walked a distance of nearly sixteen miles, as may be imagined, was somewhat faint and hungry. But the good wife of Mr. Payne showed herself not lacking in the kindly courtesy belonging to a gentlewoman, and, with true hospitality, placed before the young Normal student a delicious repast of bread and honey.

To this youthful wayfarer, with a purse reduced to a cypher, and struggling over the first rough places in the pathway of life, the simple meal was like manna in the wilderness. After chatting pleasantly with the family for an hour or more, he started again on his journey. But this time not alone; for Mr. Payne very gallantly sent his niece with the boy teacher, in whom he had become so much interested, to show him a shorter route to East Schodack "across lots." This village, two miles farther on, by the traveled highway, was only three-quarters of a mile distant by a pathway leading across the pasture lands of some adjoining farms. In the fading November afternoon the young lady and her *protegé* walked together to East Schodack—a walk which young Willard never forgot, and out of which afterwards grew a fairy fabric of romantic regard glittering with all the rainbow hues of boyish sentiment, and falling collapsed in the after-crash of life, like many another soap-bubble experience of first young days.

But he did not succeed, at that time, in securing the East Schodack School, as he had hoped to do. Nothing daunted, however, he trod reverses under foot and pushed on towards the residence of the School Commissioner whose *ipse dixit* was to award him success or failure.

Allen Barringer lived one mile from the village of Nassau, in Rensselaer County, and it was nearly nightfall when, with an anxious heart and weary with the day's journey, he knocked at the door of the comfortable country residence which had been pointed out to him as the one belonging to the School Commissioner. That gentleman himself came to the door in answer to his knock, and upon Willard's inquiry for Mr. Barringer replied:

"I am Mr. Barringer, sir; what can I do for you?"

His manner was so pleasant and his face so genial that young Glazier, at once reassured, had no difficulty in making known his business.

"I have come out here from Albany," said he, "to see if I could pass examination for a certificate, to teach in your district."

"Well, come in, come in," said Mr. Barringer, cordially, "and I will see what I can do for you. You are not going back to Albany to-night?" he asked.

"No, I shall not be able to do so," replied Willard.

"Have you friends or relatives here with whom you intend to stay?"

"No, sir."

"Then I shall be glad to have you stop with us to-night. I am a young man like yourself, living at home here with my parents, as you see, I am fond of company, and will be happy to place my room at your disposal. And as there will be no hurry about the examination, we will talk more about it after supper."

Young Glazier thanked his host for the kind proffer of entertainment, and of course acquiesced in the arrangement.

Accordingly, after the physical man had been refreshed at a well-spread supper-table, Mr. Barringer conducted his young guest to his own apartments, where they drew their easy-chairs before a comfortable fire, and entered into conversation.

"I am considerably interested in politics just now," said Mr. Barringer, and then he asked abruptly, "what is your opinion of John Brown?"

At this time the first red flash of the war that swiftly followed, had glowered athwart the political horizon, in the John Brown raid at Harper's Ferry, and against this lurid background the figure of the stern old man stood out in strong relief. It was at the period when, shut up in prison, he was writing those heroic words to his wife, those loving words of farewell to his children; when petitions poured in pleading for his life—though they were petitions all in vain—and when, naturally, partisan feeling on the subject was at its height. Willard felt that in expressing his candid convictions he might be treading on dangerous ground, and perhaps endangering his chances for success, yet he held principle so high, and honest sentiment so far above bribe, that if his certificate had depended on it he would not have hesitated to express his admiration for the brave old man who laid down his life for the slave, and whose name has since been crowned with the immortelles of fame. Therefore Willard replied with a frankness worthy of emulation that he looked upon John Brown as a conscientious, earnest, devoted man— a man whose face was firmly set in the path of duty though that path led to imprisonment and the gallows; a man much in advance of his time—one of the pioneers of free thought, suffering for the sacred cause, as pioneers in all great movements always suffer. He spoke with a modest fearlessness known sometimes to youth and to few men. Mr. Barringer replied that, though he held different views, he could not but admire Willard's frankness in avowing his own political convictions, and that this independence in principle would in nowise detract from his previously formed good opinion of him. Afterwards, Mr. Barringer examined him in the common English branches of study, besides astronomy, philosophy and algebra—studies usually taught in the public schools of Rensselaer County. In this way, with much pleasant talk dropped at intervals through the official business of examination, prefaced at length with politics and concluded with social chat, an agreeable evening passed.

Mr. Barringer at last said good-night to the young Normal student, with the remark that he would see what could be done for him in the morning.

Not much sleep visited Willard's eyes that night, with the ghost of possible defeat haunting his wakeful senses, stretched to their utmost tension of anxiety.

Would he, or would he not, receive in the morning the certificate he sought? This was the thought tossed continually up on the topmost wave of his consciousness all the night long. Morning dawned at last, much to his relief. When Mr. Barringer came to his door to announce breakfast, he handed Willard the coveted piece of paper.

"Now then," said he, cheerily, "here is your certificate, and as I am going to drive down to Albany after breakfast, if you have no particular school in view, I shall be glad to have you ride with me as far as Schodack Centre, where I have some very good friends, and will introduce you to the trustees of the district, Messrs. Brockway, Hover and Knickerbocker."

Accordingly they drove over to the residence of Milton Knickerbocker, school trustee of District No. 7, of the town of Schodack.

That gentleman thanked the School Commissioner for bringing the young teacher over, said that he would be pleased to engage him, and that it was only necessary to see another trustee, George Brockway, to make the engagement final. Mr. Knickerbocker then accompanied young Glazier to the residence of Mr. Brockway, where arrangements were made for him to teach the school at Schodack Centre. He then walked back to Albany.

Willard had said nothing to his landlady, on Lydius street, concerning his intended absence, fearing he might have to report the failure of his project, and on the evening of his return to Albany—having been away for thirty-six hours—was surprised to find that the family were just about to advertise him in the city papers, thinking some strange fate had befallen him, or that he had perhaps committed suicide.

In just one week from the time Glazier engaged his school at Schodack Centre, he returned to that place, and taught the young Schodackers successfully through the specified term, after which he went to Albany and passed the next Normal School term. On the twelfth of July following, he left Albany for the home farm, where he worked until the first of September. He then went on a prospecting tour out to Edwards, near the field of his former efforts, and canvassed for scholars at two dollars each, for a term of eight weeks. His object was to teach during the fall and winter months and return to Albany in the spring. This energetic youth of eighteen succeeded in obtaining about thirty pupils, among whom were six teachers—one of them having taught four terms.

Among the incidents of his school experience at this

time may be mentioned the fact of a series of drill tactics, originated by himself, with which he practised his pupils so thoroughly that they were enabled to go through all the regular evolutions set down in Hardee. Yet he had never seen the drill-book.

It may be regarded as one of those outcroppings of his natural bent towards the military art which he displayed from his very infancy; for true military genius, like true poetical genius, is born, not made. Of course our young tactician soon made himself known, and throughout the district he was distinguished by the title of the "Soldier-Schoolmaster."

It was an involuntary tribute yielded by public sentiment to the boy who afterwards became the "Soldier-Author."

This boy-teacher, young as he was, marshalled all his pupils into disciplined order, like the rank and file of the army, and somehow held natural words of command at his disposal whereby he wielded the human material given into his charge, as a general might wield the forces under his command. The school was his miniature world and he was its master—his diminutive kingdom wherein he was king; and within the boundary of this chosen realm his sway was absolute.

First the "Soldier-Schoolmaster," drilling his boy-pupils; then the Soldier of the Saddle, riding through shot and shell and war's fierce din on Virginia's historic fields; and last, but perhaps not least, the "Soldier-Author," winning golden opinions from press and people; through all these changes of his life, from boy to man, one characteristic shows plain and clear —his military bent. It is like the one bright stripe through a neutral ground, the one vein of ore deposit through the various stratifications of its native rock.

The Edwards Select School was continued until the first of November, when Glazier left home once more, this time in company with his sister Marjorie, bound for Troy. On arriving at that city he left his sister at the house of an old friend, Alexander McCoy, and went down into Rensselaer County a second time in search of a school, or rather two schools —one for his sister as well as one for himself. He succeeded in obtaining both of them on the same day, and went back to Troy that night. His own district was East Schodack, near Schodack Centre, where he had previously taught, and his sister secured the school two miles north of the village of Castleton and six miles distant from Albany.

The little school-house near Castleton, where his sister taught, was located in a lovely spot on a height overlooking the Hudson and commanding a fine view of the river and the surrounding scenery.

During the school term taught in their respective districts, it was Willard's habit to visit his sister once a week, on Saturday or Sunday, and on several occasions a gentleman living at East Schodack, William Westfall by name, who owned a fine horse and sleigh, loaned him the use of his establishment to drive to Castleton and return. The sleigh was provided with warm robes of fur and the horse was beyond doubt spirited, and a handsome specimen of the genus horse. But as we cannot look for absolute perfection in anything pertaining to earth, it may be stated that this animal was no exception to the universal rule. He had his fault, as young Glazier discovered—a disagreeable habit of running away every time he saw a train of cars. Perhaps the horse couldn't help it; it was no doubt an inherited disposition, descended to him through long lines of fractious ancestors, and therefore it need not be set down against him in the catalogue of wilful sins. But whether so or otherwise, this little unpleasantness in his disposition was an established fact, and unfortunately there were two railroads to cross between East Schodack and Castleton. On Glazier's first ride to Castleton with the Westfall horse and sleigh, he had just crossed the Boston and Albany Railroad when a freight-train rolled heavily by, which put the horse under excellent headway, and on reaching the Hudson River Railroad—the two tracks running very near each other—a passenger train came up behind him. This completed the aggregation of causes, and away flew the horse down the road to Castleton at break-neck speed. Fences disappeared like gray streaks in the distance; roadside cottages came in view and were swiftly left behind in the track of the foam-flecked animal. All that Glazier could do was to keep him in the road, until at length an old shed by the roadside served his purpose, and running him into it, the horse, puffing and snorting, was obliged to stop. On his return to East Schodack, Mr. Westfall asked him how he liked the horse. He replied that he thought the animal a splendid traveler. He *did* think so, beyond question.

The next Sunday young Glazier was driving again to Castleton with the same stylish turn-out; this time with his sister Marjorie in the sleigh. She had come up to East Schodack the evening before, and he was taking her back to her school. The sleighing was excellent, the day fine, and all went merry as a marriage bell until they reached the railroad. There the inevitable train of cars loomed in view, and the puff, puff of the engine, sending out great volumes of steam and its wild screech at the crossing, completely upset what few ideas of propriety and steady travel this horse may have had in his poor, bewildered head, and, with a leap and a jerk, he was once more running away on the Castleton Road as if the entire host of the infernal regions were let loose was after him.

For a little while he made things around them as lively as a pot of yeast. Away went whip, robes, mittens and everything else lying loose in the bottom of the sleigh at all calculated to yield to the vortex of a whirlwind or a runaway. But Glazier proved himself master of the situation in this as in many another event of his life, and with one hand holding his frightened sister from jumping out of the sleigh, with the other he twisted the lines firmly around his wrist and kept the horse in the road, until, at the distance of three-quarters of a mile beyond Castleton, he brought the infuriated animal to a stand-still by running him against the side of a barn. Afterwards he drove leisurely back and picked up the robes and whip and lost articles spilled during the wild runaway ride.

A broken shaft was the only result of this last adventure, which Glazier of course, put in repair before his return to East Schodack. Mr. Westfall never knew until after the close of the school term that his horse had afforded the young teacher an opportunity to tell what he knew about runaways.

The school at East Schodack closed with an exhibition exceedingly creditable to the efforts of the teacher,

A TRIBUTE TO MERIT. 117

at which Mr. Allen Barringer was present, and in a speech before the school complimented young Glazier in the highest terms. The programme of exercises was an excellent one, and was made up of original addresses, declamations, recitations and music. After the close of the school, Mr. Barringer presented Glazier with a certificate which entitled him to teach for three years, and also gave him in addition the following letter of recommendation—a tribute of which any young teacher might be justly proud, and which he carefully preserved:

"To Whom it May Concern:

"This is to certify, that I am well acquainted with Willard Glazier, he having taught school during the winters of 1859 and '60 in my Commission District. I consider him one of the most promising young teachers of my acquaintance. The school that has the good fortune to secure his services will find him one of the most capable and efficient teachers of the day.

"ALLEN BARRINGER,
"School Commissioner, Rensselaer County.
"SCHODACK, New York, 1860."

Early in the year 1860 he resumed his studies at the State Normal School, and remained at that institution until the guns of Sumter sounded their war-cry through the land.

This period was the great turning-point in Willard Glazier's life, and hereafter we encounter him in a far different *rôle*.

CHAPTER XI.

INTRODUCTION TO MILITARY LIFE.

The mutterings of war.—Enlistment.—At Camp Howe.—First experience as a soldier.—"One step to the front!"—Beyond Washington.—On guard.—Promotion.—Recruiting service.—The deserted home on Arlington Heights."—How shall I behave in the coming battle?"—The brave Bayard.—On the march.—The stratagem at Falmouth Heights.—A brilliant charge.—After the battle.

THE irresistible results of the discord so long pending between North and South accumulated day by day; and when, at length, Abraham Lincoln was elected by a large popular majority, that election was, as everybody knows, immediately followed by the calling of the Southern States Convention, the secession, one after another, of each of those States, the capture of Fort Sumter, the killing of Ellsworth, and the defeat of the Federal troops at Bull Run. All of these occurrences contributed to inflame the passions, intensify the opinions, and arouse the enthusiasm of the people of both sections to fever-heat.

It was in the whirl and torrent of this popular storm that Willard Glazier was caught up and swept into the ranks of the Union army.

His regiment, the Harris Light Cavalry, was originally intended for the regular service—to rank as the Seventh Regular Cavalry. The general government, however, concluded to limit the number of their regiments of horse to six—the reasons for which are

CAVALRY COLUMN ON THE MARCH.

given by Captain Glazier in his "Soldiers of the Saddle," as follows:

"Under the military *régime* of General Scott, the cavalry arm of the service had been almost entirely overlooked. His previous campaigns in Mexico, which consisted chiefly of the investment of walled towns and of assaults on fortresses, had not been favorable to extensive cavalry operations, and he was not disposed, at so advanced an age in life, materially to change his tactics of war."

Hence, this regiment was mustered into service as the "Second Regiment of New York Cavalry," and, as Senator Ira Harris had extended to the organization the influence of his name and purse, it soon came to be called the "Harris Light Cavalry," and retained that title throughout the whole of its eventful career. The natural tastes of young Glazier led him into this branch of the service in preference to the infantry, and we find him writing to his sister as follows:

CAMP HOWE, near SCARSDALE, NEW YORK,
August 16*th*, 1861.

MY DEAR SISTER: From the post-mark of this letter you will at once conjecture the truth ere I tell it to you, and I can fancy your saying to yourself when you glance at it: "Willard is no longer talking about becoming, but really *has* become a soldier." You are right. I am now a soldier.

Many of our home friends will doubtless wonder why I have sacrificed my professional prospects at a time when they first began to look cheering, in order to share the hardships and perils of a soldier's life. But I need not explain, to *you*, my reasons for doing so. When our country is threatened with destruction by base and designing men, in order to gratify personal ambition and love of sway, it becomes her sons to go to her rescue and avert the impending ruin. The rebelling South has yet to learn the difference between the *true principles* of the Constitution and the *delusion* of "State rights." It is as easy to die a volunteer as a drafted soldier, and in my opinion, is infinitely more honorable. I shall return to my studies as soon as the Rebellion is put down and the authority of our Government fully restored, and not *until* then.

Let me give you a sketch of our movements thus far. Having reached Troy at 3 o'clock on the afternoon of the day you and I parted, I spent the remainder of the evening until 8 o'clock in the city. At that hour we embarked for New York, and the boys had a very exciting and enthusiastic time on board the Hudson River boat. Wednesday was spent at 648 Broadway, Regimental Headquarters of the "Harris Light Cavalry;" and on that night we came by train to our present camp: or, rather, as near it as we could, for it is two miles from the nearest station. The spot is picturesque enough to be described. An old farm, surrounded by stone fences that looked like ramparts, constitutes the camp. The Hudson and Harlem rivers are in full view, and the country around is full of beauty. On the first night we *bivouacked* upon the bare sod, with no covering for our bodies but the broad canopy of heaven. It was not until late on the following afternoon that our white tents began to dot the ground and gleam whitely through the dark foliage of the trees.

Crowds of visitors from the neighboring village come out every day to see us. My health was never better, and this sort of life affords me keen enjoyment. The very roughness of it is invigorating. My present writing-desk is the top of the stone wall I have alluded to, so you must criticise neither my penmanship nor my style. I received a letter from father on Tuesday afternoon, and, thank God! I enter the service with his full approbation The discipline enforced here is rigid, our rations are good, fruit is very abundant, and to be had for the asking; so that if you will only write soon and often, there will be little else required to fill the wants of
Your affectionate brother, WILLARD.

Fortunately for their future comfort, the Harris Light Cavalry, at the very outset of its military career, was placed under the charge of a rigid and skilful disciplinarian—one Captain A. N. Duffié—who, having graduated honorably at the celebrated French military school, St. Cyr, possessed all the martial enthusiasm as well as personal peculiarities of his excitable countrymen.

The captain either was, or believed himself to be, an eloquent speaker, and his efforts at rhetorical display, added to his French accentuation of English words, became a source of great amusement to the men. He was wont to harangue them, as if they were about to enter upon a sanguinary battle. The old stone walls of the peaceful farm were pictured as bristling with the enemy's bayonets, and the boys were called on to "charge" at the hidden foe and capture him.

"One morning," says Captain Glazier, "after a week spent in drill, we were all surprised by receiving an order to 'fall into line,' and discovered that the object of this movement was to listen to a Napoleonic harangue from Captain Duffié. So loud had been our protests, so manifest our rebellious spirit on the subject of fortifying a peaceful farm on the banks of the Hudson, that the captain undoubtedly feared he might not be very zealously supported by us in his future movements, and, like Napoleon on assuming command of the Army of Italy, sought to test the devotion of his men. After amusing us a while in broken English, appealing to our patriotism and honor, he at length shouted:

"'Now, as many of you as are ready to follow me to the cannon's mouth, take one step to the front!'

"This *ruse* was perfectly successful, and the whole line took the desired step."

The time passed pleasantly enough in this camp of instruction, despite the monotony of drill and guard duty, and, by the time the order to break camp reached the men, they were well advanced in the duties of the soldier.

The regiment left Camp Howe about the end of

August, and, passing through New York, entered that most beautiful and patriotic of cities, Philadelphia, where they were royally entertained by the managers of the "Volunteer Refreshment Saloon." They at length reached Washington and encamped a half mile beyond the Capitol.

From this point Glazier writes to his mother as follows:

CAMP OREGON, WASHINGTON, D. C., August 28th, 1861.

DEAR MOTHER: I am at present seated under the branches of a large peach tree that marks the spot where two sentinels of our army, while on duty last night, were shot by the rebels. I was one of the same guard, having been assigned to such duty for the first time since entering the service. Like all other sentinels, I was obliged to walk my lonely beat with drawn sabre.

It may interest you to know where I walked my first beat. It was in front of the residence of a rabid secessionist, who is now an officer in the famous Black-Horse Cavalry. You may remember that this regiment was reported to have been utterly destroyed at Bull Run, and yet I am informed by Washingtonians that it had but two companies in the fight.

So much for newspaper gossip.

During the day I was very kindly treated by the family of this gentleman, but in the evening our camp commander came to me and said: "Take this revolver, and if you value your life, be vigilant.

"*Remember, you are not at Scarsdale now!*"

He, of course, referred to our old camp near Scarsdale, twenty-four miles from New York. Our present one is a little over half a mile from the Capitol, and from my tent I can see the dome of that building, glittering, like a ball of gold, in the sunlight.

Yesterday I paid a visit to the city. The streets were crowded with infantry, artillery and cavalry soldiers, all actively engaged in preparing for the coming conflict. An engagement seems to be close at hand. Entrenchments are being dug and batteries erected in every direction. The citizens do not apprehend any danger from an attack by the enemy.

My regiment has been attached to Brigadier-General Baker's

Brigade. It will be three weeks to-morrow since I enlisted. I have been in this camp one week, and one week was spent at Camp Howe, Scarsdale, New York.

We are being rapidly prepared for field service. Our drill is very rigid, yet I submit to the discipline willingly, and I find that hard study is as essential to the composition of a good soldier as to a good teacher. I have purchased a copy of the "Cavalry Tactics," and devote every leisure hour to its mastery. There is but one thing which gives me any serious annoyance now, and that is the question of the ways and means for the education of my brothers and sisters. I cannot assist them at present, though they will ever have my best wishes. I think Elvira and Marjorie had better teach this winter, and then, if the war should be concluded before next spring, I will make arrangements for their attendance at school again. With kindest love to all, I am your loving and dutiful son,

WILLARD.

About two months more were occupied by the Harris Light in camp-duty, scouting and foraging, but almost immediately after their arrival in Virginia, young Glazier was promoted to the rank of Corporal. Shortly after his promotion he was detailed for recruiting service and sent to the city of New York for that purpose. The great city was in a turmoil of excitement.

The "Tammany" organization carried things with a high hand, and was opposed by the equally powerful Union League. Between these two centres the current of public opinion ran in strong tides. But, in the midst of it all, the young corporal was successful in his recruiting service, and on the second day of December rejoined his comrades, who were then at Camp Palmer, Arlington Heights.

This spot was one of peculiar beauty. Its associations were hallowed. There stood the ancestral home of the Lees, whose deserted rooms seemed haunted with memories of a noble race. Its floors had echoed to the tread of youth and beauty. Its walls had witnessed gatherings of renown. From its portals rode General Lee to take command of the Richmond troops —a man who must be revered for his qualities of heart and remembered especially by the North as one who, amid all the fury of passion which the war engendered, was never betrayed into an intemperate expression towards the enemy. *Now,* the halls and porches of the quaint old building rang with the tread of armed men. Its rooms were despoiled, and that atmosphere of desolation which ever clings about a deserted home, enveloped the place. A winding roadway under thick foliaged trees, led down the Heights to the " Long Bridge," crossing the Potomac. Near the house stood an old-fashioned " well sweep " which carried a moss-covered bucket on its trips down the well, to bring up the most sparkling of water. Instinctively a feeling of sadness took possession of the heart at the mournful contrast between the past and present of this beautiful spot.

> "Ah, crueler than fire or flood
> Come steps of men of alien blood,
> And silently the treacherous air
> Closes—and keeps no token, where
> Its dead are buried."

The day of trial—the baptism of battle—seemed rapidly approaching. General McClellan, having drilled and manœuvred and viewed and reviewed the Army of the Potomac, until what had been little better than an armed and uniformed mob began to assume the aspect of a body of regulars, determined upon an advance movement. Accordingly on the third of March, 1862, the army marched upon Centreville, captured the "Quaker" guns and, much to the disgust of his followers, fell back upon his original position, instead of continuing the advance.

As the Harris Light enjoyed throughout this campaign of magnificent possibilities, the honor of being "Little Mac's" body guard, they were of course during the forward movement in high spirits. They believed it to be the initial step to a vigorous campaign in which they might hold the post of honor. But when the order to fall back came, their disappointment was great indeed. At first they were mystified, but it soon leaked out that a council of war had been held and that McClellan's plan of the Peninsular Campaign had been adopted.

It had also been determined that a section of the army should be left behind, under the command of General Irvine McDowell, to guard the approaches to Washington.

The First Pennsylvania Cavalry, under the command of General (then Colonel) George Dashiel Bayard, and the Harris Light, remained with the latter force. Under such a leader as Bayard, the men could have no fear of rusting in inactivity. He was the soul of honor, the bravest of the brave. No more gallant spirit ever took up the sword, no kinder heart ever tempered valor, no life was more stainless, no death could be more sad; for the day that was appointed for his nuptials closed over his grave.

Judson Kilpatrick, one of those restless, nervous, energetic and self-reliant spirits who believe in themselves thoroughly, and make up in activity what they lack in method, was Colonel of the Harris Light, and the dawning glory of young Bayard's fame excited a spirit of emulation, if not of envy in his heart, which found vent in a very creditable desire to equal or excel that leader in the field. The brilliant night attack on Falmouth Heights was one of the first results of this rivalry, and as it was also the initial battle in Corporal Glazier's experience, we give his own vivid description of it as it is found in "Three Years in the Federal Cavalry."

"Our instructions," he says, "were conveyed to us in a whisper. A beautiful moonlight fell upon the scene, which was as still as death; and with proud determination the two young cavalry chieftains moved forward to the night's fray. Bayard was to attack on the main road in front, but not until Kilpatrick had commenced operations on their right flank, by a detour through a narrow and neglected wood-path. As the Heights were considered well-nigh impregnable, it was necessary to resort to some stratagem, for which Kilpatrick showed a becoming aptness.

"Having approached to within hearing distance of the rebel pickets, but before we were challenged, Kilpatrick shouted with his clear voice, which sounded like a trumpet on the still night air:

"'Bring up your artillery in the centre, and infantry on the left!'

"'Well, but, Colonel,' said an honest but obtuse Captain, ' we haven't got any inf—'

"'Silence in the ranks!' commanded the leader. 'Artillery in the centre, infantry on the left!'

"The pickets caught and spread the alarm and thus greatly facilitated our hazardous enterprise.

"'Charge!' was the order which then thrilled the ranks, and echoed through the dark, dismal woods;

NIGHT ATTACK ON FALMOUTH HEIGHTS.

and the column swept up the rugged heights in the midst of blazing cannon and rattling musketry.

"So steep was the ascent that not a few saddles slipped off the horses, precipitating their riders into a creek which flowed lazily at the base of a hill; while others fell dead and dying, struck by the missiles of destruction which filled the air. But the field was won, and the enemy, driven at the point of the sabre, fled unceremoniously down the heights, through Falmouth and over the bridge which spanned the Rappahannock, burning that beautiful structure behind them, to prevent pursuit."

This engagement, while otherwise of but little importance, was valuable because it taught the enemy that the Federals could use the cavalry arm of the service as effectively as their infantry.

All accounts agree that Corporal Glazier acquitted himself very creditably in his first battle. After the action was over he accompanied his comrades to the field and contributed his best aid towards the care of the wounded and the unburied dead. Such an experience was full of painful contrast to the quiet scenes of home and school life to which he had hitherto been accustomed. In his history, as with thousands of other brave boys who missed death through many battles, this period was the sharp prelude to a long experience of successive conflicts, of weary marches seasoned with hunger, of prison starvation and the many privations which fall to the lot of the soldier, all glorified when given freely in the defence of liberty and country.

CHAPTER XII.

FIRST BATTLE OF BRANDY STATION.

The sentinel's lonely round.—General Pope in command of the army.—Is gunboat service effective?—First cavalry battle of Brandy Station.—Under a rain of bullets.—Flipper's orchard.—"Bring on the brigade, boys!"—Capture of Confederate prisoners.—Story of a revolver.—Cedar Mountain.—Burial of the dead rebel.—Retreat from the Rapidan.—The riderless horse.—Death of Captain Walters.

THE Harris Light now entered upon exciting times, and Corporal Glazier, ever at the post of duty, had little leisure for anything unconnected with the exigencies of camp and field. At that period the men of both armies were guilty of the barbarous practice of shooting solitary sentinels on their rounds, and no man went on guard at night without feeling that an inglorious death might await him in the darkness, while deprived of the power to strike a defensive blow, or to breathe a prayer.

On the twenty-second of July, 1862, a new commander was assigned the Army of Virginia in the person of General John Pope. General McClellan had lost the confidence of the Northern people by his continued disasters, and was at length superceded by General Pope, who was placed at the head of the united commands of Fremont, Banks, McDowell (and later in August), Burnside and Fitz-John Porter. General Pope commenced his duties with a ringing address to the army under his command. Among other things, he declared: "That he had heard much of 'lines of communication and retreat,' but the only *line* in his opinion, that a general should know anything about, *was the line of the enemy's retreat."* The dash of such a theory of war was extremely invigorating, and once more the hearts of the Northern people cherished and exulted in the hope that they had found the "right man for the right place." Popular enthusiasm reacted upon the army; their idol of yesterday was dethroned, and they girded their loins for a renewal of the struggle, in the full belief that, with Pope to lead them, they would write a very different chapter upon the page of History, from that which recorded their Peninsular campaign.

Here we desire to correct a statement, then current, regarding the value of the gunboat service, viz., that McClellan's army was indebted for its safety during the retreat from Malvern Hill to the gunboats stationed in James river. That this was not the case is proven by the testimony of L. L. Dabney, chief-of-staff to General T. J. Jackson. He says: "It is a fact worthy of note, that the fire of the gunboats, so much valued by the Federals, and, at one time, so much dreaded by the Confederates, had no actual influence whatever in the battle. The noise and fury doubtless produced a certain effect upon the emotions of the assailants, but this was dependent upon their novelty. The loss effected by them was trivial when compared with the ravages of the field artillery; and it was found chiefly among their own friends. Far more of their ponderous missiles fell within their own lines than within those of the Confederates. Indeed, a fire directed at an invisible foe across two or three miles of intervening hills and woods can never reach its aim, save by accident. Nor is the havoc wrought by the larger projectiles in proportion to their magnitude. Where one of them explodes against a human body it does, indeed, crush it into a frightful mass, but it is not more likely to strike more men, in the open order of field operations, than a shot of less pounds; and the wretch blown to atoms by it is not put *hors de combat* more effectually than he whose brain is penetrated by half an ounce of lead or iron. The broadside of a modern gunboat may consist of three hundred pounds of iron projected by forty pounds of powder, but it is fired from only *two* guns. The effect upon a line of men, therefore, is but one-fifteenth of that which the same metal might have had, fired from ten-pounder rifled guns."

The truth of the matter is, that so far as offensive operations in conjunction with that army were concerned, the gunboats were more ornate than useful; and it is not just that the modicum of glory (mingled with so much of disaster), won fairly upon that occasion by the land forces, should be awarded to another branch of the service.

General Pope was not permitted to remain long before an opportunity offered for practically testing his war theories. McClellan's troops had scarcely recovered breath after their retreat from before Richmond when Lee, leaving his entrenchments, boldly threw himself forward and met Pope and the Union forces, face to face on the old battle-ground of Manassas. The Harris Light, prior to the second battle of Bull Run, had been offered, and eagerly accepted,

ILLICIT TRADING ON THE RAPPAHANNOCK.

an opportunity to cross swords with the "Southern chivalry," and the result now was a desperate encounter at Brandy Station. The first action which baptized in blood this historic ground took place August twentieth, 1862. About six o'clock in the morning a heavy column of Stuart's cavalry was discovered approaching from the direction of Culpepper, and Kilpatrick received orders to check their advance. The Harris Light, acting as rear-guard of Bayard's brigade, kept the enemy in check until Bayard could form his command at a more favorable point two miles north of the station. Corporal Glazier was in the front rank of the first squadron that led the charge, and repulsed the enemy. His horse was wounded in the neck, and his saddle and canteen perforated with bullets.

The fight at Flipper's Orchard preceded that at Brandy Station by more than a month, having occurred on the Fourth of July. The Troy company of the Harris Light had been ordered, about eight o'clock in the morning of that day, to reconnoitre the Telegraph Road, south of Fredericksburg. Leaving camp, they soon came in sight of a detachment of Bath cavalry on patrol duty, escorting the Richmond mail. They learned the strength of the enemy from some colored people along the route, and also the probability that they would halt at Flipper's Orchard for refreshments. This place was on the south bank of the Po River, some twenty miles from Fredericksburg, in an angle formed by the roads leading to Bull Church and the Rappahannock. After following them for several hours, the company halted for consultation, "and," says Glazier, "our lieutenant put the question to vote, whether we should go on and capture the foe, about one hundred strong, or return to camp. The vote was unanimous for battle. I was in charge of the advance guard, having a squad of four men, and received orders to strike a gallop. Just as we came within sight of the Orchard, we saw the Confederates dismounting and making leisurely arrangements for their repast. Dashing spurs into our horses' flanks, we wheeled round the corner and along the Bull Church Road, sweeping down upon them with tremendous clatter. 'Here they are, boys!' I shouted; 'bring up the brigade!' We were about forty in number, but surprised them completely, and they fled panic-stricken. Twelve men and nine horses were captured. On reaching Dr. Flipper's house, I noticed a dismounted Confederate officer who, with others, was running across a wheat-field. I started in hot pursuit, jumping my horse over a six-rail fence to reach him. He fired upon me with both carbine and revolver, but missed his mark, and by this time I stood over him with my navy-revolver, demanding his surrender. He gave up his arms and equipments, which were speedily transferred to my own person. We made quick work of the fight, the whole affair lasting not longer than fifteen minutes. The Confederate reserves were only a short distance off at Bull Church, and we hurried back with our spoils towards the Rappahannock, fearful that we might be overtaken. My prisoner, as I afterward learned, was Lieutenant Powell, in command of the patrol. His revolver has a story of its own. It was a beautiful silver-mounted weapon, and I resolved to keep possession of it as my especial trophy, instead of turning it over to the Quartermaster's Department.

This was not an easy matter, as vigilant eyes were on the look-out for all 'munitions of war captured from the enemy,' which were consigned to a common receptacle. I therefore dug a hole in the ground of our tent and buried my treasure, where it remained until we changed our encampment. One day, some time after, I carelessly left it lying on a log, a short distance from camp, and on returning found it gone. While I stood there deploring my ill luck, I heard a succession of clear, snapping shots just beyond a rise of ground directly in front of me, and recognized the familiar report of my revolver. Going in the direction of the shots, I rescued it from the hands of a sergeant by whom it had been temporarily confiscated. After this adventure I concluded to incur no further risks with the weapon, and so packed it in a cigar-case and sent it to my sister Elvira."

The battle of Cedar Mountain, fought on the afternoon of August ninth, 1862, needs only a passing notice in connection with this record. The battalion in which Corporal Glazier served acted as body-guard to General McDowell, and arrived on the field just as the wave of battle was receding. The following morning, on passing over the slopes of Cedar Mountain, where the guns of General Banks had made sad havoc on the previous day, a dead Confederate soldier, partially unburied, attracted the attention of the troopers. At that period of the war a sentiment of extreme bitterness toward the adversary pervaded the ranks on both sides, and as the squadron swept by the men showered on the poor dead body remarks expressive of their contempt. Corporal Glazier was an exception. Moved by an impulse born of our common humanity, he returned and buried the cold, stark corpse, covering it with mother Earth; and when questioned why he gave such consideration to a miserable dead rebel, replied, that he thought any man brave enough to die for a principle, should be respected for that bravery, whether his cause were right or wrong.

On the eighteenth of the month our cavalry relieved the infantry on the line of the Rapidan, and on the nineteenth, in a sharp skirmish between Stuart's and Bayard's forces, Captain Charles Walters, of the Harris Light Cavalry, was killed. This officer was very popular in the regiment, and his death cast a gloom over all. Wrapped in a soldier's blanket his body was consigned to a soldier's grave at the solemn hour of midnight. And while the sad obsequies were being performed, orders came for the retreat to Culpepper.

> "We buried him darkly at dead of night,
> The sod with our bayonets turning
> By the struggling moonbeam's misty light,
> And our lanterns dimly burning.
> . . . . .
> "Slowly and sadly we laid him down,
> On the field of his fame fresh and gory;
> We carved not a line, we raised not a stone,
> But left him alone with his glory."

BURIAL OF CAPTAIN WALTERS AT MIDNIGHT, DURING POPE'S RETREAT.

CHAPTER XIII.

MANASSAS AND FREDERICKSBURG.

Manassas.—The flying troops.—The unknown hero.—Desperate attempt to stop the retreat.—Recruiting the decimated ranks.—Fredericksburg.—Bravery of Meagher's brigade.—The impregnable heights.—The cost of battles.—Death of Bayard.—Outline of his life.

THE plains of Manassas still speak to us. The smoke of battle that once hung over them has long since rolled away, but the blood of over forty thousand brave men of both North and South who here met, and fighting fell to rise no more, consecrates the soil. Between them and us the grass has grown green for many and many a summer, but it cannot hide the memory of their glorious deeds. From this altar of sacrifice the incense yet sweeps heavenward. The waters of Bull Run Creek swirl against their banks as of old, and, to the heedless passer-by, utter nothing of the despairing time when red carnage held awful sway, and counted its victims by the thousand; yet, if one strays hitherward who can listen to the mystic language of the waves, they will reword their burden of death and of dark disaster which " followed fast and followed faster," and at last overtook the devoted Northern army, and made wild confusion and wilder flight.

No general description of the battle need be given here. That portion only which concerns the subject of this biography, now promoted to the rank of Sergeant, will be set in the framework of these pages. Concerning the part which he took in the action, and which occurred under his own observation, he says:

"On the eventful thirtieth—it was August, 1862— our artillery occupied the crest of a hill a short distance beyond Bull Run Creek, the cavalry regiments under Bayard being stationed next, and the infantry drawn up in line behind the cavalry.

"A short time before the battle opened, I was sent to a distant part of the field to deliver an order. An ominous stillness pervaded the ranks. The pickets as I passed them were silent, with faces firmly set towards the front, and the shadow of coming battle hovered portentously, like a cloud with veiled lightnings, over the Union lines.

"It was the calm which precedes a storm, and the thunderbolts of war fell fast and heavy when the storm at length broke over our heads. I had just taken my place in the cavalry ranks when a shell from the enemy's guns whizzed over our heads with a long and spiteful shriek. One of the horses attached to a caisson was in the path of the fiery missile, and the next instant the animal's head was severed entirely from his neck. The deathly silence was now broken, and more shot and shell followed in quick succession, plowing through the startled air and falling with destructive force among the Union troops. This iron hail from the guns of the enemy was composed in part of old pieces of chain and broken iron rails, as well as the shot and shell ordinarily used. Our artillery soon replied, but from some unexplained cause the Union troops in this portion of our line broke and fled in panic before a shot had been fired from the muskets of the enemy. This battle, like the first Bull Run, had been well planned, and every effort which good generalship and good judgment could dictate in order to insure success, had been made by Generals Pope and McDowell.

"At this crisis of affairs, the cavalry under Bayard and Kilpatrick were ordered to the rear, to stem, if possible, the tide of retreat, but the effort was well nigh fruitless. Regiment after regiment surged by in one continuous and almost resistless wave. A cheer was heard to go up from the Confederate ranks as Stuart's cavalry charged us, and though we returned the charge it did not stop the panic which had taken possession of our troops.

"One of its causes was undoubtedly the supposition that the enemy was executing a flank movement on our left. In forty-five minutes from the beginning of the battle, this part of the army was in full retreat; but the determined stand made by Heintzelman, and also one or two heroic attempts to stop the backward-surging wave, saved our forces from utter rout and possible capture.

"As soon as the Union batteries were taken by the enemy, they were turned upon us, in addition to their own guns, and afterwards, on came Stuart in a headlong charge with one of those hideous yells peculiar to the Southern 'chivalry.' With thousands of others who were rapidly retiring, I had recrossed Bull Run Creek when my attention was arrested by a mounted officer who sprang out from the mass of flying men, and waving his sword above his head, called on every one, irrespective of regiment, to rally around him and face the foe. He wore no golden leaf—no silver star. He was appealing to officers higher in command than himself, who, mixed with the crowd, were hurrying by. His manner, tense with excitement, was strung up to the pitch of heroism, and his presence was like an inspiration, as he stood outside the mass, a mark for the bullets of the enemy.

"I halted, filled with admiration for so noble an example of valor, and then rode rapidly towards him. Seeing me, he galloped forward to meet me and asked my aid in making a stand against the enemy.

"'Sergeant,' said he, 'you are just in time. As you are mounted, you can be of great service in rallying these men for a stand on this ground.'

"'Lieutenant,' I replied, 'they will not listen to the wearer of these chevrons.'

"'Tear off your chevrons,' said this unknown hero, —'the infantry will not know you from a field officer—and get as many men to turn their muskets to the front as you can.'

"'Lieutenant,' I responded, 'I will do all I can to help you,' and the insignia of non-commissioned rank was immediately stripped from my sleeves.

"I put myself under his command and fought with him until he gave the order to retire. While he was talking with me he was at the same time calling on the men to make a stand, telling them they could easily hold the position. He seemed to take in the situation at a glance.

"The enemy having advanced to the first crest of hills, were throwing their infantry forward with full force, and with the three thousand or more of men who rallied around this heroic officer, a stand was made on the rising ground north of Bull Run from which the advance of the enemy was opposed. We held this position for half an hour, which gave considerable time for reorganization.

"While riding along the line, helping my unknown superior as best I could, my horse was shot—the first experience of this kind which had befallen me.

"Just as the disaster was occurring which culminated in retreat, General McDowell, on his white horse, galloped up to the guns behind which Heintzelman was blazing destruction on the Confederates. Alighting from his horse he sighted the guns and gave a personal superintendence to this part of the action. An artillery captain, standing by his battery while his horses were shot down, his pieces in part disabled, and the infantry deserting him, shed tears in consequence.

"'You need not feel badly over this affair,' said the general, 'General McDowell is responsible for this misfortune. Stand by your guns as long as you can. If the general is blamed, *your* bravery will be praised.'

"Was there a touch of irony in this remark which met in advance the grumblings and questionings of the future? Was it the sarcasm of a man who, having done his utmost, could not yet prevent disaster, and who knew that an unthinking public sometimes measured loyalty by success?

"Later in the day our regiment—the 'Harris Light Cavalry'—lost a squadron. Most of them were killed.

"In the deepening twilight we charged the enemy just as they were forming for a similar attack on us. They were compelled to halt, and Pope was thus enabled to discover their position and arrange for the next day's defence.

"On the night of the thirtieth, the enemy occupied the battle-field and buried the dead of both armies. And thus it was that Bull Run again ran red with patriot blood and witnessed the retreat of the Union battalions.

"By what strange fatality General Pope was allowed to struggle on alone against an army twice the size of the Federal force, has not been satisfactorily explained. One is almost tempted to believe, with astrologists, that baleful stars sometimes preside with malign influence over the destinies of battles, as they are said to do over individuals and nations."

After the battle of Manassas, the Harris Light Cavalry was so reduced in material that it was ordered into camp at Hall's Hill, near Washington, with a view of recruiting its wasted strength and numbers. They remained at that point until November, when they were again moved forward to form the principal picket line along the front, prior to the Federal disaster at Fredericksburg.

Burnside, having strongly secured the mountain passes in the neighborhood, in order to conceal from Lee his real object, made a *feint* in the direction of Gordonsville; but the keen eye of the Confederate generalissimo penetrated his true design and took measures to defeat its accomplishment. Upon the eighth of this month, a lively encounter between the Harris Light and a detachment of Confederate cavalry resulted in the defeat of the latter, and soon after, the regiment joined the main army.

As all know, the battle of Fredericksburg was fought and lost during the three days intervening between the thirteenth and sixteenth of December. Burnside's gallant army, in the midst of darkness, rain and tempestuous wind, came reeling back from a conflict of terrible ferocity and fatality. Six times in one day Meagher's gallant Irishmen were literally hurled against Marye's Heights, a point of almost impregnable strength, and which, even if carried, would still have exposed them to the commanding fire of other and stronger Confederate positions.

Twenty times had charge and counter-charge swept the tide of battle to and fro—at what terrible cost, the killed and wounded, strewing the ground like leaves in the forest, made answer. Twelve thousand men lay dead on the field when the battle ended, and one thousand prisoners were taken, besides nine thousand stand of arms.

Although this battle seems to have been well planned by General Burnside, a want of capacity to meet unforeseen emergencies doubtless contributed to his defeat. He committed a fatal error at a critical moment, by sending General Franklin an equivocal *recommendation*, instead of an *order* to attack the enemy in force. The enemy, however, though having nobly held their ground, could not boast of having advanced their lines by so much as a foot. There were, indeed, but few even of the Confederate officers, who knew they had been victorious, and the amazement of their army was beyond description when the gray dawn of the fourteenth of December revealed the deserted camps of the Federals, who had withdrawn their entire command during the night to the north side of the river.

Had General Franklin brought his men into action, as he should have done, at the critical moment when the issue of the fight was trembling in the balance, the fortunes of this day would have terminated differently. Had the splendid divisions of brave Phil. Kearney or "Fighting Joe. Hooker" been ordered into the arena, and lent the inspiration of their presence to this hour of need, the scales of victory would have turned in an opposite direction.

The "might have beens" always grow thickly from the soil of defeat.

Among the lamented dead of this day's havoc, no loss was more keenly felt than that of Major-General George Dashiel Bayard. He was standing among a group of officers around the trunk of an old tree, near the headquarters of Generals Franklin and Smith, when the enemy suddenly began to shell a battery near by, and one of the deadly missiles struck this gallant leader. He was carried to the field-hospital, mortally wounded.

Quietly turning to the surgeon who examined his ghastly wounds, he asked "if there was any hope." On being informed that there was none, he proceeded with undisturbed composure, and without a murmur of pain, to dictate three letters. One of these was to his affianced bride. This day, it was said, had been appointed for his wedding. The time-hands marked the hour of eight when this letter was finished, and, as he uttered its closing words, his spirit fled from the shattered body and left it only cold and tenantless clay. He was but twenty-eight years of age, of prepossessing appearance and manners, with as brave a soul as ever defended the flag of the Union, and a capacity for military usefulness equal to any man in the service.

Gradually he had arisen from one position of honor and responsibility to another, proving himself tried and true in each promotion, while his cavalry comrades especially were watching the developments of his growing power with unabating enthusiasm.

Briefly, the outlines of his history are as follows:

He was born December eighteenth, 1835, at Seneca Falls, New York, from whence, in 1842, he removed with his parents to Fairfield, Iowa. From this place he went to the Dorris Military Institute at St. Louis, Missouri, where he remained eighteen months.

The family then removed to the East, and settled at Morristown, New Jersey. From Morristown, he entered West Point Academy. When twenty years of age, he graduated with the highest honors, and, strange to say, it was through the offices of Jefferson Davis, then Secretary of War, that he was at once assigned to a cavalry regiment as second lieutenant. His subsequent career, so full of brilliance and the true spirit of heroism, is better known to the country.

Watered by the dews of hallowed remembrance, his fame, as a sweet flower, still exhales its fragrance, and finds rich soil in the hearts of the people.

> "How sleep the brave who sink to rest,
> By all their country's wishes blest?
> When Spring, with dewy fingers cold,
> Returns to deck their hallowed mould,
> She there shall dress a sweeter sod
> Than Fancy's feet have ever trod.
>
> . . . . .
>
> "By fairy hands their knell is rung,
> By forms unseen their dirge is sung,
> There Honor comes, a pilgrim gray,
> To bless the turf that wraps their clay.
> And Freedom shall awhile repair,
> To dwell a weeping hermit there."

CHAPTER XIV.

UNWRITTEN HISTORY.

"What boots a weapon in a withered hand?"—A thunderbolt wasted.—War upon hen-roosts.—A bit of unpublished history.—A fierce fight with Hampton's cavalry.—In one red burial blent.—From camp to home.—Troubles never come singly.—The combat.—The capture.—A superfluity of Confederate politeness.—Lights and shadows.

WHILE the events we have narrated were occurring, the "Harris Light" was not idle. Under the command of their favorite Kilpatrick, they made a dashing raid, and completely encircled the rebels under Lee, penetrating to within seven miles of Richmond. Such duties as were assigned them were effectively performed, and yet, General Hooker's object in detaching his cavalry from the main army remained unaccomplished, either by reason of General Stoneman's want of comprehension, or want of energy. This general, instead of hurling his thirteen thousand troopers like a thunderbolt upon the body of the Confederates, divided and frittered away the strength under his command by detaching and scattering it into mere scouting parties, to "raid on smoke-houses and capture hen-roosts." General Hooker was very naturally exasperated by this conduct. The detachment from the main army of such a splendid body of horse, was a measure he had taken after mature deliberation, and with the view of cutting off Lee's communications with Richmond; thus precluding the possibility of his being reinforced during the grand attack which Hooker contemplated upon that leader at Chancelorsville.

The Federal general attributed the loss of that battle in a great degree to Stoneman's failure to carry out the spirit of his orders. In a letter to the author, long after that field of carnage had bloomed and blossomed with the flowers and fruits of Peace, when the heart-burning and fever engendered by the contest had subsided, and it was possible to obtain access to men's judgments, General Hooker wrote: "Soon after Stonewall Jackson started to turn my right (a project of which I was informed by a prisoner), I despatched a courier to my right corps commander informing him of the intended movement, and instructing him to put himself in readiness to receive the attack. This dispatch was dated at nine o'clock A. M., and yet, when 'Stonewall' did attack, the men of this corps had their arms stacked some distance from them, and were busily engaged in cooking their supper. When the attack came these men ran like a flock of sheep. *This*, in a wooded country, where a *corps* ought to be able to check the advance of a large army. To make this more clear, I must tell you that the corps commander, General Howard, received the dispatch while on his bed, and, after reading it, put it in his pocket, where it remained until after the battle of Gettysburg, without communicating its contents to his division commander, or to any one!!! My opinion is that not a gun of ours was fired upon Stonewall Jackson's force until he had passed nearly into the centre of my army. Judge, if you can, of the consternation throughout that army caused by this exhibition of negligence and cowardice. One word more, in regard to the cavalry.

I had to have, under the seniority rule of the service, a wooden man for its commander. If you will turn to the first volume of the Report of the Committee on the Conduct of the War, you will find my instructions to General Stoneman, and then you will see the mistake that I made in informing him of the strength and position of the enemy he would be likely to encounter on his raid, as that officer only made use of the information to avoid the foe. He traveled at night, made extensive detours, and did not interrupt the traffic on the railroads between Lee's army and Richmond for a single day. As he was charged to make this duty his especial object of accomplishment over all others, he had twelve thousand sabres, double the force the enemy could collect from all quarters. I had men enough with me to have won Chancellorsville without the cavalry and other corps, but of what use could a field of battle have been to me when the enemy could fall back a few miles and post himself on a field possessing still greater advantages to him? General Grant did this, and is entitled to all the merit of his soldiership from a grateful country. I believe if he had sacrificed every officer and soldier of his command in the attainment of this object, the country would have applauded him. When I crossed the Rappahannock I aimed to capture General Lee's whole army and thus end the war, by manœuvring, and not by butchery."

While his superior in command did little that was practically useful with the cavalry, Kilpatrick covered his little band with glory, and gave the people of Richmond a scare as great as Stuart administered to our Quaker friends in Pennsylvania during his famous foray into the border counties of the Keystone State.

THE "HARRIS LIGHT" AT ALDIE. 147

Their return was almost immediately followed by the second grand cavalry battle of Brandy Station, June ninth, 1863, a struggle as hotly contested as any that occurred during the war. In this encounter Sergeant Willard Glazier took part, leading the first platoon of the first battalion that crossed the Rappahannock. Matters were now assuming a warlike aspect. The Valley of the Shenandoah groaned beneath the tramp of the main army of the Confederacy, under Lee. The Federal general, Pleasanton, and the Confederate general, Stuart, were in fierce conflict among the Blue Ridge mountains.

At Aldie, on the seventeenth of June, 1863, the "Harris Light" led the division under Kilpatrick, Glazier's squadron again being the advance guard, his place at the head of the long column which wound down the road. As they came upon Aldie, the enemy's advance, under W. H. F. Lee, was unexpectedly encountered. But Kilpatrick was equal to the occasion. Dashing to the front, his voice rang out, "Form platoons! trot! march!" Down through the streets they charged, and along the Middleburg Road, leading over the low hill beyond. This position was gained so quickly and gallantly that Fitzhugh Lee, taken by surprise, made no opposition to the brilliant advance, though immediately afterward he fought for two hours to regain the lost position, while the guns of his batteries blazed destruction upon the Federal cavalry. The latter, however, handsomely repelled the attack.

On the crest of the hill there was a field of haystacks, inclosed in a barricade of rails. Behind these the enemy occupied a strong position, and their sharpshooters had annoyed Kilpatrick's lines to such an extent as to prevent their advance on the left. It was well known to the officers of the "Harris Light" that their regiment had not met Kilpatrick's expectations on the field of Brandy Station, and on the morning of this battle they had asked their general for "an opportunity to retrieve their reputation." This chance came soon enough. Kilpatrick, ordering forward a battalion of the "Harris Light," and giving the men a few words of encouragement, turned to Major McIrvin and pointing to the field of haystacks, said: "Major, there is the opportunity you ask for! Go take that position!" Away dashed the "Harris Light," and in a moment the enemy was reached and the struggle began. The horses could not leap the barricade, the men dismounted, scaled the barriers, and with drawn sabres rushed furiously upon the hidden foe, who quickly called for quarter. Aldie was by far the most bloody cavalry battle of the war. The rebel "chivalry" was beaten; Kilpatrick from this moment took a proud stand among the most famous of the Union cavalry generals, and the fame of the regiment was greatly enhanced. To quote our young soldier in "Battles for the Union:" "Many a brave soul suffered death's sad eclipse at Aldie, and many escaped the storm of bullets when to escape was miraculous. In looking back upon that desperate day, I have often wondered by what strange fatality I passed through its rain of fire unhurt; but the field which brought a harvest of death to so many others marked an era in my own humble, military history, which I recall with pride and pleasure, for from the Battle of Aldie I date my first commission. The mantle of rank which fell from one whom death had garnered on that ground dropped upon my shoulders, and I was proud and grateful to wear it in my country's service. I feel proud also of having been a participant in the 'Battle of the Haystacks,' where the glorious squadrons of the 'Harris Light' swept into the mad conflict with the same invincible bravery that distinguished them on the field of Brandy Station. Every soldier of the saddle who there fought under Kilpatrick may justly glory in the laurels won at Aldie."

In the same month followed the engagements of Middleburg and Upperville, in each of which the "Harris Light" participated with great éclat, charging in face of the enemy's guns, forming in platoon under fire, and routing him in splendid style. At Upperville, Kilpatrick received orders to charge the town. With drawn sabres and shouts which made the mountains and plains resound, they rushed upon the foe. The encounter was terrific. The enemy's horse were driven through the village of Paris, and finally through Ashby's Gap upon their own infantry columns in the Shenandoah Valley. At Rector's Cross-Roads, where Kilpatrick ordered the "Harris Light" to charge the enemy's battery, as they were forming a fatal bullet pierced Glazier's horse, and it fell dead under him. Fortunately he was not dragged down in the horse's fall, and as he struck the ground, a riderless horse belonging to an Indiana company came up. His owner, a sergeant, had been shot dead, and, rapidly mounting the horse, Glazier rode forward with his regiment as they valiantly charged the enemy's position.

These actions were succeeded by the battle of Gettysburg (July first, second and third), in which the disasters of Chancelorsville and Fredericksburg were fully retrieved, and the rebel army, under Lee, received a blow so staggering in its effects as to result in a loss of prestige, and all hope in the ultimate success of their cause. Prior to this battle the Confederates had warred upon the North aggressively; thenceforward they were compelled to act upon the defensive. During the progress of this great and (so far as the ultimate fate of the Confederacy was concerned) decisive battle, the cavalry, including the brigade to which our subject was attached, performed brilliant service. They held Stuart's force effectually at bay, and while the retreat of the rebel army was in progress their services were in constant requisition. On the first day of the battle, General John Buford, commanding the Third Cavalry Division, was in position on the Chambersburg Pike, about two miles west of the village. Early in the forenoon the vanguard of the rebel army appeared in front of them, and the dauntless troopers charged the enemy vigorously, and drove them back upon their reserves.

The second day of the battle was spent by the cavalry in hard, bold and bloody work, in collision with their old antagonists, Stuart, Lee and Hampton. Charge succeeded charge; the carbine, pistol and sabre were used by turns; the artillery thundering long after the infantry around Gettysburg had sunk to rest exhausted with the carnage of the weary day. Stuart, however, was driven back on his supports, and badly beaten.

Upon the third day the sun rose bright and warm upon the bleached forms of the dead strewn over the bloody field; upon the wounded, and upon long, glistening lines of armed men ready to renew the conflict. Each antagonist, rousing every element of power, seemed resolved upon victory or death. Finally victory saluted the Union banners, and with great loss the rebel army sounded the retreat. "Thus," says Glazier in his "Battles for the Union"—"the Battle of Gettysburg ended—the bloody turning-point of the rebellion —the bloody baptism of the redeemed republic. Nearly twenty thousand men from the Union ranks had been killed and wounded, and a larger number of the rebels, making the enormous aggregate of at least forty thousand, whose blood was shed to fertilize the Tree of Liberty."

During this sanguinary battle, the cavalry were in daily and hourly conflict with the enemy's well-trained horse under their respective dashing leaders. The sabre was no "useless ornament," but a deadly weapon, and "dead cavalrymen" and their dead chargers, were sufficiently numerous to have drawn forth an exclamation of approval from even so exacting a commander as "Fighting Joe Hooker." Haggerstown, Boonsboro', Williamsport and Falling Waters, all attested the great efficiency of the cavalry arm, and at the end of the month it was an assured, confident, and capable body of dragoons, that, according to Captain Glazier, "crossed the Rapidan for, as they believed, the purpose of a continued advance movement against the enemy."

And here, parenthetically, we may observe, that he, and other recent writers (Mr. Lossing being an exception), are scarcely accurate in so designating the river crossed by them as the Rapidan. It was the *chief tributary of the Rappahannock*, while two sister streams, which together form the Pamunkey, are known to local topography as the North and South Rapid Anna rivers.

It was a pleasant locality, and the "Harris Light" encamped there for several weeks, having no occupation more exciting or belligerent than picket duty. Duties of a more stirring character, were, however, awaiting them, and as these are intimately associated with the career of the subject of this history, the delineation of whose life is the purpose of the writer, we will give them something more than a cursory notice.

We will first, however, take the opportunity of introducing a letter from our young cavalryman to his parents, illustrative in some measure of his intelligence and soldierly qualities, while it is no less so of his sense of filial duty:

> Headquarters Harris Light Cavalry,
> Near HARTWOOD CHURCH, VA.
> *August* 22*d*, 1863.

DEAR FATHER AND MOTHER:

Another birthday has rolled around, and finds me still in the army. Two years have passed since we were lying quietly in camp near Washington. Little did I think at that time that the insurrection, which was then in process of organization, was of such mighty magnitude as to be able to continue in its treacherous designs until now. Newspaper quacks and mercenary correspondents kept facts from the public, and published falsehoods in their stead. Experience has at last taught us the true state of things, and we now feel that the great work of putting down the rebellion is to be accomplished only by energy, perseverance and unity. Our cause never looked more favorable than to-day. It is no longer a rumor that Vicksburg and Port-Hudson have fallen, but a stern reality, an actual and glorious victory to our arms, and a sure exposition of the waning strength of the ill-fated Confederacy. Charleston and Mobile must soon follow the example of the West, and then the Army of the Potomac will strike the final blow in Virginia.

Kilpatrick's cavalry is now watching the movements of the enemy on the Rappahannock—his head-quarters being near Hartwood Church. I have seen nothing that would interest you much, save a few expeditions amongst the bushwhackers of Stafford County.

It may not be uninteresting to you to learn that I have just been promoted to a lieutenancy, my commission to date from the seven-

teenth of June. I have received four successive promotions since
my enlistment. Your son can boast that his Colonel says he has
earned his commission. Political or monied influence has had
nothing to do with it. I have been in command of a platoon or
company ever since the thirteenth of last April, and have very frequently been in charge of a squadron. I conclude by asking you to
remember me kindly to all my friends.

And believe me, as ever, your dutiful son,
WILLARD.

It will be remembered that the greater part of the spring of this year (1863), that is, from the time the Federal army moved from its winter-quarters in Stafford and King George counties, and all the early summer, were passed by the belligerent forces in efforts to compel their adversaries to fall back on their respective capitals. The people and the press on both sides were clamoring for the accomplishment of *something definite*, and when Vicksburg fell, and on the stricken field of Gettysburg, victory perched on the Union banner, our hopes seemed on the point of realization, but the fall of the leaf found the hostile armies still confronting each other. Lee's force, though fearfully shattered, maintained its organization, and to all appearance had lost little of its former self-reliance. General Meade, perhaps the most scientific strategist of all the generals who had held the chief command of the Army of the Potomac, was severely criticised, simply because he declined by "raw Haste, half-sister to Delay," to hazard the ultimate fruition of his well-laid plans; and Captain Glazier, it must be admitted, was one of his adverse critics. We think the censure was uncalled for. Wellington had but one Waterloo, and although to him was due the victory, it was the fresh army of Blucher that pursued the retreating French, and made defeat irretrievable. But whenever Lee, or McClellan, Jackson, or Meade obtained a hard-earned victory, the people, on either side, were dissatisfied because their triumph was not followed up by, at once and forever, annihilating the foe!

CHAPTER XV.

FROM BATTLE-FIELD TO PRISON.

A situation to try the stoutest hearts.—Hail Columbia!—Every man a hero.—Kilpatrick's ingenuity.—A pen-picture from "Soldiers of the Saddle."—Glazier thanked by his general.—Cessation of hostilities.—A black day.—Fitzhugh Lee proposes to crush Kilpatrick.—Kil's audacity.—Capture of Lieutenant Glazier.—Petty tyranny.—"Here, Yank, hand me that thar hat, and overcoat, and boots."

AT this period of the war, the cavalry was separated into three divisions. Buford with his division fell back by the way of Stevensburg, and Gregg by Sulphur Springs; leaving Kilpatrick with the brigades of Custer and Davies, which included the "Harris Light," on the main thoroughfare along the railroad line. "No sooner," says Glazier, "had Kilpatrick moved out of Culpepper, than Hampton's cavalry division made a furious attack upon the 'Harris Light,' then acting as rear-guard, with the evident design of breaking through upon the main column to disperse, or delay it, so as to enable a flanking force to intercept our retreat. Gallantly repelling this assault, the command, on the eleventh of October, advanced to Brandy Station, where an accumulation of formidable difficulties threatened our annihilation." It appears that Fitzhugh Lee, with the flower of the Confederate cavalry, had possession of the only road upon which it was possible for Kilpatrick to retire, while Stuart, at the head of another body of cavalry, supported by artillery well posted on a long line of hills, completely covered the Federal left. His right was exposed to a galling fire from sharp-shooters hidden behind the forest; "while just behind them was Hampton's legion threatening speedy destruction to its surrounded foe." Here was a situation to try the stoutest hearts. Nothing daunted, however, by this terrific array of an enemy very much his superior in numbers, Kilpatrick displayed that decision and daring which ever characterized him. "His preparations for a grand charge," for he had determined to cut his way out of this *cul-de-sac*, "were soon completed. Forming his division into three lines of battle, he assigned the right to General Davies, the left to General Custer; and placing himself, with General Pleasanton, in the centre, advanced with terrible determination to the contest. Approaching to within a few yards of the enemy's lines, he ordered the band to strike up a national air, to whose stirring strains was added the blast of scores of bugles ringing out the 'charge.' Brave hearts became braver, and weak ones waxed stronger, until 'pride of country had touched this raging sea of thought, and emotion kindled an unconquerable principle that affirmed every man a hero until death.'" The troops filled the air with their battle-cry, and hurled themselves on their unequal foe. "So swiftly swept forward this tide of animated power that the Confederates broke and fled, and Kilpatrick thus escaped a disaster which had seemed inevitable."

"No one"—we quote from "Soldiers of the Saddle,"—"who looked upon that wonderful panorama, can ever forget it. On the great field were riderless horses and dying men; clouds of dirt from solid shot

LIEUTENANT GLAZIER AT BRANDY STATION.

"Come on, boys! We must break that line."

and bursting shells, broken caissons, and overturned ambulances; and long lines of dragoons dashing into the charge, with their drawn and firmly grasped sabres glistening in the light of the declining sun; while far beyond the scene of tumult were the dark green forests skirting the distant Rappahannock."

In this action Glazier, who occupied the post of volunteer aide to General Davies, had his horse shot under him, received a sabre-stroke on the shoulder, two bullets in his hat, and had his scabbard split by a shot or shell. His conduct was such as to obtain for him the thanks of his general and a promise of early promotion. This was the fourth battle of Brandy Station in which the Harris Light Cavalry had been engaged. The first occurred on August the twentieth, 1862, the second on June ninth, the third on September twelfth, and this last action on October eleventh, 1863. They were followed by a number of spirited engagements between the Federal cavalry and the cavaliers of the South—the former under Generals Buford and Kilpatrick, and the latter under Stuart and Wade Hampton. In all of these both sides behaved gallantly, the result being the masterly retreat of the Federals across the Rappahannock to the old battle-ground of Bull Run, where they made a protracted halt.

From this time until the fifteenth of October, nothing of sufficient importance transpired to require mention here. Upon that day an indecisive battle was fought at Bristoe Station, which was followed by another calm that continued until the nineteenth of October—a black day in the calendar of Willard Glazier's life.

Far away among the peaceful hills of his native

State there fell upon his father's house a sorrow such as its inmates had never known before. Not that this family had escaped the ordinary bereavements of human life. On the contrary, two little children had been taken from them at intervals of time which seemed to them cruelly brief. But the death of an infant, while a sad, is a beautiful thing to witness. There is no flower that blooms on a baby grave that does not speak to the world-worn heart, of *Immortality*. The grief, therefore, is gentle in its touch. But with the ebb of a maturer life the sorrow is of a different character, and when the physician announced to this worthy couple that their daughter, Elvira, would die, they were stunned by the blow, and when the event came " they refused " like Rachel " to be comforted." The child that is going from us is, for the time, the favorite, and these afflicted parents could not realize that she who had grown up among them, the ewe lamb of their flock, could be torn from their loving arms, and go down, like coarser clay, to the dark grave. She was so good, so gentle, so loving to her kindred, that their simple hearts could not understand how God could let her die, in the very bloom and beauty of her maidenhood. But though crushed, they bowed their heads in submission. Their hearts were almost broken, but they rebelled not against the Hand that chastened them. Why is it that such examples of tender feeling and unquestioning faith are seldom found in cities? Is it that " the memories which peaceful country scenes call up, are not of this world; nor of *its* thoughts and hopes ? " That "their gentle influences teach us how to weave fresh garlands for the graves of those we love, purify our thoughts, and beat down old enmities and hatreds ? " And that "beneath all this there lingers in the least reflective mind, a vague and half-formed consciousness of having held such feelings long before, which calls up solemn thoughts of distant times to come, and bends down pride and worldliness before it?" The physician had said that Elvira would not live another day, and the mother sat down to the sad task of writing the mournful news to her soldier son. Meanwhile beyond the Rappahannock, a scene was on the eve of being enacted, which was destined to inflict upon her a pain as poignant as that she was now about to bestow.

The night of October eighteenth was passed by Kilpatrick's command at Gainesville, but the first faint streak of dawn saw him and his faithful followers in the saddle, booted, spurred, and equipped for some enterprise as yet unexplained to them, but evidently, in their leader's estimation, one of " pith and moment." At the word of command, the force, including the " Harris Light," moved forward at a quick trot, taking the road to Warrenton, and anticipating a brush with Stuart's cavalry who, during the previous ten hours, had thrown out videttes in their immediate front.

The surprise of the Federals was great to find their advance unimpeded, and that, instead of offering opposition, the Confederates fell back as rapidly as their opponents approached. On they dashed, unopposed and unobstructed, until Buckland Mills was reached. At this point they found themselves checked, and in a manner that somewhat astounded them. As they arrived within a stone's throw of that village, Fitzhugh Lee, with his magnificent following, struck their flank. That astute and valiant officer, it appears, had cut his way through the Federal infantry at Thoroughfare-Gap, and accompanied by a battery of flying artillery, swept down upon Kilpatrick, designing to crush him at a blow. General Stuart, taking in the situation, and keenly anxious to profit by the advantage thus afforded him, instantly turned upon and charged the Federals in his front, while, as if to make their utter annihilation a certainty, the rebel General Gordon, with a third body of men (his proximity at that moment not being suspected), bore down fiercely on their left, threatening to cut Kilpatrick's division in two.

Kilpatrick possessed an extraordinary amount of ingenuity in devising means of escape from a dangerous position. In the present case his plan was formed in an instant, and executed as soon as formed. He immediately changed his front, and, without the slightest hesitation, headed a mad and desperate charge upon Fitzhugh Lee's advancing column. The merit of the movement lay in its audacity; it was the only one that promised the remotest chance of escape to the entrapped Federals. Executed with great rapidity and desperate decision, the movement resulted in the salvation of the greater portion of his command. It so happened, however, that the "Harris Light," originally, be it remembered, forming the vanguard of Kilpatrick's force, was by this manœuvre thrown round upon the rear, and Stuart, who was now the pursuer instead of the pursued, had a fine opportunity of attacking them with his full force, at a great disadvantage to the former—an opportunity he was not slow to avail himself of.

Kilpatrick's men met the assault manfully, retiring

CAVALRY FIGHT AT NEW BALTIMORE—LIEUTENANT GLAZIER TAKEN PRISONER.

slowly, until at length, upon the brow of a small hill, they turned at bay, and for a time formed a living rampart between their retreating comrades and the enemy. Every attempt to approach and penetrate their line proved instant death to their assailants, and General Stuart, seeing no chance of otherwise dislodging them, determined to charge in person, and crush them with an entire division. Glazier, who had already emptied two saddles, sat coolly upon his horse, reloading as this formidable body came sweeping down. By this time, experience of the vicissitudes of a soldier's career, and possibly the fact that he had hitherto been very fortunate in the numerous conflicts in which his regiment had been engaged, left him quite composed under fire. Singling out one of Stuart's men, he covered that cavalier with his revolver, and probably, in another instant, would have ended his career ; but, just as his finger gave the final pressure upon the trigger, his horse, riddled with bullets, fell dead under him, the shot flew wide of its mark, and he fell to the ground.

His first sensation was of a dense cloud between himself and the sky, and next of being crushed by tramping hoofs, whole squadrons of horse passing over his body as he lay prone and helpless. A vague, dreamy sensation of being a mass of wounds and bruises was succeeded by utter darkness and oblivion. How long he continued in this comatose state he never knew. Raised from the ground, a terrible sense of acute bodily pain gradually crept over him, as he found himself hurried along at a rapid pace. Where he was going, who had him in charge, what he had done, whether he was in this or some other world, were matters of which he had no more conception than the dead charger he had ridden. Pain, pain, nothing but intense pain, absorbed the whole of his faculties. Gradually his full consciousness returned. He remembered the fierce onset of the enemy, his fall from his horse, and at once concluded that he was a prisoner in the hands of the enemy! Very soon after, he discovered that, in addition to being deprived of his arms, he had been stripped of his watch and other valuables.

One of the great annoyances to which a newly captured prisoner was subjected, arose from the fact that skulkers and sneaks, in order to secure safe positions, coveted and sought the privilege of quartering them. In his own words Glazier says:

"The woods in the vicinity were full of skulkers, and, in order to make a show of having something to do, they would make their appearance in the rear of the fighting column, and devote themselves sedulously to guarding the prisoners." He adds, that "privates, corporals and sergeants, in turn, had them in charge;" and that "each in succession would call them into line, count them in an officious manner, and issue orders according to their liking," until some sneak of higher rank came along, assumed the superior command, and in a tone of authority, would say to the other poltroons: "Gentlemen, your services are much needed at the front. Go, and do your duty like soldiers." The result would be an exchange of tyrants, but no diminution of the petty tyranny. At dusk the prisoners were marched to, and lodged in, the jail at Warrenton.

ROBBING PRISONERS. 163

Like all Federal soldiers who fell into the enemy's hands, Glazier complains very bitterly of the small persecutions inflicted by the officers and men of the Home Guard, and unfortunately these mongrels—a cross between a civilian and a soldier—were their chief custodians during that night, and signalized themselves after their fashion. They deprived the prisoners of their clothing, and, in truth, everything of the slightest value in the eyes of a thief. One of these swashbucklers attempted to reduce our young hero's wardrobe to an Arkansas basis, namely, a straw-hat and a pair of spurs, with what success the following dialogue, taken mainly from "The Capture, Prison-Pen, and Escape," will indicate.

"Here, Yank," said the guard, "hand me that thar hat, and over-coat, and boots."

"No, sir, I won't; they are my property. You have no right to take them from me."

"I have," said the guard. "We have authority from General Stuart to take from you prisoners whatever we d—d choose."

"That I doubt," said the captive, "and if you are a gentleman you won't be guilty of stripping a defenceless prisoner."

"I'll show you my authority, you d—d blue-belly," said the ruffian, drawing his revolver. "Now, take off that coat, or I'll blow your brains out."

By this time Glazier's Northern blood was up, and he grew desperate, so he angrily answered:

"Blow away then! It is as well to be without brains as without clothing."

So the fellow, who was evidently a contemptible blusterer, whom General Stuart, had he been aware of his conduct, would have drummed out of the army, not willing to risk the consequences of actual violence—sneaked away.

While this little incident was occurring at Warrenton jail, a very different event was transpiring at his father's house. His sister was dying. It was a peaceful, hopeful death—the death of a Christian—of one who in her young life had never by word or deed injured man or woman. Many weeks elapsed before her imprisoned brother heard of her death, and when the intelligence at length reached him, he was overwhelmed with grief at her loss.

Upon the morning following the day of his capture, in that dense darkness that precedes the dawn, the prisoners started on their tramp toward Culpepper, and as the day broke, and the sun mounted above the eastern hills, their march, which extended to full thirty miles, became a weary and exhausting journey. Themselves on foot, and compelled to keep up with the pace of mounted men, it was a tiresome task; but to do so under the burning rays of a Southern sun was nearly impossible. To make matters worse, in the present case, the Confederates having sustained a defeat at Bristoe and Rappahannock Station, the guard was not in the most amiable humor; in addition to which they were compelled to use haste in order to avoid capture by the victorious Federals. Glazier gave no thought to his present discomfort, and to use his own words, "felt relieved when he heard of the successes of his comrades." Still the annoyance of this compulsory tramp was felt keenly. The prisoners "being encumbered with heavy high-heeled cavalry boots," and their feet having become tender from contact with the mud and water through which they marched, soon became a mass of blisters, and their sufferings from this cause alone were intense. Six of the poor fellows succumbed, unable to proceed. After a journey attended with much mental depression, and bodily agony, the former increased by the barbarous contumely flung at them by men who emerged from roadside inns, to stare at them as they passed, the prisoners, including the subject of our story, entered Richmond, and were at once introduced to the amenities of "Libby Prison."

CHAPTER XVI.

LIBBY PRISON.

"All ye who enter here abandon hope."—Auld lang syne.—Major Turner.—Hope deferred maketh the heart sick.—Stoicism.—Glazier enters the prison-hospital.—A charnel-house.—Rebel surgeons.—Prison correspondence.—Specimen of a regulation letter.—The tailor's joke.—A Roland for an Oliver.—News of death.—Schemes for escape.—The freemasonry of misfortune.—Plot and counter-plot.—The pursuit of pleasure under difficulties.

IT does not come within the scope of the present work to enter into a detailed description of the sufferings of the Union prisoners in this place of durance: those who have a taste for such gloomy themes may gratify it by reading the first work by our young soldier-author, entitled "The Capture, Prison-Pen and Escape," in which the horrors of that house of misery are eloquently described. We may, however, say this much, that if the testimony of eye-witnesses is to be credited, it was a fearful place, and one over whose portals the words of Dante might have been appropriately inscribed, "All ye who enter here abandon hope."

Of some thousand Northern officers confined here, Glazier, of course, met several from his own corps, who had been previously captured. He at first felt his condition very acutely. His roving life amid the magnificent scenery of Virginia, Maryland and Penn-

LIBBY PRISON.

sylvania was now exchanged for the gloomy and monotonous routine of a prison; but he writes under date of October twenty-eighth, in a more reconciled and hopeful strain "I am gradually," he says, "becoming accustomed to this dungeon life, and I presume I shall fall into the habit of enjoying myself at times. 'How use doth breed a habit in a man.' Indeed he can accommodate himself to almost any clime or any circumstance of life, a gift of adaptation no other living thing possesses in any such degree." Of one man, in the midst of all his philosophy, our hero speaks very bitterly. We allude to Major Turner, military warden of the prison. He describes him as possessed of a vindictive, depraved, and fiendish nature, and moralizes over the man and his career in this wise:

"There is nothing more terrible than a human soul grown powerful in sin, and left to the horrible machinations of the evil one, and its own evil promptings. Demons developed from germs that might have produced seraphs, become rank growths, drinking in the healthful stimulants of life and reproducing them in hideous forms of vice and crime.

"'Souls made of fire, and children of the sun,
With whom revenge is virtue.'

"Thus we see a soul coming pure and plastic from its Maker's hand, yet afterward standing before the world, stained and hardened."

Slowly and wearily the days and weeks passed on in "Libby," leaving its drear monotony unbroken, except when the rumor of a prospect of being exchanged came to flush the faces of the captives with a hope destined not to be fulfilled while Willard Glazier was in Richmond. The result was that he at length abandoned all hope of being exchanged, and for a time tried hard to cultivate and "grow into the luxury of indifference." His experience told him that "however reprehensible" it might be in ordinary life, "stoicism, under the circumstances in which he then found himself, was an actual necessity." His mind appears at this time to have sustained him under many extreme bodily privations. But despite all his philosophy and cultivated resignation of spirit, despite the mental resources which he fortunately possessed in no small degree, and which enabled him to occupy his time profitably, while others were pacing up and down the room like caged beasts feeding upon their own hearts, his bodily health was materially impaired. The first winter month, with its frosty atmosphere, and fierce northern blasts, instead of bringing invigoration to his wasted frame, left him more debilitated, and upon the eighth of December he succumbed to a disease which had been encroaching upon him for some time, and requested to be sent to the hospital. His sensations were far from pleasant when, for the first time in his life, he found himself seriously ill among strangers, and in that most dismal of all dismal places, a Prison Infirmary. "Once in the hospital," he writes, "I found myself soon subjected to its peculiar influences. There was the ominous stillness, broken only by the choking cough, or labored groan; the chilling dread, as though one were in the immediate presence of death, and under the ban of silence; and the anxious yearning—the almost frantic yearning one feels in the contemplation of suffering which he is powerless to alleviate. And worse than all, at last came the hardened feeling which a familiarity with such scenes produces. This is nothing but an immense charnel-house. We are constantly in the midst of the dead and dying. Nearly every day some of our comrades, and on some days several of them, are borne away coffinless and unshrouded to their unmarked graves. Nor flower, nor cross, nor hallowed token, gives grace to the dead, or beauty to the grave. I am well aware that in time of war, on the field of carnage, in camp, where the pestilential fever rages, or in the crowded prisons of the enemy, human life is but little valued. Yet there are moments amidst all these scenes, when the importance of life and the terrors of death, seem to force themselves upon the mind of every man, with a power which cannot be resisted."

It is pleasant to find that here, as generally in the world, with members of the learned professions, the surgeons were humane and kind; and remonstrated with the authorities whenever remonstrance on behalf of the poor sufferers was needed. Of course they could not "minister to a mind diseased, pluck from the memory a rooted sorrow," or,

"With some sweet oblivious antidote, cleanse
The choked bosom of that perilous stuff
That weighs upon the heart;"

but gracious words and sympathizing looks, and the knowledge that he was once more in the hands of *gentlemen*, were a source of great comfort to the patient, after having been brought into daily and hourly contact with the familiars of Major Turner. Another gratifying circumstance was, that the Federal surgeons held as prisoners were permitted to attend upon their sick compatriots when they expressed a wish to do so, and that, of course, was very frequently. Even an hospital has its little events, which although they appear very trifling in the retrospect, are of considerable importance at the time of their occurrence. Here these little episodes were not infrequent. At one time it was the destruction of a box of dainties sent by the Federal Sanitary Commission for the prisoners; at another, it was the excitement incident to an exchange of the surgeons held in captivity; and again, it was the surreptitious acquisition by some of the patients of a daily newspaper, and the guarded dissemination of such items as it might contain among his fellow-sufferers; but greatest of all in importance was the receipt of a letter from HOME. Even when surrounded by all the incidents of home life, the postman is ever a welcome visitor; but in the midst of such a dreary captivity as these men were undergoing, a letter from *home* was like a message from heaven.

Their correspondence had, however, its sad as well as its cheerful aspect. The prisoners were restricted in writing their letters to six lines, by an arbitrary order from Major Turner, and much ingenuity was exercised in the effort to crowd into these six lines the thousand and one messages many of the writers desired to send to mothers, wives, sisters and sweethearts. Here is a genuine specimen of a "regulation" letter from a fond husband to the wife of his bosom:

MY DEAR WIFE: Yours received—no hope of exchange—send corn-starch—want socks—no money—rheumatism in left shoulder—pickles very good—send sausages—God bless you—Kiss the baby—Hail Columbia! Your devoted husband,
A. D. S.

But the "rule of six" was successfully evaded for a considerable time, by the manufacture and use of invisible ink. The trick was however at last discovered, and the way in which Glazier tells the story is so amusing, that we are tempted to give it in his own words:

"A certain captain writing to a fair and undoubtedly dear friend, could not brook the idea of being limited to six lines, when he had so much to communicate; so resorting to the use of the invisible ink, he comfortably filled the sheet with 'soft and winning words,' and then fearing lest his *inamorata* would not discover the secret he added this postscript:

"'P. S.—Now, my dear, read this over, and then bake it in the oven and read it again.'

"This was too much. The rebels thinking if the letter would improve by baking it might be well to improve it at once, accordingly held it over the fire. This brought to light four closely written pages of the tenderest and most heart-rending sentiment."

Ever after all letters sent out by the prisoners were carefully inspected and subjected to the "ordeal by fire," so that, to use the expressive language of an old soldier, "that game was played."

Among Glazier's fellow-prisoners at this time was a certain Major Halsted. He was one of those social anomalies that are not infrequently met with in this country, a man of obscure origin, a member of a very humble calling, prior to entering the army, and yet possessing the personal appearance and manners of a man of distinction. He really belonged to that terribly maligned craft of whose followers it is popularly said, "It takes nine to make a man,"—he was a tailor.

Upon this fact some of the little wits of the prison, forgetting that one of the bravest of Napoleon's generals, and one of the most intrepid of America's sons, had both followed the same occupation, were in the habit of jokingly asking him to repair their old and dilapidated clothes.

When this jest was first indulged in, those who knew the undaunted spirit and somewhat irascible temper of the major, expected to hear him blaze out upon the perpetrator of the *mauvaise plaisantrie*, or possibly knock him down. To their surprise, however, he did neither. For a single moment a gleam of passionate wrath shot up in his eyes, but it was instantly suppressed, and he joined in the laugh against himself. The man who first attacked him in this coarse way was a bold, reckless dare-devil, who did it out of pure brutishness. Seeing, however, that the victim did not appear at all shocked or hurt, other, better-natured fellows, followed in the wake, and the jest of asking the major to patch a pair of breeches or mend a coat, became somewhat threadbare by repetition.

It happened, however, that one day the rebel surgeon accidentally ripped his coat across the breast, and turning to Major M. said, he would give him a bottle of wine if he would mend it. "Yes, sir," said the major, "if you will furnish me with a needle, thread, and a few other indispensables, I will take the whole suit and make it look very different." He added, "the fact is, I would rather do anything than rust in idleness in this d—d prison." Finding that he spoke seriously, and as if it were an ordinary business, the Confederate sawbones, who had a lively appreciation of Yankee handicraft, accepted the proposition, and all next day the major was hard at work clipping and scouring and pressing the surgeon's uniform, every now and then the owner thereof passing by and smiling approval; and it was remarked that his face wore that complacent expression common to all good men when they have furnished employment for idle hands—and it is not going to cost them anything.

The same evening, however, when the work, so neatly done, was finished, the major very quietly slipped it upon his own dignified person, and taking with him a fellow-prisoner as "hospital steward," coolly walked past the guard, remarking, to the great consternation of that personage, "My friend, there are unmistakable indications of *cerebro-spinal meningitis* in your eyes. Come over to the hospital as soon as you are relieved, and I will see what can be done for you," walked out into the street, and neither he nor the "hospital steward" was heard of again until they reached the Federal lines.

The devices resorted to, to effect an escape, were as ingenious as they were numerous, and for a short time the most popular and successful *ruse* was for the prisoners to get into the hospital, simulate death, and, while left unguarded in the dead-house, to escape. The difference, however, between the tally of the deaths and the burials ultimately attracted the attention of the authorities, and that was stopped.

It will be remembered that while young Glazier was fighting his last fight prior to his capture upon the nineteenth of October, the family at home were gathered around his sister's dying bed, when her gentle spirit winged its flight to heaven. From that day until the twenty-ninth of November, he had received no news of his family, and consequently, up to that time, was ignorant of her decease. It had been his habit, during the weary hours of his prison life, to overcome the dangerous disposition that is common to all human beings when in trouble—to brood over their misfortunes by fixing their thoughts upon the loved ones at home. His imagination constantly conjured up before his mind's eye pictures of the parents, his sisters and brothers, and placed them amid the rustic surroundings of his boyhood's home. Even while in the hospital, and tossing with fever upon his bed, the visions which haunted him were not visions of red-handed war, but of quiet country life, where his kindred filled their several spheres of duty. He had never thought of them, except collectively. Although he had, from time to time, felt apprehensive that "Elvi" was somewhat delicate, he never had the slightest fear that her life was thereby endangered. Hence, when the sad news arrived, it came as a terrible surprise. His sisters had been the objects of his peculiar care. The relation he had borne to them, young as he was, was that of a father, as well as brother. He never wearied of planning schemes for their intellectual improvement. He made it his peculiar care that they should be thoroughly educated, and that, while intellectually robust, none of the soft down and bloom of true womanhood should be brushed away in the process. They were his memory's "good angels" even in sleep; for what must have been his dreams in the midst of such surroundings, if he had not had them to think of!

The shock on thus learning of his sister's death was a very great one to young Glazier, and his reflections for a time were bitter. He alludes to the subject himself in this way: "In the very midst of death I am permitted to drag out a weary life, while dear ones in a land of health, freedom and plenty are struck down by the fatal shaft. Her death occurred on the nineteenth of October, the very day of my capture. I was thrust into prison, and doubly bound to the groveling discomforts of earth, while *she* was released from the prison-house of clay, and received, I trust, into the joyous freedom of heaven. Our lives are all in the hands of Him who doeth all things well. He appoints us a period of existence, and appoints a moment to depart. All other influences are subordinate to His will. 'What can preserve our lives, and what destroy!'"

From the moment he realized that he was in the hands of the enemy, after the battle of New Baltimore, Glazier had made up his mind to exercise sleepless vigilance in seeking for opportunities of escape. He pondered over the matter until he became a complete enthusiast in his efforts to master the minute details of the construction and topography of the place of his confinement, and, by the exercise of that natural freemasonry which enables kindred spirits to recognize each other, soon effected an understanding upon the subject with certain of the more daring of his companions in misfortune. One of these gentlemen was a Lieutenant Tresouthick, an officer of the Eighteenth Pennsylvania Cavalry. In order to comprehend the plan which they finally determined to carry out, it will be necessary to premise that Libby Prison was a three-story structure, built over very ample cellarage; that the stories were each divided into three compartments, as was the cellar; and that these spaces were all of equal size in length and breadth. For the purpose of conveying a clear conception of the *locus in quo* of the proposed effort, the reader should also be informed that the hospital occupied the first floor; that Lieutenant Tresouthick was one of the occupants of the room immediately above it; and that there were sinks built against the exterior wall of the same height as each story, and running the entire length of the building. The lieutenant's plan was, that "he should feign sickness and get into the hospital," says our hero, in describing the scheme; "and that I, in the meanwhile, should, with a saw-backed knife, cut a board out of the sink large enough to let us through." This looked feasible enough, and the two conspirators were beginning to felicitate themselves upon their approaching freedom, when they discovered that any such opening as they proposed, would let them out "directly opposite the guard," so *that* plan had to be dropped. Glazier then proposed a plan of operations, promising better and safer results. It was, that Tresouthick should still carry out his original idea of a feigned sickness and consequent admission to the hospital; that he (Glazier) should procure a piece of rope, eight or ten feet long, and then, "some dark, rainy night," the pair should "steal down into the basement"— the outer doors of which were "not locked until ten o'clock"—and await their opportunity. That, when they once reached the exterior of the building, and the sentry's back was turned, they should rush past him on either side, and, with the rope, trip him up, in the hope of being beyond the reach of his musket before he could fire. This was approved by the lieutenant.

and they made up their minds to try it. Of course, it was necessary that Lieutenant Tresouthick's illness should come on very gradually, and progress naturally from bad to worse, until he became a fit subject for the hospital, so that some time was occupied in preliminary operations before any steps could be taken for the execution of their plan.

Meanwhile, through the kindness of one of the surgeons, young Glazier was furnished with some reading matter, a very great luxury to a man in his situation and of his tastes. In his more serious hours he re-read the Bible, and committed to memory daily a portion of "Saint Matthew's Gospel;" and for relaxation read "Napoleon and his Marshals." This with an occasional game at chess, checkers, or dominos, games in which the invalids were permitted to indulge, made the hours pass much more pleasantly than those spent in the convalescent department. It is true their chess-board was made with chalk upon the floor, the "men" being pieces wrought out of bone saved from their soup, and the "checkers" old buttons ripped from their scanty wardrobe. But these rude implements afforded as much real sport as if they had been constructed of ivory or gold. The scene must at all times have been grimly grotesque in this place, for all the trades and professions had their representatives there, and the lawyers held mock courts, politicians formed caucuses, gamblers started a square game of faro, and even some ministers of the gospel gathered together a few each day, who listened to words of hope and comfort from their lips.

On the eighth of December Glazier made this note in his diary: "Getting into the hospital is no easy matter, but Tresouthick is becoming more and more sick, and has good hopes." But

> "The best o' plans o' mice and men
> Gang aft aglee;"

and all hope of escape for our two worthies was interrupted by the inconvenient fact that a couple of their comrades anticipated them in point of time, and by so doing aroused the guards to such a state of vigilance, that our over-sanguine boys saw there was no chance for them. Consequently Lieutenant Tresouthick's illness vanished as it had come, and he was soon pronounced convalescent.

CHAPTER XVII.

PRISON LIFE.

Mournful news.—How a brave man dies.—New Year's Day.—Jolly under unfavorable circumstances.—Major Turner pays his respects.—Punishment for singing " villainous Yankee songs."—Confederate General John Morgan.—Plans for escape.—Digging their way to freedom.—" Post No., 1, All's well."— Yankee ingenuity.—The tunnel ready.—Muscle the trump card.—No respect to rank.—*Sauve qui peut!*—A strategic movement.—" Guards! guards!"— Absentees from muster.— Disappointed hopes.—Savage treatment of prisoners.—Was the prison mined?

THE Richmond papers occasionally found their way into the hands of the prisoners, and the following mournful item of news is transcribed from one of them. The writer of the ensuing letter was a man about thirty years of age, who was accused by the rebel authorities of having acted as a spy on behalf of the Union government. A gloom hung over the prison for some days after the reading of the article:

CASTLE THUNDER, RICHMOND, Virginia.

DEAR FATHER:—By permission and through the courtesy of Captain Alexander, I am enabled to write you a few lines. You, who before this have heard from me in regard to my situation here, can, I trust, bear it, when I tell you that my days on earth are soon ended.

Last Saturday I was court-martialed, and this evening, a short time since, I received notice of my sentence by Captain Alexander, who has since shown me every kindness consistent with his duty.

Writing to my dear parents, I feel there can be no greater comfort after such tidings, than to tell you that I trust, by the mercy of our Heavenly Father, to die the death of a Christian.

For more than a year, since the commencement of my confinement, I have been trying to serve him in my own feeble way, and I do not fear to go to Him.

I would have loved to see you all again; God saw best not; why should we mourn? Comfort your hearts, my dear parents, by thoughts of God's mercy unto your son, and bow with reverence beneath the hand of Him who "doeth all things well."

* * * I sent a ring to my wife by a clergyman, Monday last; I also sent a telegram to yourself, which will arrive too late, as the time of my execution is set for the day after to-morrow.

Dear parents: there are but few more moments left me; I will try to think often of you; God bless and comfort you; remember me kindly and respectfully to all my dear friends and relatives. Tell Kitty I hope to meet her again. Take care of Freddy for me; put him often in remembrance of me.

Dear mother, good-bye. God comfort you, my mother, and bless you with the love of happy children. Farewell, my father; we meet again by God's mercy.

SPENCER KELLOGG.

The following account of the execution is from a Richmond paper:

"At eleven o'clock yesterday forenoon, a detail of one hundred men from the City Battalion, marched from Castle Thunder with Spencer Kellogg, the recently condemned spy, in custody.

"The cavalcade reached the scene of execution about half-past twelve o'clock, where, as usual, a vast concourse of people, of both sexes and all ages, were congregated. After a few moments spent in preliminary arrangements, the prisoner was escorted, under guard, to the gallows. While seated in the hack awaiting the perfection of the arrangements for his execution, he conversed freely with the utmost *nonchalance* with Dr. Burrows, frequently smiling at some remark made either by himself or the minister.

"Arriving under the gallows, the charges preferred against the accused and the sentence of the court-martial were read. A short but impressive prayer was then offered by the minister, at the conclusion of which the condemned man, unaccompanied, mounted the scaffold.

"In a few moments Detective Capehart followed, and commenced to adjust the rope over the neck of the condemned, in which he assisted, all the while talking with the officer. On taking off his hat, to admit the noose over his head, he threw it one side, and falling off the scaffold, it struck a gentleman beneath, when the prisoner turned quickly, and bowing, said: 'Excuse me, sir!'

"A negro next came on the scaffold with a ladder, and proceeded to fasten the rope to the upper beam, the prisoner meanwhile regarding him with the greatest composure. The rope being fastened, the negro was in the act of coming down, when the prisoner, looking up at the rope, remarked: 'This will not break my neck! It is not more than a foot fall! Doctor, I wish you would come up and arrange this thing!' The rope was then arranged to his satisfaction, and the cloth cap placed over his head.

"The condemned man then bowed his head, and engaged a few seconds in prayer, at the conclusion of which he raised himself, and standing perfectly erect, pronounced in a clear voice: 'All ready!'

"The drop fell, and the condemned man was launched into eternity!"

Kellogg is said by his captors to have died with the conviction that he had furnished more valuable information, in the character of a spy, to the Federal government than any other ten men in the service. But this has been denied by his friends at the North, who assert that he was innocent of the charge.

With baseless rumors of a soon-to-be-effected cartel of exchange; the drawing of lots for the selection of hostages, upon whom the Confederacy proposed to retaliate for the punishment inflicted upon three Confederates by the Federal authorities who had sentenced them to imprisonment in the Illinois State Prison; listening to yarns spun by real or pretended veterans; playing games of chance; holding spirited debates; reading letters from home; occasionally poring over the newspaper procured by stealth; or meditating plans of escape—the balance of the year 1863 wore on to its close, and still Willard Glazier was a prisoner of war, with no prospect whatever of a speedy release. Then came New-Year's Day, January first, 1864, and some little attempt was made to get up a New-Year's dinner—though no extra rations had been issued. They did their best, however, like Mark Tapley, to be "jolly under unfavorable circumstances."

Nothing occurred out of the usual routine until the twenty-fourth of January, when, as the prisoners, including Glazier, were singing "The Star-Spangled Banner," "Rally Round the Flag, Boys," etc., the door leading into the street was suddenly flung open, and a squad of armed men filed in. Turner was at their head, and quickly crossing the room and placing himself at the door leading up-stairs, to prevent any of the prisoners from making their escape, began: "Now you d—d boisterous scoundrels, I'll teach you to begin your d—d howling in this building again. I want you to understand that you must not drive people crazy out in the streets with your villainous Yankee songs." He then turned to his men and ordered them to "Take their stations around the d—d rascals, and shoot the first man that dared to stir out of his tracks." Having completed which arrangement, he added to his helpless victims: "Now, d—n you, stay here until twelve o'clock to-night, and make a bit of noise or move from your place, if you dare." And he kept them there until the appointed hour, standing and in silence. "The fires went out early in the evening, and the cold became intense. Some managed to get blankets from their friends," in the apartment above, "but the guards soon put a stop to that. One man called down to a friend through a knot-hole in the floor, asking him if he wanted a blanket. The guard heard him, cocked his gun, and aimed at the hole; but a call from below gave the man warning and he fled." And all this for singing a song written by a Southerner, in praise of the flag under whose ægis Major Turner was nurtured and received his military education! It is quite possible that a song identified with the cause of their supposed enemy might have produced a commotion among the ignorant rabble in the street, and hence it is perhaps unfair to blame the commander of the prison for prohibiting the loud singing, which partook somewhat of the nature of defiance; but he could certainly have attained his object as effectually in a manner becoming an officer and a gentleman. Even the victims of the First French Revolution were permitted to express in song through the bars of the Temple sentiments of utter scorn for their enemies, and when the Jacobins in their turn marched to the guillotine they did so, singing the "Marseillaise."

A great sensation was created among the prisoners on the twenty-fifth of the month on account of a visit made to "Libby" by the famous raider, General John Morgan, whom Glazier described as a "large, fine-looking officer, wearing a full beard and a rebel uniform, trimmed with the usual amount of gold braid;" but something far more interesting than the visit of any man, however famous, began to absorb the attention of our imprisoned hero at this time. He had never ceased to rack his brain with schemes looking to his escape. A life of captivity was indescribably wearisome to him. He not only taxed his own ingenuity in the effort to discover some feasible plan, but eagerly entered into the schemes of others. The result, however, so far as he was individually concerned, was by no means in accordance with his hopes; but, as he has given the details in his "Capture, Prison-Pen, and Escape," we cannot do better (even at the risk of quoting from that work more freely than we had intended) than to let our readers have it in his own words, thus:

"Early in the winter, Colonel Thomas E. Rose, of the Seventy-seventh Pennsylvania Volunteers, conceived a plan of escape, and organized a secret company of twenty-seven, who were to dig their way to freedom.

"Colonel Rose was well calculated to superintend this work, for he had served in the Mexican War, was taken prisoner by the Mexicans, and after a short confinement, escaped by tunneling from the prison a sufficient distance to be clear of the guards. He had served his apprenticeship and was now prepared to manage and direct. After thorough organization of our company, with secresy well enjoined, we adopted the following plan of operations:

"In the basement of the building just below our cook-room, was a small unoccupied cellar, which had been closed since our arrival, and was never entered. From this room or cellar arose a large chimney, which passed through the cook-room, and so to the top of the building. Our first work was to make a hole in the chimney from the kitchen, which opening we could easily conceal by means of some slop-barrels. These barrels we managed to empty ourselves so that all danger of detection from this point was carefully avoided. A short ladder which our Confederate jailers had brought into the rooms for the purpose of raising their flag on the building, was used to make our descent into the dark room below. Inquiry was made for the ladder, but as no one seemed to know anything about it, it was inferred that it had been converted into fuel. At the foot of the ladder another opening was made through the chimney wall leading into the underground basement room. By removing a few stones from the wall of this place, we were in a situation to commence the work of tunneling. The only implements in our possession were an old trowel and the half of a canteen. The arduous labor was commenced with only the fragment of a canteen, but with this the progress was so slow that even the most patient was disheartened. Fortunately for us a mason came in to repair the prison walls, and going to dinner before he had finished his work, left his trowel, which in his absence most mysteriously disappeared. To him it may have been of little account, to us it was a godsend. With the aid of this implement we were enabled to make more rapid progress; were greatly encouraged, and worked night and day with ceaseless energy. Two of our number were kept in the tunnel almost constantly. One, by a vigorous use of the trowel and canteen, would advance slowly, placing the loosened earth in an old blanket, which the other would convey out of the tunnel into a corner of the room, whence the tunnel started. Our course was due east, under the street, where constantly paced the sentinels, who at every hour of the night were wont to cry: 'Post No. 1; all's well!'—'Post No. 2; all's well!' etc. Little did they dream that Yankee ingenuity and perseverance were perforating the solid earth under their feet, and opening a path to freedom.

"As we progressed in our work we experienced great difficulty from the want of pure air to breathe, and to sustain our candles, which refused to burn. Consequently, one of our party was compelled to stand at the opening, fanning pure air into the tunnel with his hat. Our atmospheric difficulties were the more increased by the small size of the hole, which was a little less than two feet in diameter, quite irregular in consequence of large stones, and descended in a line below the horizontal. This severe labor was carried on without much interruption for more than three weeks, when, at last, the plan came near being a failure on account of a sad mistake in our measurement. Our intention was to reach the yard of an old shed, or warehouse, in which were then stored the boxes sent us by the Christian and Sanitary Commissions, and by our friends at the North.

"Thinking we had reached the desired point, an opening was made to the surface, when it was found we were still in the street, outside the fence, and within a few yards of the sentries. Not discovered by this mishap, the hole was quickly filled with a pair of old pants and some straw, and the work of excavation continued to the spot intended.

"The selection of this point was very fortunate, as the guards used to skulk about this building at night for the purpose of plundering the boxes, and on the night of the escape, as it happened, they saw every man that came out; but, supposing them to be friends, only whispered to each other, that 'the boys were going through the *Yankee boxes* mighty fast.'

"These whisperings," adds Captain Glazier, "were distinctly heard by some of our men. The tunnel was about sixty-five feet in length, and was ready for use February ninth, 1864.

"The company of diggers had arranged that they should make their egress first, and inform the others just as they were going out. But each man had a particular friend whom he wished to notify, and, as we were seen packing our clothing, it soon became suspected among our fellow-prisoners that something unusual was in the wind. Curiosity, once on the alert, soon discovered the secret, and then all were jubilant with the hope of escape, and forthwith commenced packing their poor wardrobes. But egress was so slow that it soon became evident to the cool calculator that, at best, but a comparatively small proportion of our number would be fortunate enough to take their departure from 'Libby' before daylight would forbid any further efforts in that direction.

"In order to get down the chimney, as well as along the tunnel, it was necessary to do so *in puris naturalibus*, wrap our clothing in a bundle, and push it on before us. As soon as it was seen that only a few could possibly get out, many, and in fact most, became selfish, and thought only of attaining their own liberty. All rushed for the mouth of the tunnel, each man seemingly determined to be first out. By this movement, the organization formed by the pioneers or working party was broken up, and the workmen, who were to have had the first opportunity to escape, were not more favorably situated than those who had never borne a hand in the digging. At the entrance to the tunnel were hundreds eagerly awaiting their turn.

"Through the intense anxiety and excitement that arose, there was a rush and a crowd, each one being eager to improve the opportunity. Muscle was the trump card, and won. The weak had to step aside, or rather they were pushed aside without apology. No respect was paid to rank or name. A long-armed second lieutenant had no scruple in taking hold of a pair of shoulders that wore eagles, and pushing them out of the way. It was *sauve qui peut*, and no standing aside for betters—no deference to age, and gray hairs ceased to be honored. Mere physical force was the test of championship. Those poor weak ones who gravitated to the outskirts of such an eager crowding mass—just as the light kernels will find their way to the top of a shaken measure of wheat—doubtless thought, as they felt themselves crowded further and further from the door of egress:

"'Oh, it is excellent
To have a giant's strength, but 'tis tyrannous
To use it like a giant!'

"I made several attempts," Glazier continues, "to assert what I considered my rights, but as I had not, at that time, much muscle to back my claims, they were not recognized, and thus I spent the whole night in a bootless struggle for freedom.

"In digging the tunnel we had encountered a large root which we could not well remove, and the passage at this point was very narrow. Lieutenant Wallace F. Randolph, Fifth United States Artillery, a corpulent fellow, was caught fast by the root. There was a man before him, and another behind, which almost entirely excluded atmospheric circulation, and before they could pull him out of his unfortunate predicament, Randolph was almost dead. He was, however, successful at last. This blockade greatly retarded the line of march, and made the crowd within still more desperate.

"Some of the outsiders in the struggle, who despaired of accomplishing anything by strength, had recourse to a stratagem. There had been considerable noise during the struggle for position, and the guards were expected to make their appearance at any moment. The outsiders, taking advantage of this apprehension, went to the farther end of the cook-room, and, in the darkness, made a racket with pots and kettles, which sounded very much like the clashing of fire-arms; while some of their number in the crowd sang out: 'Guards! guards!' In an instant every man was gone from the tunnel, and a frantic rush took place for the single stairway by about five hundred men. Such a struggling and pressing I have never elsewhere seen, or participated in. We neither walked up, nor ran up, but were literally lifted from our feet, and propelled along in a solid mass up the passage, and made our entrance through the door at the head of the stairs as though shot from a cannon—most of us not stopping until we struck the wall on the opposite side of the room. While this was going on, the scamps who had given the false alarm were quietly passing out of the tunnel! The *ruse* was soon discovered, however, and, in a few minutes, there was as great a jam at the entrance of the tunnel as ever. But, so eager and unthinking were we, that within half an hour, the same trick was played on us again by others and then followed another stampede up the stairs. It is a wonder this affair was not stopped by the guards, but they had no suspicion whatever of what was going on. This was probably owing to the fact that great noises in the cook-room were common throughout the night as well as day. It is however reported that one of the sentinels was heard to call out jocosely to a comrade on the next beat, 'Hello, Billy! there goes somebody's coffee-pot, sure.'

"This struggle continued until morning, when the opening in the chimney was covered, and we went to our several quarters. Here a muster was called to discover how many had made their escape, when it was found that one hundred and fifteen were missing. Arrangements were at once made to account for their absence, and certain men were designated who were to cross the room slyly during roll-call, and be counted twice.

"For some reason the authorities were late that morning, and did not make their appearance until about ten o'clock. On the roll being called the men, according to arrangement, attempted to cross the room, but the movement was discovered, and so the count showed one hundred and fifteen short. The clerk thought he had made a mistake, and counted again, but with the same result. The authorities also thought there must be some error in the count, and joked little Ross, the prison clerk, who was none of the brightest, because he could not count a thousand Yankees!

"We were now marched from one room to another, and counted one by one, but still there were one hundred and fifteen short of the complement. We, of course, pretended to be as much surprised as the authorities. They next sent for Major Turner, and he counted us two or three times, but with an equally unsatisfactory result. He demanded of us where they had gone, and how they got out; but not a man knew.

"The escape was at once made public, and the papers were filled with the news, and the most strenuous measures at once adopted to ensure the recapture of the runaways. The authorities were terribly exasperated, and as a first step, arrested the guards and threw them into Castle Thunder, concluding as a matter of course, that they had been bribed. This set the guards thinking, and one of them remembered he had seen an unusual number of men in the lot near the Yankee boxes. Latouche, the prison adjutant, hearing of this, just before nightfall went and discovered the locality of the opening. Next, they questioned the prisoners as to *where* in the building it began, but could obtain no satisfaction, and not until after a long search, did they discover the opening in the chimney."

So the "patient toil and vigil long" of poor Glazier went for nothing. The Confederate authorities seem to have treated the matter very good-humoredly, frankly expressed their surprise at the ingenuity and patience of the subterranean engineers, and manfully set about the task of recapturing the fugitives. Forty-eight were brought in during the next two days, but at the same time it leaked out among the prisoners that the Unionists under General Kilpatrick were within the outer line of fortifications, engaging the rebels, as it was conjectured, with the view of rescuing the prisoners. The consequence was, there was much excitement among the latter, for the boom of cannon sounded distinctly in their ears, and that sound was accepted as the music that heralded their approaching freedom.

All such hopes, however, were doomed to disappointment. The object of the expedition, which was a combined movement from different points by General Kilpatrick and Colonel Dahlgren, was defeated in consequence of the treachery of a negro guide, employed by the latter officer, and one of the effects of this man's treason was the death of that gallant young soldier. The only result that followed to the prisoners was that the rebels became more exasperated than ever, and unfortunately for their reputation, they seem, with regard to the treatment of the few prisoners that fell into their hands on this occasion, to have behaved rather like savage than civilized people. Not satisfied with the perpetration of acts of cruelty upon these particular prisoners, they (according to Captain Glazier's information) undermined the prison building, and stored beneath the foundation a sufficient quantity of powder to blow it into fragments. This proceeding he says they called, with more force than elegance,

THE HOLE IN THE FLOOR.

"preparing the Yankees for hell;" and Major Turner very grimly informed them that if any further attempt at escape were made, or efforts for their rescue, the prison would be blown to atoms! It is not surprising that at such a time, and under the circumstances, the prisoners looked upon this threat as meant in sober reality; but in all probability (or at least let us hope), it was used simply as a means of discouraging attempts upon the part of the incarcerated men, to regain their liberty by their own efforts or that of their friends.

The raiders captured in the expedition under Kilpatrick and Dahlgren had been thrust into a cell directly beneath the room in which Glazier was confined. Contrivances were made to open communication with them for the purpose, if possible, of alleviating their sufferings, as it was well known that food was issued to them in very niggardly quantities, and every indignity the rebels could devise inflicted upon them. After much effort, by the aid of a knife, a hole was cut in the floor, sufficiently large to pass a man's hand, and through this hole Glazier, for several weeks, was instrumental in furnishing the captives with a share of his own and his companions' rations, which were eagerly grasped and devoured by the starving men. No single act of our hero's life afforded him more real happiness than the service he was thus enabled to render the brave men who had lost their liberty in the noble effort to capture the prison and release its inmates.

CHAPTER XVIII.

DANVILLE.—MACON.—SAVANNAH.

Belle Boyd, the Confederate spy.—National characteristics.—Colonel Mosby.—Richmond to Danville.—Sleeping spoon-fashion.—Glazier's "corrective point" suffers.—Saltatory entrance to a railroad car.—Colonel Joselyn.—Sympathy of North Carolinians.—Ingenious efforts to escape.—Augusta.—Macon.—Turner again!—"Carelessness" with firearms.—Tunneling.—Religious revival.—Order from Confederate War Department.—Murder!—Fourth of July.—Macon to Savannah.—Camp Davidson.—More tunneling.

THE celebrated Confederate spy, Belle Boyd, paid a visit to "Libby" in the latter part of March, and her presence created much comment among the prisoners. She was not that ideal of grace and gentleness which

"Untutored youth,
Unlearned in the world's false subtleties,"

enthrones within the temple of his heart, but was, notwithstanding, a remarkable woman. With much of the enthusiasm that characterized *"La Pucelle,"* she appears to have combined a considerable allowance of shrewdness, or common sense; a mixture of qualities, by the way, of more common occurrence than is generally supposed, among the northern and southern people of our continent. There is little difference between the "peartness" of the one, and the "smartness" of the other; or the "high tone" of the South, and the *nonchalance* of the North. The common *national* characteristic of the people of both sections, however, is the power of adapting themselves to every variety of circumstance. No matter what the importance, or the insignificance of the occasion, or event, upon which they perceive that their opportunity for the attainment of a desired object depends, they are ready at the right moment to seize and turn it to account; and while, to-day, the banks of the Ganges or the Tigris are made to yield up to them the fruits of their industry and produce, to-morrow, when a modification of the law of demand and supply prevails, we find the same men following the tide of fortune through humbler but equally useful channels. We are pre-eminently a practical people, and that this characteristic to some extent destroys the poetic aspect of American life, cannot be gainsaid. The homes of our infancy, the graves of our kindred, the hills upon whose summits we first felt the glory of the morning, the altar at which we first knelt in prayer, the rustic nook where we listened for the one step to which our boyish hearts beat sweetest time; have no power to trammel our migratory proclivities, or to check our local inconstancy. The sentiments with which such objects are indissolubly connected, are but tendrils clinging round the parent nest, and the wings of the new-fledged bird, bursting them asunder, he soars out into the world to contend and battle with its storms.

One of the least attractive illustrations of this spirit of unrest, is where it extends to our women, and Miss Belle Boyd's is in our estimation a case in point.

> "Unknown to her the rigid rule,
>   The dull restraint, the chiding frown,
> The weary torture of the school;
>   The taming of wild nature down.

> Her only lore, the legends told
> Around the soldiers' fire; at night
> Stars rose and set, and seasons rolled;
> Flowers bloomed, and snowflakes fell,
> Unquestioned, in her sight!"

Her career was full of adventure and intrepid daring, and she served the disloyal cause she espoused faithfully and to the bitter end; and then, like other wandering stars of the unholy strife, sank into the oblivion of private life. From the time of Miss Boyd's visit until the seventh of May, Willard Glazier continued to lead the same dull life at Libby Prison. The monotony of the hours was unbroken by any circumstance more exciting than a visit from the celebrated partisan chief, Mosby, who is described by Glazier as a *preux chevalier*, at that time about twenty-eight years of age, in figure, slight, with straight fair hair and closely shaven face, except that "a faded German moustache overshadowed his upper lip." It does not appear that he was recognized as a welcome visitor, although he jocularly remarked to some of the prisoners who had been captured by his own troopers that he was "glad to see them there."

Time! what wonders dost thou work. But a few years have passed, and Mosby, who was erst so malignant a rebel, that even the poor, but loyal, prisoners, presented him the cold shoulder, is now a confidential friend of General U. S. Grant! Longstreet again swears by the Star-Spangled Banner; and Beauregard, hero of Sumter and Bull Run, is now an advocate of perfect equality between the black and white races of his Southern State of Louisiana!

The visit of Colonel Mosby was the last memorable

GLAZIER ATTEMPTS TO ESCAPE. 197

incident of our hero's sojourn in Libby. Upon the seventh of May following, the prisoners were removed thence to Danville, Virginia. Several, in the course of this transit, effected their escape, but the great majority were safely conveyed to their new place of durance. The change made no improvement in their unhappy condition. True, the rations furnished at Danville were of somewhat better quality, and more liberal in quantity, but the discipline was equally Draconian, and the penalty of its slightest infraction— Death! The chief source of misery among the captives was want of room, the men being compelled to sleep "spoon-fashion," and in detachments, many being compelled to stand up awake while their comrades slept as best they could.

This condition of things, however, did not last long. Early upon the morning of the twelfth, the prisoners were once more marched out and started southward. After a journey of twenty-four hours in cattle cars, exposed most of the time to a drenching rain, they were disembarked and tramped another twelve miles to Greensboro. Here the mass of weary, wet, and hopeless patriots were about to be driven, pell-mell, like a herd of cattle, into a train of filthy cars, when young Glazier thought he espied a chance of giving his captors the slip. He waited until it appeared to him that the guard was sufficiently occupied with other duties to overlook his whereabouts, and then slipped behind a log, where in an instant he lay upon the ground apparently fast asleep, trusting in the confusion attendant upon the departure of the train to escape observation. But luck was against him. The only result was the infliction upon that portion of his body which some mothers consider the "corrective point" of their children, of sundry unceremonious kicks, which, coming from such boots as the "C. S. A." at that time supplied to their soldiers, were felt to be more persuasive than agreeable. Of course it became necessary to awaken from his profound slumber slowly, which made the *kicks* still more persuasive, and by the time he was erect, the cars were filled and the doors all closed. The guards therefore insisted upon his effecting an entrance through the small window, which he did with certain vigorous assistance from behind, and landed upon the head and shoulders of Lieutenant-Colonel Joselyn, of the Fifteenth Massachusetts Infantry, who passed him around in such a way that the other occupants of the car were moved to sundry objurgations at the expense of our young friend more forcible than polite, and partaking little of the nature of a hospitable reception! However, this is a world of compromises, and Glazier soon found his level among his fellow-captives.

Their route took them through a portion of North Carolina, where for the first time they met with unmistakable proofs of sympathy. At one city, on learning there were Yankee prisoners in town, the citizens came out in large numbers. Many attempted to converse with them, but were forced back at the point of the bayonet. The prisoners then struck up the "Star-Spangled Banner," and "Rally Round the Flag, Boys," and in each interlude could see white handkerchiefs waiving in the breeze, demonstrations that so exasperated the Virginia guard that they sent a detail to drive "the d—d tar-heels" from the field.

The contiguity of friends of course presented a strong temptation to some to strike for liberty. Every

TUNNELING—THE NARROW PATH TO FREEDOM.

device promising the least chance of escape was therefore resorted to. Among the most ingenious of these was one so graphically described by young Glazier that we make no apology for again using his language:

"The night being very dark," he writes, "and the soil where we were huddled together very sandy and light, many of the prisoners dug holes in the ground and there buried themselves, hoping thus to escape the observation of the guard when we should be marched from the field to the cars. Unfortunately, however, the scheme was exposed by one of the guard who accidentally stumbled into one of the holes, in the bottom of which he beheld a live 'Yankee.' Struck with amazement, he shouted out: 'Oh, my God, Captain, here be a Yankee buried alive!' Great excitement was the natural consequence. A general search ensued, torch-lights were used, and the trees and ground thoroughly inspected. This investigation brought to light several holes of a similar character, each having deposited therein a Federal prisoner. The guards were very angry and went about shouting, 'Run them through! Pick up the d—d hounds!' but their captain, a good-natured sort of man, stopped all this. 'No,' said he, 'the d—d Yankees have a right to escape if they can. Let them alone. I'll risk their getting away from me!'"

Some of the burrowers did escape, however, and several others hid themselves in the foliage and were left behind.

After this nothing eventful occurred upon the way, and on the fifteenth of the same month, the whole party arrived in Augusta, Georgia, and found the home guards, to whose custody they were consigned, a bad lot. From that city they were soon after removed to

Macon. Up to this period, amid all the mortifications of their condition, notwithstanding their tiresome rides and weary marches; despite the chagrin they naturally felt when well-laid plans of escape were frustrated by accidents beyond the power of men to foresee, they still had one source of consolation—there was at least one drop of balm in Gilead—*for had they not gotten rid of—Turner!*

Judge, then, of their mingled horror and despair when they reached the front gate of Camp Oglethorpe, their future prison, to find that monster before them, lounging gracefully against the gate entrance, and evidently delighted with the idea of being in a condition to shock his former victims with his presence.

The laugh, however, was not entirely his, for, upon mustering them, he discovered that forty-seven had escaped. Smothering his wrath upon this subject, he welcomed the remainder to their prison-house, with the gratifying intelligence that *it had its dead-line*, and all who approached it had better be ready to meet the contingencies of a future state of rewards and punishments!

After horrifying them with his presence, he shortly after took himself off, and not long afterward, to their great relief, was ordered back to Richmond.

Before the week had expired, Glazier had an opportunity of estimating how *careless* (?) some of his custodians were in handling their firearms, being an eye-witness of an attempt by a sentinel to shoot Lieutenant Barker, of the First Rhode Island Cavalry. The bullet, kinder than the boy who sped it on its errand (for this guard was not over fourteen years of age), passed over the old man's head. As the latter noted the direction of the lad's aim, and heard the whistle of the bullet above him, he very temperately asked the somewhat unnecessary question, "What are you shooting at?" "I am shooting at you, you d—d old cuss." "What are you shooting at me for?" mildly inquired the lieutenant. "Because you had your hands on the deadline," answered the boy. At this moment the sergeant of the guard came up, and taking the precocious ruffian by the collar, shook him with considerable energy, and demanded of him very fiercely, "What the devil are you shooting at that prisoner for, you little scoundrel?" The boy replied that the prisoner had his hands on the dead-line. Whereupon the sergeant shook him again, told him he was a liar, and that the lieutenant was not within twenty feet of the dead-line, and consigned him to the custody of the corporal of the guard, who marched the young monster away.

Captain Glazier states that he was within ten feet of the lieutenant when the shot was fired, and that the latter *was not within thirty feet of the fatal line.* The incident was not very exhilarating upon the threshold of his new abode, and the prisoners naturally felt greatly exasperated when they heard the particulars.

An order was promulgated next morning by the officer commanding, Captain W. K. Tabb, directing that "any of their number not in ranks at roll-call should be shot," which was not calculated to make them think more kindly of their jailers. The fact is, that the prisoners, in pursuance of a settled determination to lose no opportunity of escape that seemed at all possible, had been again making experiments in *tunneling,* and this atrocious order was intended as a measure of precaution against similar schemes in future.

Thus excluded from the relief afforded by such hopeful occupation, their poor captives had to find other employment for their leisure hours, and at this time a kind of religious revival took place among them, and if human prayer could have effected the destruction of the Confederacy, that organization would certainly have crumbled into dust forthwith. The enthusiasm was so great that at times the exercises bordered upon tumult, and greatly incensed their less fervent guards. At one time a huge Western man poured forth such a rhapsody in favor of Grant and Sherman, and garnished it with such pungent denunciations of Jefferson Davis, and other Confederate magnates, that one of the jailers commented thus: "D—d smart praying, but it won't do! It won't do!"

On the morning of the tenth of August, an order from the Confederate War Department was read before the entire garrison of Camp Oglethorpe, and caused much excitement. This order directed that a detail of fifty prisoners, selected from officers of the highest rank, should be forwarded to Charleston, in order that they might be placed under the fire of the siege guns with which the beleaguering Union forces were attempting the reduction of that city. The order further directed that Generals Scammon, Wessels, Seymour, Schuyler and Heckman should be included in the number. The mandate was of course at once executed, and the departure of the devoted band was the signal for a wild burst of indignant reprobation of the Confederate authorities. It happened also, at this time, that one of the sentinels shot and mortally wounded a prisoner. The victim's name was Otto Grierson, and he had been a general favorite. The excuse assigned for the murder was that he was endeavoring to escape, but his comrades declared that at the time the shot was fired, he was fully sixteen feet from the dead-line, and had made no attempt to escape. Young Glazier and others joined in a formal report of the facts to the officer in command, but the only result was that the murderer received promotion, and was granted a furlough!

If the statements of Captain Glazier regarding this and other contemporaneous outrages are to be relied upon (and he is very strongly corroborated), the officers commanding this military prison sadly abused their trust. Even the highest of those officials indulged in such petty exhibitions of puerile spite as to be altogether unworthy of his station, or even the name of an American.

On the arrival of the Fourth of July, the prisoners very naturally determined, as far as their limited resources would permit, to celebrate the occasion. Accordingly, in true American fashion, a meeting was called, at which speeches of a patriotic character were made, songs sung, and a miniature flag, containing the full number of stars and stripes, which one of their number had concealed about his person, was produced, and became an object of much interest. Instead of magnanimously ignoring all this harmless enthusiasm, the commander of the prison marched in a regiment of soldiers and violently dispersed the meeting!

On the twenty-seventh of July, six hundred prisoners were counted out, as they supposed to be added to the others under fire at Charleston, but really for removal to Camp Davidson, at Savannah, Georgia.

This change was for the better. In the first place,

in lieu of the Sahara of shadeless sand and clay of their former prison grounds, they found at "Davidson" a number of fine oaks, beneath the shade of which they were permitted to recline in peace. In addition to this, and a matter of infinitely greater importance, their guards were officered by *gentlemen*. Captain Glazier states that the authorities here issued tents, cooking utensils, and decent rations, and adds this tribute to their generally manly conduct toward the prisoners: "The troops here have seen service, and there is nothing like the battle-field and the suffering there experienced to teach soldiers humanity toward each other. Whenever attempts are made to escape, they give us to understand that they would do the same themselves, under like circumstances, but are still compelled to punish such infractions of discipline. They politely ask our pardon for inspecting our quarters, and in a manner as gentlemanly as possible, remove our blankets from the floor of our tents in their search for incipient *tunnels*. All this is very gratifying and tends to assuage the bitter hatred which former brutality has engendered. These Georgia boys will be long remembered, and may look for the utmost kindness and consideration from us if the chances of war ever reverse our situations."

This is a record for Georgia nobler far than any she ever gained upon the battle-field, albeit her sons were always in the van. All honor to them! Such victories are well worth the winning.

But pleasant as their Georgia quarters were by comparison with former experiences, the captives were afflicted with the *malade du pays*—the home-sickness that tugged at their hearts, and bade them again and again risk death for the chance of freedom. Tunnel after tunnel was attempted, and one, constructed by a select band (sworn to secrecy), was upon the eve of completion, when a straggling cow blundered upon the frail covering of turf, and became so securely imbedded in the falling earth that she could not extricate herself. Her bellowing attracted the attention of the sentinel, the plot was discovered, and, of course, frustrated.

Despite such disappointments, however, when the time came, as it soon did, for the prisoners to leave Savannah, they did so with sentiments of gratitude for the comparatively humane treatment they had received at the hands of the Georgians, not unmingled, however, with apprehensions concerning their future, for it was openly rumored that they were destined to join their former fellow-prisoners now under fire of Gilmore's siege guns at Charleston.

CHAPTER XIX.

UNDER FIRE AT CHARLESTON.

Under siege.—Charleston Jail.—The Stars and Stripes.—Federal compliments.—Under the guns.—Roper Hospital.—Yellow Jack.—Sisters of Charity.—Rebel Christianity.—A Byronic stanza.—Charleston to Columbia.—"Camp Sorghum."—Nemesis.—Another dash for liberty.—Murder of Lieutenants Young and Parker.—Studying topography.—A vaticination.—Back to reality.

THE next we see of Lieutenant Glazier is in the city of Charleston, South Carolina, on the twelfth of September, 1864. Coming Street on the morning of that day was crowded with people of every variety of calling, from the priest and sister of charity, out on their merciful errands, to the riff-raff and *sans-culottes* out on no errand at all but to help the excitement. The city was under siege.

At the end of the street a body of six hundred emaciated, broken-spirited, ragged men, escorted by a strong guard, marched along, and the busiest of the pedestrians paused to gaze upon them as they passed. Coarse and scurrilous was the greeting the captives received from the motley and shameless groups. A few of the more respectable citizens, however, spoke words of grace to them, and some added hopeful predictions of the final triumph of the Union cause. The prisoners were hurried forward to the yard of Charleston Jail, where for the first time in many weary months they beheld the glorious flag of their country floating in the breeze over Morris Island. Weak as they were

CHARLESTON JAIL—CHARLESTON, SOUTH CAROLINA.

the patriotic sentiment was still strong within them, and they gave one rousing cheer! Some, despite the curses of their guard, dancing like children, while others wept tears of joy.

The jail, as Captain Glazier describes it, was a large octagonal building of four stories, surmounted by a tower. In the rear was a large workshop, in appearance like a bastile, where some of the prisoners were confined. As a lugubrious accessory to his own quarters, he had a remarkably clear view of a gallows, erected directly in front of his fragment of a tent. "The ground floor of the jail was occupied by ordinary criminal convicts; the second story by Confederate officers and soldiers, under punishment for military offences; the third by negro prisoners, and the fourth by Federal and Confederate deserters, and it is complimentary to the good sense of the rebels that deserters from *either* side were treated by them with equal severity." He gives a sad account of the terrible condition of the negro soldiers and their officers who were captured at Fort Wagner, and says the hospital at this place was "a lazar-house of indescribable misery."

On the twenty-second of September, Glazier makes the following note on the progress of the siege:

"Shelling is kept up vigorously. From sixty to a hundred huge, smoking two-hundred-pounders convey Federal compliments daily to the doomed city."

It appears, however, that, for the most part, the destructive effects of this bombardment were confined to what was known as the "burnt district," and caused little damage to the occupied portion of the city.

Seven days after the above entry in his journal his

heart was gladdened by an order for removal, with his fellow-prisoner and messmate, Lieutenant Richardson, to Roper Hospital; a place much more tolerable as to its situation and appointments, though still within shot-range of the bombarding force. Prior to the transfer, a written parole was obtained from each, in which they pledged themselves, while in their new quarters, to make no attempt to escape.

Here our prisoner found opportunity under the usual restrictions for writing the following letter home:

[Only one page allowed.]

> C. S. Military Prison,
> Charleston, South Carolina,
> Roper Hospital, *October 4th*, 1864.

My Dear Mother:

For a long time you have doubtless waited with anxiety some intelligence of your absent son, which would tell you of his health, and his prospects of release from the disagreeable restraints of prison life; and I am now delighted to find this opportunity of writing to you. Since my last letter, which was dated at Libby Prison, I have been confined at Danville, Virginia; Macon and Savannah, Georgia; and at this point. My health for the most part has been very poor, which I attribute to the inactivity of prison life. I have also suffered much for want of clothing. I have a pair of shoes on to-day that I bought more than a year ago; have run about barefoot for days and weeks during the past summer; many of our officers have been compelled to do the same. I do not look for a *general exchange* before winter, though I hope and pray that it may take place to-morrow. There is now an opportunity for sending boxes to prisoners. I should be glad to receive one from home if convenient. Please give my love to all the family circle. Remember me to my friends, and believe me ever

> Your affectionate son,
> Willard.

The days passed anxiously with Glazier, when the yellow fever began its inroads upon the prisoners.

He had now, at the same moment, to face death at the hands of man, and by the pestilence—a condition of things to which the bravest spirit might succumb. One great source of consolation was derived from the visits of the Sisters of Charity, who were always found where suffering and peril prevailed. Writing of these angelic women, Captain Glazier says:—" Confined as we are, so far away from every home comfort and influence, and from all that makes life worth living, how quickly do we notice the first kind word, the passing friendly glance! Can any prisoner confined here ever forget the 'Sisters of Charity?' Ask the poor private now suffering in the loathsome hospital so near us, while burning with fever, or racked with pain, if he can forget the kind look, the gracious word given him by that sister. Many are the bunches of grapes—many the sip of their pure juice, that the sufferer gets from her hands. They seem, they *are* 'ministering angels;' and while all around us are our avowed enemies, they remain true to every instinct of womanhood. They dare lift the finger to help, they do relieve many a sufferer. All through the South our sick and wounded soldiers have had reason to bless the 'Sisters of Charity.' They have ministered to their wants and performed those kind womanly offices which are better to the sick than medicine, and are so peculiarly soothing to the dying. These noble women have attended their sick-beds when other *Christian* ladies of the South looked on unpityingly, and turned away without even tendering the cheap charity of a kind word. *They* have done what others were too scornful and cruel to do—they have done what others did not dare do. They were, for some inscrutable reason, permitted to bestow their charities wherever charities were needed. Their bounties were bestowed indiscriminately on Federal and Confederate sufferers, and evidenced a broad philanthropy untainted by party-feeling or religious bigotry. Many a poor soldier has followed them from ward to ward with tearful eyes. . . . . . Were other Christian denominations in the South as active in aiding us as the Catholics have been, I might have some faith in 'Rebel Christianity.'"

This is no mean tribute to the beneficent influences of the Catholic church, albeit the pen of a Protestant records it; but the facts fully justify him. Protestant England had *one*—the Church of Rome has her *legions* of Florence Nightingales. They are found in the camp, and the hospital, and the prison—wherever human sympathy can palliate human suffering; they are to be found where even wives and mothers flee before the dreaded pestilence, and these ministers of divine love, like light and air, and the dews of Heaven, visit alike the rich and poor, the sinner and the saint; the only claim they recognize being the claim of suffering and misfortune.

Willard Glazier remained *under the guns* of his friends until the fifth of October, and during his sojourn here had various opportunities of forming an acquaintance with vagrant shot and shell that struck or exploded near the hospital building, but fortunately did no greater damage to its inmates than create "a scare."

What was much more serious was the prevalence of the deadly fever, which was of a most malignant type, and carried off, among its many victims, the Confederate commander and his adjutant. The prisoners therefore were removed—the authorities assigning as their reason for the step, the "danger to which they would be exposed on account of the fever;" and although, at the time, it appeared an anomaly to the prisoners, "after bringing them there to be murdered by their own guns, to remove them for the purpose of saving them from death in another shape,"—yet it is possible such was the case. At all events they were removed, and their "Poet Laureate"—Lieutenant Ogden, of Wisconsin—wrote a farewell poem, containing among others, the following "Byronic" stanza:

> "Thy Sanctuaries are forsaken now;
>   Dark mould and moss cling to thy fretted towers;
>   Deep rents and seams, where struggling lichens grow,
>   And no sweet voice of prayer at vestal hour;
>   But voice of screaming shot and bursting shell,
>   Thy deep damnation and thy doom foretell.
>   The 'fire' has left a pile of broken walls,
>   And Night-hags revel in thy ruined halls!"

Who will say that a dread Nemesis has not overtaken the metropolis of the Palmetto State? Streets covered with grass, once the busy scenes of commerce and industry, in this city of secession which was formerly the head and front of treason and rebellion!

Escorted by the Thirty-second Georgia Volunteers, Glazier and his fifteen hundred companions were marched through the principal streets of the city to the depot, where they took the cars for Columbia, the State capital. None will ever forget the parade of ragged and bearded men through King Street. But the Georgian guards, while strictly attentive to duty, showed the politeness and demeanor of gentlemen. He says of them, at this point in the history of his imprisonment, "the Georgia troops seem to be by far the most civil and gentlemanly of all the Southern army. They were the most respectable in appearance, most intelligent and liberal in conversation, and to a greater extent than others, recognized the principle that a man is a man under whatever circumstances he may be placed, and is entitled to humane treatment. They very generally addressed the prisoners as 'gentlemen.'"

The same kind of unventilated and filthy cattle-cars were employed in their transportation as had been used in their various previous removals. All suffered from want of water, air and space. The arrival of the captives at Columbia took place in the midst of a drenching rain-storm, and during the entire night, with scarcely any clothing, no rations, and no shelter, they were exposed to the merciless elements, while not twenty yards off, in front of their camping ground, glared the muzzles of a park of loaded artillery. The prisoners, being in a starving condition, looked the picture of despair. A discovery however was made of some bacon suspended to the rafters of the building that enclosed them, in one corner separated by a partition. As the famished men looked through the bars of a window and saw this tempting food, their eyes watered, and their inventive faculties were aroused. Hooks, strings and poles were brought into requisition, and in a short time most of the meat, by Yankee talent, was transferred from the rafters of the building to the stomachs of the prisoners!

The day following, they were moved to a spot about

two miles from the town, and bivouacked in an open field, without any shelter whatever. Surrounded by the usual cordon of sentries, and menaced with the customary "dead-line," they were turned loose to provide for themselves, neither axe, spade, nor cooking utensils being provided them. Two days after their arrival some corn-meal and *sorghum* were issued, the latter a substitute for molasses. A great many suffered from diarrhœa and dysentery in consequence, and the place from this circumstance acquired the sobriquet of "Camp Sorghum."

They had no quarters to protect them from the cold November storms, only huts constructed by themselves of brush and pine boughs. The treatment at "Camp Sorghum" was so exceptionally brutal, that almost every dark night starving men would run the guard and risk their lives to escape dying by inches. Sometimes as many as thirty or forty would run in one night. Generally some daring fellow would act as *forlorn hope* and rush past the sentries, drawing their fire, at the imminent risk of forfeiting his own life, his comrades joining him before the guards could reload their rifles. The latter would then fire a volley into the camp, killing or wounding some of the prisoners. Lieutenant Young, of the Fourth Pennsylvania Cavalry, was thus shot dead whilst sitting at his hut, and according to Captain Glazier, "no reason for this atrocity was apparent, and none was assigned by the guards." The poor young fellow had been a prisoner twenty-two months. About this time the guards accidentally killed two of their own men, in their reckless and savage shooting, and afterwards observed more care in firing at the prisoners.

Hounds were kept near the prison to track escaped fugitives. Lieutenant Parker, while attempting to escape, was so much torn and bitten by these dogs that he died the day after his recapture.

Mingled with thoughts of home, and the friends gathered around loved firesides, there had by this time arisen in young Glazier's mind a stern determination to win his freedom, or, in the effort, lose his life.

As the weather grew colder, the possession of wood became a matter of necessity, and some of the prisoners were paroled to pass beyond the lines, and gather such broken branches and pieces of bark in the neighboring woods as they could carry back into camp. Glazier availed himself of this privilege, and stored up an abundance of fuel. But a more important acquisition than fuel to him was the knowledge he obtained of the topography of the surrounding country. One great difficulty he foresaw in getting away arose from the sorry condition of his shoes, which were nearly soleless. He succeeded, however, in obtaining the rim of an old regulation-hat, and out of this fashioned a serviceable pair of soles for his worn-out brogans, and thus removed one obstacle from his path.

We need feel no surprise that he and many of his companions thought no risk too great to run for the chance of effecting their escape. Their treatment by this time had become so bad as to be almost unendurable. For example, to avoid being frozen to death, they were compelled to run around all night, and only when the sun arose in the morning dare they venture to recline themselves on the ground to sleep. The truth is, that our friend, in common with many of his comrades, had arrived at the desperate conclusion that no fate, even death by shooting, or by hounds, could be worse than the misery and suffering he was now enduring. It was not alone that they were starved and shelterless, sick and unattended, nearly naked, with no hope of being clad; it was not alone that they were immersed, day and night, in filth and squalor like hogs, with no prospect of relief to cheer them; but, in addition to all this suffering of their own, they were compelled to witness the sufferings of others—to hear their sighs and groans, and look upon faces that hard usage and despair had made ghastly and terrible. They would greet in the morning a man sick and emaciated perhaps, but still a human being, erect and in God's image, who, in the evening of the same day, would disappear from among them, making a desperate dash for freedom. The next day a broken, nerveless, shivering wretch would be dragged into their midst, blood-stained, faint, and with the gashes of a bloodhound's teeth covering his face and throat!

Thus it was that existence became unbearable. Their own sufferings were hard, but to continue for many long months looking upon the sufferings of others added to their misery beyond endurance. Accordingly, when Thanksgiving-day arrived, and the excitement created by Sherman's "march to the sea" had reached its highest point, Glazier and a fellow-prisoner, named Lieutenant Lemon, determined that *they* would wait no longer the slow process of tunneling, but make a bold effort for liberty—or die in the attempt.

"It was customary," says the former, "to extend the guard-line in the morning for the purpose of allowing prisoners (as previously stated) to collect fuel on a piece of timbered land just opposite the camp, and it was our intention this morning to take a shovel, when permitted to pass to the woods, and make a hole in the ground large enough to receive our two 'skeletons,' and then enlist the services of some friend, who would cover us up with brush and leaves, so that, when the guard was withdrawn, we would be left without the camp." The plan looked feasible, and, if successful, it would not be a difficult matter to reach Augusta, Georgia, at which point they hoped to find themselves within Sherman's lines. The fates, however, decreed otherwise. Their scheme was rendered abortive by the simple fact, that upon that particular morning, the line was not extended at all. Why it was not, is purely a matter of conjecture. Possibly, "the morning being unusually cold and raw," the guard did not care to leave their own snug tents along the line of the encampment, with no greater inducement than that of increasing the comfort of their Yankee prisoners, who, for that day, were left without any fires at all; but, be this as it may, the guard-line was not extended as was usual, and thus the plot of our young friends was frustrated for the time being. They agreed to "watch, pray *and act*" at the very first opportunity that presented. It was not long before that opportunity came.

Early upon the day following that of their disappointment, the conspirators arranged that each should make a reconnaissance of the lines, discover the weak points of the enemy, and, that being accomplished, rendezvous at a given spot, ready to act upon any likely plan that might suggest itself to them. Glazier had become a tolerably expert physiognomist, and

THE ESCAPE FROM COLUMBIA—CROSSING THE DEAD LINE.

singled out an unsophisticated-looking giant, who was patrolling a certain beat, as the best man among the line of sentries on whom to practise an imposition. This individual was evidently a good-natured lout, not long in the service, and very much resembling our conception of "Jonas Chuzzlewit," in respect to his having been "put away and forgotten for half a century." It is only necessary to add that his owners "had stuck a musket in his hand, and placed him on guard." Yet there was some pluck in him. He was just the sort of man who, led by a good officer, would fight like a lion, but whose animal instincts had so befogged his intellect that, if left to his own resources, he would be as likely to ruin friend as foe.

When Glazier rejoined his comrade, he described this man, and the friends agreed that they would boldly cross the "dead-line" immediately in front of him, be ready to answer promptly his challenge, and, by the audacity of their movement, attempt to deceive him in regard to their real character and purpose. With such a man as they had to deal with, this scheme was certain to result in one of two things: he would let them pass, or he would kill them both; therefore, courage and *sang-froid* were matters of first necessity.

Accordingly, with the utmost coolness, and laughing and chatting together, they sauntered up to and upon the fatal line. The sentinel looked at them in amazement. He then brought his piece to bear upon Glazier, completely covering his person, and, with the usual order to "Halt!" added: "Whar in hell are you going, Yanks?" As if his dignity was seriously offended by this demand, our hero answered this question by asking another: "Do you halt paroled prisoners here?" "His meek 'No, sir!'" Glazier relates, "was not yet lost in the distance when I boldly crossed the dreaded line, adding: 'Then let my friend in the rear follow me;' and so we passed, while the sentinel murmured 'All right!' And right it was, for now we were free, breathing the fresh air, untainted by the breath of hundreds of famishing, diseased and dying men."

They could not proceed very far without falling in with numbers of the paroled prisoners and their guards. This they did, but their presence excited no suspicion or comment, as they assumed to belong to the party. They applied themselves to gathering wood and piling it apparently for transportation, and gradually crept on and on until they reached a point beyond the vision of the gray-jackets, when off they started at the top of their speed; and although before long they were compelled to reduce their pace, they put several miles behind them in a space of time that at any other period of their lives, or under any other circumstances, would have seemed impossible. Pausing to regain breath, they turned, and *Columbia* was no longer within sight. This, in itself, was a relief, for the place was associated in their minds with the intense misery they had suffered within its boundaries.

Could these men have *foreseen* the not very distant future, they would have known that every sigh and groan that cruelty had wrung from them in that place of torture would be avenged; they would have seen loyal soldiers swarming in its streets, their old comrades in misery torn from the grasp of their merciless jailers, and the soulless "Southern Chivalry" thrust into

A GLIMPSE OF THE FUTURE. 219

their place; they would have seen red-handed vengeance doom that city of blood to destruction, and the glaring tongues of fire lap up the costly goods and edifices of its vile and relentless citizens, and those who had no mercy for them in their wretchedness and famine, now awe-struck on finding that the men they had so barbarously trampled upon had now the power and the will to retort upon them with interest; they would have seen brothers in arms, who until now had been merciful to their enemies when in their power, suddenly transformed into ravenous wolves, fierce and terrible in their righteous wrath at the treatment their less fortunate brothers had met with in this city of blood. The Avenger had come! and not one house but would fall a smouldering heap of ruins. They would have foreseen this city ablaze with burning homes for its sins against humanity; its men, so lately drunk with pride and satiated with cruelty to their countrymen; its women divested of all womanly attributes, and invested with those of demons, *now* all cowed and humbled in the dust! They would have seen one noted instance of the interference of a just Providence that occurred amid all this dreadful saturnalia—a woman, pale, but beautiful of feature, delicate of form, madly rushing to and fro in front of her blazing house, crying for her child that lay within it. They would have seen a poor, emaciated prisoner, roused to exhibit strength and courage by the hope of saving life, rush in and drag the cradle and its innocent living freight from the very jaws of death, while burning rafters crashed and fell upon him; they would have seen him place the babe in its mother's arms, and they would have seen that mother turn with streaming eyes to thank the saviour of her child, *and then start back conscience-smitten, and scream and fall, seeing in her child's preserver a man who in the prison had once implored her for a piece of bread because he was starving, and she spat upon him because he was of Northern race!!* Could they have seen the future of the coming months, they would have seen all this and more. But no such prevision was vouchsafed them. Their thoughts were now of themselves. They felt that the shade of a deadly peril encompassed them. Columbia and its prison were hidden from their sight, but still they were so near that at any moment the hounds might scent them, and if recaptured, all the horrors they had undergone would be light compared with the fate they must submit to in the future.

Fortunately for the purpose of our fugitives, the settlements, whether towns or villages, in that part of the country, were " few and far between." The residences of the planters were also distant from each other and few in number, and the ravines and swamps which abound there, while in many respects disagreeable and dangerous lurking spots, were still the safest refuges for hunted men. The wilder the country, the better it promised to Glazier and his comrade fleeing for their lives. Their greatest fear was the dreaded bloodhound. Our friends knew they could defeat most of the devices of human ingenuity in tracking them, but they were apprehensive that the instinct of the brutes, which a depraved humanity had enlisted in its service, might render abortive all their plans and precautions. They did their best, however, to baffle their canine foes, and nightfall found them hurrying forward on the Lexington Court-house Road.

THE ESCAPE—FED BY NEGROES IN A SWAMP.

CHAPTER XX.

THE ESCAPE FROM COLUMBIA.

Mysterious voices.—"I reckon deys Yankees."—"Who comes there?"—The Lady of the Manor.—A weird spectacle.—The struggle through the swamp.—A reflection on Southern swamps in general.—Tired nature's sweet restorer.

THE attention of the fugitives was suddenly arrested by the sound of human voices in their immediate rear. It occurred to both at once to discover as quickly as possible if the speakers were white or black, and they accordingly listened in the hope of learning their race by their dialect. This was by no means easy, the vernacular of the poorer class of whites in that section of the country very much resembling the ordinary language of the negroes. The comrades, therefore, concluded to risk a halt until the strangers came up. Glazier then saluted them with the remark that it was "a pleasant night," with the view of drawing them out before committing himself. "Indeed 'tis!" was the reply. This failed to convey the desired information as to the color of the strangers, and they thought it wiser to hurry forward than prolong the conversation at some risk to their safety. Before they had advanced many steps, however, they were agreeably surprised by hearing one of the same party remark to another, "I reckon deys Yankees," followed by the response, "Golly, I hope to God dey is!" Glazier immediately turned and inquired, "Do you know who I am?" "I reckon I dunno yer, massa," was the reply. "Have you ever seen a Yankee?" asked Glazier. "Lord bress yer, marser, I've seen a right smart heap ov um down at Clumby." "Well," said Glazier, "do we look like them?" "How'n de debbil can I tell dat in de dark, marser?" answered the now unmistakable negro, "but I spec' yer talk jest like' em." "We are Yankees," responded Glazier, "and have just escaped from Columbia. My good fellow, can't you do something for us?" "Ob course!" said our colored friend, promptly. "I'll do all I can for you, marster. I no nigga if I didn't 'sist de Yankees."

The fugitives had heard so much from their fellow-prisoners of the sympathy exhibited by the colored people of the South for Federal soldiers, that they hesitated not for a moment to place the fullest confidence in these humble friends. They thereupon explained their precise situation, and told them the story of their recent escape. They also learned from the negroes that they were returning to their masters, having come from Columbia, where they had been working upon a new prison stockade, now abandoned on account of the expected approach of General Sherman.

The name of their "Master" was Steadman, and, slave-fashion, one of the men was named "Ben Steadman." They were directing their steps to Mr. Steadman's plantation on the Augusta Road, and the fugitives therefore decided to keep in their company and use them as guides. In the nature of things, unless guided by some one accustomed to traveling in a country so bare of landmarks, they would lose ground continually, even if they ever reached their destination.

One of the negroes with that shrewdness engendered by slavery, in which cunning is the only protection against injury; and strength and courage count for nothing; suggested that so large a party would attract attention, and the safety of the two officers might be endangered. It was therefore finally determined that Ben should act as guide, and the other darkies take a different route home. Another advantage to be derived from dividing the party was that in the event of the fugitives being pursued, the double trail would mystify the hounds. Ere long Ben reached a bridle-path, which plunged into the wood, and as it offered superior advantages on account of its narrowness and privacy, and from the fact of its leading to the plantation of a well-known planter and therefore less likely to be suspected of being the road taken by escaped prisoners, the little party concluded that this was their safest route. They therefore hurried forward upon their way, Ben preceding them in the double capacity of guide and scout. A few miles from its commencement this path led to a blind road, which Ben informed them was seldom traveled by any in the night-time but men of his own race, so they turned into it, and had become quite joyful and careless, when suddenly the challenge, "Who goes there?" rang out in the stillness, and the next moment Ben was halted by the sentry of a Confederate picket consisting of eight men, who had bivouacked just off the road. Ben boldly advanced, and our two friends, it must be admitted, with more discretion than valor, started off like lightning, their "guide" meanwhile amusing the guard with a description of how "Dem two oder dam niggas got skeered, kase dey thought Mars Sentinel must be a dam Yank!"

No harm could come to Ben, as he was in a condition to prove that two other negroes had left Columbia with him, and the fugitives therefore feeling that *he* was safe, concealed themselves among the brush and awaited events. Ben shortly passed their place of hiding, in custody, *en route* to the Reserve, and our friends were not a little amused, despite their danger, to hear Ben's vigorous denunciation of "dem two cowardly niggas," who had taken to their heels!

A few moments only elapsed before they were made aware, by certain unmistakable tokens, that they were in dangerous proximity to the Confederate encampment, and although nearly famished, for they had eaten nothing since morning, it was deemed safest to lie *perdu ;* so, thanking the good providence which had sped them thus far on their journey, they lay down and slept.

The enemy's camp, which upon closer inspection, turned out to be simply the resting-place of a local patrol, unconnected with any regular command, broke up early in the morning, and Glazier and his companion once more had a clear road. Although hungry from long fasting, they ran swiftly over the swampy ground, and felt so elated to find themselves again in a state of freedom, that they laughed and joked like boys released from school, and pushed on until the verge of an extensive morass was reached and passed, and they found themselves in a section of country well wooded and watered, the alternate hills and vales presenting a pleasing variety to the eye.

There was here also a public road, but it would have been dangerous to travel thereon, and they therefore strode on beneath the trees and umbrageous undergrowth of the wood. Having had no breakfast,

T OF KNOWLEDGE UNDER DIFFICULTIES.

"blueberries" were not precisely the diet they would have selected for dinner, but as *necessitas non habet leges*, they quietly munched their berries, and we may hope felt grateful that matters were no worse. After a while they made a sudden detour, crossing the highroad, and by so doing, again broke the trail. Next they came to a clearing, but the sight of the planter leaning against a fence, soon sent them back to the friendly shelter of the wood. Late in the afternoon they came to a large plantation on the border of which was a copse, in which they lay down and watched for the opportunity of communicating with some of the house slaves. At the expiration of about an hour, a lady, probably the mistress of the estate, passed within a few yards of them, accompanied by a troupe of merry children. They however went on their way, utterly unconscious of the close proximity of two terrible Yankees!

Here our fugitives remained quietly concealed until night, and then cautiously crept away. They proceeded onward until they found themselves near a junction of cross-roads. Arrived at this junction, matters looked serious. Unlike mariners, they had no compass; unlike Indians, they were inexpert at discerning a trail; and what was more appalling, they distinctly saw reared up against the moonlit sky—a gallows! Our two friends approached this object very cautiously. It was not an unusual thing to hang spies, and not unfrequently those *mistaken* for spies, but to hang them on a regularly constructed gibbet was not usual; and therefore while Lemon insisted that the black and skeleton-like object that loomed against the horizon was a gallows, he still entertained some doubt upon the subject, and determined to satisfy himself by a closer inspection.

The weird object before them proved to be an innocent guide-board—the article of all others they most needed at that moment. Like the celebrated laws of Nero, however, the *directions* were posted very high, but Lemon being tall, our hero mounted on his shoulders and by the light of the moon deciphered the inscription. They had now no difficulty in choosing their way. On they pushed therefore; and during the black darkness of the night, crept through the tangled underwood, and over swamps where loathsome, crawling things that shun by day the presence of man, now seemed to seek his acquaintance. How mysterious are these dense untrodden forests of the South! The very air one breathes is living. Throughout the day a million chirping, whirring, twittering sounds, salute the ear. The short grass beneath the forest trees moves, writhes, and creeps with microscopic life, until the brain grows dizzy at the sight. At night it is no less marvellous to hear the myriad denizens of the swamps and woods; and terrible when your tread on some soft, velvety substance reveals a sleeping snake, who, at the same moment, attacks you with his poisonous fang, mayhap, fatally.

It is a singular, but well-accredited fact, that these great Southern swamps have been yearly deteriorating, while the surrounding country has been growing in civilization. Old writers tell us that the reptile life now infesting them in such rank luxuriance had scarcely any existence one hundred years ago. Colonel Byrd writes of the "Dismal Swamp:" "Since the surveyors have entered the Dismal Swamp they have seen no living creature; neither bird, beast, insect nor reptile, came to view. Not even a turkey-buzzard will venture to fly over it, no more than the Italian vulture will venture to fly over the filthy lake of Avernus; or the birds of the Holy Land over the Salt Sea where Sodom and Gomorrah once stood." And yet, in the present day, insect and reptile life swarms there in every form through all the hours of the day and night!

Our fugitive friends, however, felt little inclination to philosophize upon this subject. The hope of coming liberty strengthened their limbs, and they bent all their energy to the task of moving forward; walking, running, creeping, until the dawn of day approached, when weary and footsore they sought some secure spot and lay down and slept—perchance to dream of "Home, sweet Home"—perchance of "Camp Sorghum," and its "chivalric" guards—perchance of the dreadful blood-hounds whose fatal scent might even then be on their trail!

CHAPTER XXI.

LOYALTY OF THE NEGROES.

Startled by hounds.—An unpleasant predicament.—A Christian gentlewoman.—Appeal to Mrs. Colonel Taylor.—"She did all she could."—A meal fit for the gods.—Aunt Katy.—"Lor' bress ye, marsters!"—Uncle Zeb's prayer.—Hoe-cake and pinders.—Woodcraft *versus* astronomy.—Canine foes.—Characteristics of the slave.—Meeting escaped prisoners.—Danger.—Retreat and concealment.

IT is the morning of November twenty-eighth, 1864. The sun has just risen above the eastern hills, and his slanting beams fall upon the goodly heritage of Colonel Alexander Taylor, "C. S. A." There are, as yet, none of the usual features here of a war-stricken country; everything around is rich and substantial. The residence is a stately mansion in the Elizabethan style, and the lady who, accompanied by two sweet children, walks the broad piazza, is evidently a refined gentlewoman. The colonel himself, like a gallant (but mistaken) knight, has "gone to the wars."

She marvels what makes "Rupert," a noble hound, that but a moment ago stretched himself at full length across the hallway, rise and bound over the lawn, barking loudly and fiercely as he runs. She calls him—at first gently, and then peremptorily, until the old hound with evident reluctance obeys the summons, and crouches at her feet. She then directs a negro, whose tokens of age and long service are as pronounced as those of his canine rival, to find out what there is in the clump of trees beyond the north hedge, to excite "Rupert's" anger. The venerable negro, with the deliberateness of his race, proceeds in the direction indicated, but is saved the necessity of much exertion, by the startling appearance of a young soldier in a motley uniform of gray and blue—his coat of one color—his nether garments of another! He advances boldly toward the house, and the lady scrutinizes the intruder. The result of her examination shows her visitor to be a slight, but sinewy young man, with a frank and honest expression, and seemingly not more than eighteen years of age. The motley stranger drew near, and bowing gracefully saluted her with, "Good-morning, madam."

The lady at once returned the salutation with a genial smile, that sent a thrill of pleasure and confidence to his heart. Without further ceremony he thereupon frankly and fearlessly informed Mrs. Taylor that he and his companion were escaped Union prisoners; that they were in a condition of starvation; and appealed respectfully but most urgently to her as a woman, for humanity's sake, to assist them in their sore need by giving them food. She at first hesitated, startled by such a request from such a source. Her husband, she said, was an officer in the Confederate service, and if it became known that she had assisted those whom his government counted enemies, it would possibly bring reproach upon him. Our young hero (for he it was) then addressed her somewhat after the fashion of the unfortunate Ulysses in his appeal to the goddess Calypso; recounted his misfortunes briefly, touched on the terrible fate that awaited him and his companion, should they be recaptured, and all doubtless in such moving terms that, like Desdemona, the lady must have thought, if she did not exclaim:

"'Twas pitiful—'twas wondrous pitiful!"

This is evident from the fact that she scarcely awaited the end of his story, before assuring him that "she would do all she could," following up that assurance in a few moments by offering the manly and polite youth before her an abundant supply of fresh and excellent food; which, she took the precaution of adding, was for himself and his comrade, fearing possibly, from Glazier's famished look, he might consume it all himself! She further assured her visitor that she would keep the secret of his having been there; while he, in return, protested that should the varying fortunes of war give him the opportunity of serving her husband, he would do so at the risk of his life. With his haversack amply replenished, an appetite like a wolf, faith in the goodness of God strengthened, and belief in the perfection of some, at least, of the fairest portion of creation greatly confirmed by this interview, he rejoined Lieutenant Lemon, and the comrades proceeded forthwith to the meal that was enjoyed with a zest known only to the starving. Before reclining himself under the glittering stars, Glazier made this entry in his diary: "Oh! ye who sleep on beds of down, in your curtained chambers, and rise at your leisure to feast upon the good things provided . . . you never knew the luxury of a night of *rest*, nor the sweets of a meal seasoned by hunger, and the grateful remembrance that it was provided by woman's kindly heart, which, wherever it may beat, sooner or later responds to the tale of misfortune."

After a sleep so profound as to extend several hours beyond the time they had agreed upon as best adapted for the resumption of their journey, they found themselves much refreshed and strengthened, so much so that by sunrise they had reached a small stream known as Black Creek, one of the tributaries of the North Edisto River. Here, in crossing a bridge, they very opportunely encountered a colored laborer, who was on his way to work, and who cheerfully turned aside to guide them to a hut, where he assured them they could remain in safety throughout the day. The proprietor of this refuge for hunted wayfarers was a certain "Aunt Katy"—an aged negress, whose heart and hut, and such fare as her scanty larder contained, were always at the disposal of the distressed. Hearing that the strangers were Union soldiers who had escaped from Columbia, she approached them with the following salutation: "Gor A'mighty bress yer, marsters; dis is de yeah ob jubilee, shua, when de Yankees come to Aunt Katy's. Come in, marsters, come in!"

Accordingly they entered, and, by some occult process, the fact of their presence soon became known to the entire slave population of the neighborhood, who came flocking in throughout the day. Such an important occasion would have been incomplete without a prayer-meeting, Aunt Katy herself being a pillar of the Colored Methodist Church, and it was not long before the whole assemblage were on their knees, invoking every imaginable blessing upon the cause of the Union and its defenders, and every evil upon its opponents. Among other things Captain Glazier records, as a feature of this impromptu prayer-meeting, is the petition of a venerable prototype of "Uncle

Tom," named Zebulon, "who appeared to be a ruling spirit in the party." This good man's enthusiasm burst forth as follows:

"Oh Lor' Gor A'mighty! We'se you-ah chillen as much as de white folks am, and we spec yo to heah us widout delay, Lor'; cause we all is in right smart ob a hurry. Dese yere gemmen has runned away from de Seceshers, and wants ter git back to de Norf! Dey has no time to wait! Ef it's 'cordin' to de des'nation of great heben to help 'em et'll be 'bout necessary for dat ar help to come soon.

"De hounds and de rebels is on dar track. Take de smell out of de dogs' noses, O Lor'! and let 'Gypshun darkness come down ober de eyesights of de rebels. Comfoozle 'em, O Lor'! dey is cruel, and makes haste to shed blood. Dey has long 'pressed de black man, and groun' him in de dust, and now I reck'n dey 'spects dat dey am agwine to serve de Yankees in de same way.

"'Sist dese gemmen in time ob trouble, and lift 'em fru all danger on to de udder side ob Jordan dry-shod.

"And raise de radiance ob your face on all de Yankees what's shut up in de Souf. Send some Moses, O Lor'! to guide 'em frue de Red Sea ob 'flickshun into de promised land.

"Send Mr. Sherman's company sweepin' down frue dese yere parts to scare de rebels till dey flee like de Midians, and slew darselves to sabe dar lives.

"Let a little de best of heben's best judgments res' on Massa Lincum, and may de year ob Jubilee come sure.

"O Lor'! bless de gin'rals ob de Norf—O Lor'! bless de kunnels—O Lor'! bless de brigerdeers—O

UNCLE ZEB'S PRAYER.

Lor'! bless de capt'ins—O Lor'! bless de Yankees right smart. O Lor'! eberlastin'. Amen."

This very pertinent supplication and much more in the same vein, was listened to with marked approval by the audience—a sonorous and prolonged "Amen!" in which our friends heartily participated, greeting the conclusion of Uncle Zeb's prayer. Our subject, in describing the particulars of his escape, remarks that, notwithstanding the fact that the secret of their retreat was known to some thirty or forty of these poor slaves, neither he nor his companion entertained the shadow of a doubt that the secret would be safe with them; and adds that, in addition to their good faith, they possessed a remarkable talent for concealment.

The Steadman plantation was only three miles from Aunt Katy's hut, and accordingly, Ben being sent for, soon made his appearance, and proffered his valuable services as guide. The offer was thankfully accepted; but, despite the preference of Glazier and his companion for the swamp as the safest place of concealment, Ben prevailed upon them to visit his cabin, where they were hospitably entertained by his wife and children. Having been duly inspected as curiosities "from de Norf," our friends were pleased to hear Ben instruct his little daughter to run up to the house of his mistress and "snatch a paper." She soon afterward came running back with the Augusta *Constitutionalist*, published that morning.

Having gathered from the newspaper a sufficiently intelligible idea of the relative position of Sherman and his opponents, the fugitives bade farewell to the family, and proceeded upon their way, crossing the river by ten o'clock; and shortly after—Ben having parted from them—in consequence of the complicated directions of *numerous blind-roads*, became confused, and, instead of pushing forward beyond the South Edisto, as they had planned to do, they halted early in the afternoon and "pitched their tent" for the remainder of the day and night—said *tent* having the sky for its roof as usual.

Their camping-ground upon this occasion was in the heart of a dense pine wood, where, notwithstanding the grim and spectral surroundings, they slept soundly until after midnight, and then arose refreshed and ready for another day's march on the road to freedom. Hoe-cake and pinders (*anglicè*, peanuts) formed their only repast, which they found sufficiently luxurious under the circumstances.

It now became necessary to find their bearings. There was no star plainly visible, and they had not yet learned to take the moon as a guide. Moreover, the heavenly bodies in Southern latitudes have so different an appearance from those seen at the North, that they were frequently in doubt as to the points of the compass. "I remember," writes Captain Glazier, "that it caused me great grief to find that the North Star was much nearer the horizon, and seemed to have lost that prominence which is given to it in higher latitudes, where it is a guide, standing far above tree-top and mountain."

What the lofty stars failed to teach, however, they learned from humbler signs. Glazier, in his youth, acquired the lesson in woodcraft, that moss hangs heaviest upon the northern side of tree trunks; and then the streams in this part of the continent, for the most part, flow towards the southeast, so that our friends were not altogether without indications of their position with regard to the points of the compass.

They were greatly annoyed by a serious obstacle to their safe progress, which presented itself in the shape of a vast multitude of dogs, of all sizes and every variety of breed. There were dogs of high degree, dogs of low degree, and mongrel curs of no degree; and all these animals were in possession of one ambition in common, namely, to nose out and hunt a Yankee!

Consequently, from the deep-mouthed baying of the blood-hound, or the mastiff, to the sniff and snarl of the rat-terrier, their music was not agreeable to the fugitives, who had, however, to contend with this difficulty, and surmount it.

Confining themselves to the pathless forest, the roads were now frequently lost sight of for miles. Occasionally, in the effort to shun the high-road, they would come suddenly upon a dwelling, and the inevitable lank, yellow dog would pounce out upon them, and add wings to their feet.

It was always a pleasant interruption of their lonely tramp to meet any negroes. These people, so patient under oppression, so humble under correction, were ever faithful and devoted to those whom they believed to be the friends of their race. Our hero, of course, had rare opportunities of observing the characteristics of this people. Simple, harmless and gentle, crimes of violence among them were very rare, and the cruelties practised upon them seem rather to have opened their hearts to sympathy than to have hardened them into vindictiveness.

With the aid of many of these devoted people,

Glazier and his friend reached and crossed the North Edisto, the latter a task of some magnitude. The river, at the point where they reached it, is not a single stream, but a maze of creeks and bayous, all of which it was necessary to cross in order to attain the opposite bank of what is known as the South Edisto River.

While passing over a bridge that spanned one of the creeks, Glazier heard footsteps upon another bridge in their rear; and so trained and acute does the ear of man become when disciplined in such a school of perilous experiences, that he knew at once they had nothing to fear from those who followed; for, instead of the bold, firm tread of the man who hunts, it was the uncertain, hesitating, half-halting step of the hunted.

"Escaped prisoners," whispered our two friends simultaneously, and Glazier, stepping boldly forth, gave the challenge, "Who goes there!"

"With a trembling start," says our fugitive hero, "the foremost man replied, 'Friends!'"

"'Halt, friends! and advance one,'" commanded Lieutenant Glazier.

Very cautiously, and with the manner of one ready to turn at any moment and dash into the recesses of the swamp, one of the strangers came forward to within a few feet of his interrogator, and craning his body over, peered nervously into his face. Thereupon a mutual recognition as Federals was the result, and Lemon discovered that one of the new comers had been a fellow-prisoner with himself. This made matters pleasant, and although it was mutually agreed that it would be wise to separate, and take different routes, both parties unconsciously protracted the meeting until they were startled into caution by perceiving almost directly in front of them, surrounding a large fire, a Confederate encampment. "It proved to be a squad of tax-gatherers, going about the country with quartermasters' wagons, collecting supplies."

Further progress was now impossible. The enemy occupied the only practicable road in front, and they were flanked on both sides by large ponds of water. Our party thereupon stealthily retreated into the woods, where they finally concluded to make themselves contented for the remainder of the night.

CHAPTER XXII.

PROGRESS OF THE FUGITIVES.

Parting company.—Thirst and no water.—Hoping for the end.—The boy and the chicken.—Conversation of ladies overheard.—The fugitives pursued.—The sleeping village.—Captain Bryant.—The *alba sus.*—Justifiable murder, and a delicious meal.—Darkies and their prayers.—Man proposes; God disposes.—An adventure.—*A ruse de guerre.*—Across the Savannah.

ON emerging from their place of concealment, the following morning, the road proved to be once more open. The tax-collectors had departed. Warned by the experience of the previous night the newly found friends reluctantly parted company, Glazier and Lemon pursuing a separate route from the others.

Our friends had suffered much in various ways since they shook the dust of Columbia from their feet, but now a dire misfortune overtook them in the total absence of water. The waters of the swamps were poisonous, and their longing desire and hope were that they might soon come upon a spring or stream to slake their burning thirst, which threatened to unfit them for the exertion necessary.

The land, in the region of country they had now entered, was waste and arid—for the most part sand, a few stunted trees being the sole vegetation. These trees had nothing pleasant in their appearance, as forest trees usually have. The branches seemed destitute of sap, as the leaves were of verdure; they had not reached maturity, and yet possessed none of the lithe grace of saplings.

Our fugitives were parched, fevered, and weak before they emerged from this inhospitable tract of country, but at length reached a point where the vegetation was fresher, and finally, to their great joy, discovered a spring. Here, to use Glazier's own words, they realized "the value of cold water to a thirsty soul." "The stream ran through a ravine nearly a hundred feet in depth, while high up on the banks were groves of pines."

After their passage though the "Desert," they were in excellent condition to appreciate the wild and solemn grandeur of the spot they had now reached, and for a considerable time they could not make up their minds to leave the place. At length, however, they resumed their journey. December second found the two friends still far from their destination, and by no means out of danger. It was one week only since they bade adieu to Columbia, and yet many weeks seemed to them to have passed. Still they were making considerable progress, and had by this time reached a swamp near Aiken, South Carolina.

Having journeyed all night since quitting the secluded ravine, they were ready once more to cast themselves upon the soft moss under a venerable tree, near which was a gurgling spring. Here they slept soundly until dawn, when a colored boy passing down a road which came within their range of vision attracted attention. The boy was carrying a basket, and they were suffering very seriously again from hunger. Lemon followed, and called to him: "Hold on, my boy; I want to see you!" The lad muttered something, but the only word they could distinguish was "chicken!" He then ran off as fast as his legs would carry him. The lieutenant, with great emphasis, endeavored to reassure him, but it was of no use. He ran as if a legion of evil spirits was at his heels, and Lemon returned to his comrade very much disappointed and chagrined. "Now they are sure to overtake us," said he, "we shall be prisoners again before night!"

"Never fear," was the reply of his cooler companion; "as long as there is a swamp in the neighborhood, we'll lead them a lively dance."

So the friends gathered up their belongings, and in a few minutes put a considerable distance between themselves and their resting-place of the previous night. Finally they concealed themselves in a swamp about a mile distant. A road bordered the margin of their sanctuary so closely, that they distinctly overheard a conversation between three ladies who passed. The chasing of a negro boy by a Yankee was the topic of their discourse.

This information made our friends more cautious, and it is well they were so, for, towards evening, several mounted men armed with guns were seen by them upon the main road leading to Aiken; their evident purpose being to intercept the fugitives, of whose presence in their neighborhood the boy had made report.

Forewarned was forearmed, and our hero and his companion determined to give the enemy a wide berth. Again, therefore, plunging into the recesses of a neighboring swamp, they went quietly to sleep, and slept until midnight, when Glazier awoke to see thousands of stars glittering through the spectral

A SLEEPING VILLAGE.

branches of the pines, and away off toward the western horizon, a flood of silvery effulgence from the waning moon.

Entranced by the beauty of the scene, he awoke his comrade, and all around being buried in profound silence, they proceeded on their way. It was not long before they found themselves upon the outskirts of the village of Aiken, and no practicable path upon either side presenting itself, but one resource remained, namely, to steal cautiously through, although this involved the imminent risk of discovery. On, therefore, they walked until they came to the border of the village. They found it dumb with sleep. Not a sound disturbed the silence. The very dogs, their usually sleepless foes, appeared for once to have become wearied and gone to rest.

There is something solemn about a sleeping town. The solitude of the swamp and wood is solemn; but the ghostly stillness of a town, where all its inhabitants lie buried in sleep, and no sign or sound proclaims the presence of life in man or beast, is of so weird a character as to produce a sensation of awe, akin to fear. The shadows that enwrapped them as they came beneath the buildings, and the fitful gleams of moonlight that fell upon them when streets were crossed, seemed not lights and shadows at all, but strange, intangible things. And when at length they reached the outer limit of the village, and the distant woods were seen by the moon's rays, our travellers felt as if they had been wandering in a graveyard, where the tombs were houses, and they wished they were in the swamp again, where such uncanny fancies never troubled them. When the toad and lizard, snakes and other loathsome things, crawled around their swampy bed, they cared nothing; but the dead silence of a cloudless night, brooding over a swarm of their fellow-beings, brought with it a feeling they could not account for or understand; and therefore it was with a sense of great relief they found themselves at the outer edge of the town.

Their satisfaction, however, was somewhat moderated when, at a sudden turn of the road, they abruptly came upon a man and a boy, who were picking their way with such velvety tread that the two parties were face to face before either was aware of the proximity of the other. The strangers appeared to be the more alarmed, for they were just making a secret and rapid detour with the view of debouching into a side street, when, feeling sure that none but fugitives would be so anxious to escape an interview, Glazier hailed them:

"Don't be uneasy, boys! We're friends! We're Yankees!"

His conjecture proved correct. The strangers were Captain Bryant, of the Fifth New York Cavalry, and a friend. "They had," says Captain Glazier, "a negro guide, who was to secrete them in a hut until the next night, when they were to proceed, as we had done, and reach the line of freedom by the nearest route."

The interview was brief, the parties differing as to which was the most expedient route, and the discussion terminated by each taking the one he thought best. Glazier and his comrade made off to a swamp, and upon securing a safe resting-place, were overjoyed to find a venerable sow and her litter approaching. They greeted the porcine mother, says our friend, "otherwise than did wandering Æneas the *alba sus* lying under the hollow trees of ancient Italy," for, "enticing them with crumbs of hoe-cake," they both in unison struck a juvenile porker on the head with a heavy cane, and then Uncle Zeb's mammoth knife came into requisition, and did good service. Over the embers of a fire kindled in a hole in the ground, they roasted the little fellow, and made a delicious meal.

They had scarcely finished their unexpected feast, when again the thud of an axe in the distance smote on their ears, and Glazier crept cautiously out to reconnoitre. The wood-cutter proved to be a colored lad, and having a vivid recollection of their scampering friend of "chicken" fame, he hailed him in this wise: "Hello, Sambo!"

This manner of salute left the party addressed in doubt as to the colors under which the young white stranger served. Off went his hat, therefore, and he stood grinning and waiting to hear more. Our hero walked quickly up to him, and frankly explained the situation, concluding, as usual, with a request for information and aid. Both were promptly tendered, and shortly after, the fugitives were concealed in a cornfodder house. Here, in the evening, a motley and humorous delegation of darkies waited upon them and after ventilating their sage opinions upon the conduct of the war, organized a prayer-meeting; and, if the fervor of human prayer availeth, they doubtless damaged the cause of Secession materially that evening.

The topographical knowledge of these well-meaning friends appears to have been at fault, for had Glazier followed the route they advised, instead of striking the railroad running from Charleston to Augusta, on the west side of Aiken, which would have enabled them, by pursuing it to the westward, to reach Augusta, they struck it on the east side, and consequently by mistake followed it towards Charleston, precisely the place to which they did *not* want to go.

"How far is it, my boy, by this road, to Drainside?" asked a mud-splashed traveler of a shrewd lad by the roadside.

"If you keep on the way you are heading, and can manage the Atlantic and Pacific on horseback," replied the boy, "it is 23,999 miles. If you turn your horse's head and go right back, it is one mile."

Our friends were in a somewhat similar condition. Soon, however, in the darkness, they came to a small village, where a freight train was in waiting for an early start. They tried to conceal themselves on board this train, but very fortunately for their safety they could not find a hiding-place in or under the cars, and shortly afterwards discovered that Charleston was its destination and not Augusta. Had they boarded this train they would certainly have been recaptured in Charleston and sent back to imprisonment. "A merciful Providence interposed," Glazier writes. "Thus 'man proposes,' often to his own ruin, but 'God disposes,' always to His own glory, and the good of his creatures."

A blood-hound was on their track in the course of the night, the deep bayings being plainly audible, but his scent being at fault, the trail of the fugitives was lost, and he shortly barked himself out of hearing.

When daybreak came and a passenger train filled with rebel soldiers and recruits swept past them, setting up a savage yell at sight of the pedestrians, it was feared by the latter that the train might be stopped with a view to their capture, so they once more concealed themselves in the wood.

The sound of heavy cannonading reassured them as to the proximity of Federal troops; but, where was Augusta? Accurate information on this point was absolutely essential before further progress was made; and Lemon was commissioned to obtain it. He was so far successful that he learned from some negro wood-choppers—much to the chagrin of both—that they had been walking all night in the opposite direction from Augusta, that is, on the direct road to Charleston! They also learned, what was much more cheering, that they could cross the Savannah River, at a point twenty miles below Augusta, at Point Comfort; that Sherman was making straight for Savannah, and therefore their chances of ultimately falling in with his army were by no means impaired.

No time was lost in moving forward in the direction indicated, and during the night our hero met with an adventure which we cannot do better than relate in his own words; he says: "We came to a fork in the road, and after debating some time as to which course we should pursue, I leaped over the fence and made for a negro hut, while several hounds from the plantation house followed hard on my track. I managed, by some tall running, to come in a few feet ahead, and bolted into the shanty without warning or formality, slamming the door behind me to keep out the dogs. A great stupid negro was standing before the fire, his hands and face buried in fresh pork and hoe-cake, which he was making poor work at eating. His broad, fat countenance glistened with an unguent distilled partly from within and partly from without. Turning my eyes from the negro to the untidy hearth, they were greeted, as were also my olfactories, with a skillet of pork frying over the coals.

"Without troubling him to answer any questions, I opened the mouth of my haversack and poured into it the dripping contents of the skillet. I next observed that the ashes on the hearth had a suspiciously fat appearance, and, taking the tongs, began raking among them. My suspicions were verified, for two plump-looking hoe-cakes came to light, which were also deposited in the haversack.

"Looking around still farther I saw what I had not observed before, *Dinah's black head*, as she peered out from among the bed-clothes, rolling two of the most astonished white eyes that ever asked the question, 'What's you g'wine to do next?' Not seeing any practical way in which I could answer her mute question, I said to Sambo, 'Call the dogs into the house.' This he did hastily. I then asked, 'Uncle, what road must *this rebel* take for Tinker Creek?' 'De right han' one, out dar', I reckon,' he answered. Again bidding him keep the hounds in the house till morning, I rushed out to the road and joined my companion. We made lively work for about three miles, after which we took it more leisurely, stopping to rest and refresh ourselves at every stream that crossed the road."

The winter was by this time fairly upon them, and sleeping in the open air by no means a pleasant experience. They therefore made long marches, and by the aid of an occasional friendly push from their negro allies at length arrived in the vicinity of Point Comfort. This was on the seventh of December, and the twelfth day of their pilgrimage. After being somewhat alarmed by the proximity of a pack of dogs, with which some boys were hunting, they escaped discovery,

THE ESCAPE—CROSSING THE SAVANNAH AT MIDNIGHT.

and securing another negro for a guide they on the same night found themselves upon the banks of the Savannah River.

A colored man's cabin, as usual, sheltered them during the day, and their host and his dusky neighbors (many of whom flocked around to see the Yankees, as was their custom) proving to be fishermen well acquainted with the river, our friends prevailed upon one of their number to undertake the task of carrying them across. The first difficulty that presented itself was, where to find a boat; but their host remembered, he said, a place upon one of the tributaries of the Savannah where one lay, not exactly in good sailing trim it is true, for the authorities had ordered the destruction of boats along all the streams where escaped prisoners were likely to seek a passage, and this craft had not escaped their vigilance; but he thought, by the liberal use of pitch and cotton, materials easily obtainable in that neighborhood, it could be made sufficiently water-tight to answer their purpose. Accordingly, accompanied by their friendly Charon, with his pitch-pot and cotton, they reached the spot indicated and found the boat.

It was in a very dilapidated state, but "all night long the faithful fellows worked, caulking and pitching," while the fugitives "lay concealed in an old hollow beech log."

It was midnight before he had finished his task, and launched the boat into the stream. She looked very shaky, but the extemporized shipwright reassured them by saying confidently:

"She's ready, massa. I'll soon land you in Georgey."

They were scarcely, however, in the boat before she commenced to leak; there was no help for it, so our adventurers betook themselves to bailing the water out as fast as it entered, and the zealous negro pulled away with all his might. They kept her afloat until within a short distance of the wished-for shore, and then, seeing that if they did not quit her she would certainly quit them, the two passengers leaped out, and managed with some difficulty to ascend the beach.

CHAPTER XXIII.

THE PERILS OF AN ESCAPE.

Alligators.—A detachment of Southern chivalry.—A scare.—Repairs neatly executed.—Misery and despair.—Virtue its own reward.—Hunger and desperation.—Audacity.—A Confederate officer.—"A good Union man."—" Two sights and a jambye."—A narrow escape.

CAPTAIN GLAZIER and his companion were not insensible to the danger they incurred of being drawn under the water by an alligator; animals they knew to be numerous and voracious in that river, and were therefore not slow in quitting its banks. So, bidding a hearty good-bye to their humble companion, who was already busy re-caulking his boat for the home voyage, they once more plunged into the recesses of the swamps, intending to push forward as far as possible before the morning dawned.

They wended their way through a Southern cypress swamp. Some distance back from the river they could perceive a large plantation-house, with its out-buildings and accessories, protected by groups of oak and beech ; but they dared not approach it. Under the far-reaching and sheltering cypress they pursued their way.

The cypress here attains considerable height, the branches issuing from a trunk formed like a cone; but occasionally they are to be seen of very stunted growth. Around the full-sized tree are frequently to be found a whole family of dwarfs, nature having arrested their growth when from one to ten feet high. These would present an unsightly look, were it not for the mantle of Spanish moss that envelopes, and gives them a graceful and picturesque appearance.

Large alligators lay along the bayous, and on every prostrate log, watching the movements of Glazier and his companion. "They were," he says, "apparently pleased at our misfortunes, and sent towards us loving, hungry glances." As soon as approached, these "wardens of the marshes" would hobble to the edge of a bayou, and allow themselves to fall in; their eyes remaining above water blinking at the invaders, as if inviting them to follow. They were probably, as Glazier observes, "a detachment of Southern chivalry doing duty on their own grounds."

Finally, emerging from the swamp they entered a corn-field, and discovered a delicious spring; and not far off, a friendly negro. They arranged to meet him here at eight o'clock, at which hour he returned and piloted them to some of his friends a short distance off. They were several times upon the point of being discovered—once by a planter, and again by a number of white children, who, attended by their nurse, and a pack of curs, approached within a few feet of their hiding-place. Our friends gradually edged themselves towards a thicket, which was distant about four miles from Briar Creek, the latter being eighteen miles from Millen—the junction of the Augusta branch and the main line of the Central Railway of Georgia.

At this thicket, feeling very weary, our fugitives threw themselves on the ground, and were soon asleep. Nothing occurred to disturb their slumber; but, on awaking, their consternation was great to find themselves guarded by sentinels! Four large hounds stood looking down at them with an air of responsibility for their safe-keeping; snuffing occasionally at their persons, to discover, probably, if they had the scent of game. This indicated an alarming condition of things. And the fear fell upon them that the owner of the hounds had discovered them while they slept, and they were again prisoners. But their alarm soon subsided. No human being appeared; and the dogs seemed to consider their responsibility at an end, now that the slumberers were awake; and walking around them in the most natural manner, with much show of dignity, trooped away without even a parting salute, but greatly to the relief of our alarmed friends. They were soon after confronted by another source of affright. This was the approach of a large cavalry patrol, which came so near their place of concealment, that they were compelled to forego a fire, cold as it was, and eat their sweet potatoes raw—the only rations left them. They however escaped observation.

They knew nothing of the whereabouts of General Sherman; but certain unmistakable indications satisfied them that they were now approaching the scene of military operations. Bridges destroyed, while others were under the guard of bodies of soldiers; large herds of stock driven by the planters themselves to the recesses of the swamps and forests for protection; the hurrying across country of men on horseback and afoot, and the general appearance of excitement and unrest that prevailed around them, convinced Glazier and his companion that the formidable Sherman was not very distant.

It was hard to be deprived of the comfort of a fire at such an inclement season, for the weather had become intensely cold, and rain fell incessantly. A merciful Providence, however, directed their steps towards a spot where an aged negro was cutting wood and warming himself at a fire by turns, and they were thus enabled to thaw their frozen garments and gather some warmth in their numbed limbs. With the aid of the old negro, they improvised a rude tent by means of their blankets, and on leaving for his supper, he promised to return in the evening with some hoe-cakes. This promise he faithfully fulfilled, and remained to cobble Glazier's shoes into a condition of comparative comfort. During the day the shoes had threatened to part company with their owner and leave him barefoot.

The aforesaid shoes having been subjected to the process of repair, our hero at first demurred to their liberal dimensions, but learned, partly from the cobbler and partly from experience, that as the *'possum skin* (which formed the uppers) began to dry, it acquired the hardness and durability of *horn;* and hence, extra space became necessary. The shoes lasted him till the end of his adventures, and are still preserved as a memento of auld lang syne.

The following day was passed in the swamp, a wretched, dispiriting, drizzling rain, falling from morn till night, bringing the temperature down to zero. They recommenced their journey at dark despite the weather; preferring to push ahead rather than seek shelter again, with their friends, and so delay their progress. Thus they tramped wearily along, until the small town of Alexander was reached, and by this time their condition had become so desperate, that they knocked at the first cabin they came to. A white woman, in reply to their inquiry, which was the road to Millen, said "she did not know." And now, for the first time since their escape from Columbia, a feeling of despair took possession of them. They were cold, hungry, worn out, nearly naked, and shelterless, and such were their misery and despair, that had they not suddenly stumbled upon a large frame building used by negro laborers on the railroad, they would have been recaptured from utter powerlessness to seek concealment, or have fallen by the wayside and died.

Here, however, they met with a generous reception, and obtained the information they sought. After exchanging some kind words with these humble people, who heartily sympathized with them, Glazier and his comrade proceeded on their way.

Everything went satisfactorily until they unexpectedly came upon the banks of a considerable stream, and, after a careful search, failed to discover any practicable means of crossing it, except by fording. The fact of its being fordable gave rise to an incident with a *moral*, and as the gallant captain relates the story we will quote his own words:

"Sitting," he writes, "on a log, and ruminating over our chances, a very selfish piece of strategy suggested itself. Accordingly, I said to Lemon, 'There is no use of both getting wet; we can carry each other over these streams. If you will carry me over this, I will carry you over the next.' I said, 'these streams,' although only one was before us, and the most prominent thought in my mind was that, in all probability, there would be no other.

"Lemon somehow failed to see the point, and consented. Accordingly, taking off our shoes, I mounted on the lieutenant's shoulders, as school-boys sometimes carry each other, and he staggered through the stream with me, doing no worse than wetting my feet. This worked well. I congratulated myself, and gave a generous sympathy to Lemon in his shiverings. The chances were ten to one, I thought, that the carrying business was at an end, when suddenly another stream, wider than the first, rose up in the darkness before us. There was no use in wincing, and I stripped for the task. The lieutenant ascended to the position he had fairly earned. I plunged into the water. The middle of the stream was reached in safety, when, through no fault of mine, either the water became too deep, or my back became too weak for the burden, and the consequence was, the worthy gentleman was nearly as well soaked as myself when we reached the opposite shore. Selfishness, as well as virtue, sometimes brings its own reward."

They crossed three other streams during the night, but, by mutual consent, the carrying contract was canceled, and each did his own wading. "Thus," adds the captain, "another grand scheme for human elevation fell to the ground!"

Weary and wet to the skin, they persevered in their onward course, until they reached another cypress swamp, and discovered a road through it, which had evidently been the scene of a recently fought battle. Fences and buildings were razed to the ground, while fragments of military equipments were scattered about profusely—broken muskets, spent cartridges, and dead cattle; all told the story of a late conflict.

Our fugitives had no means of learning at the time any particulars of the supposed fight, but were afterward informed that less than a week previous to their being on the spot, General Kilpatrick's cavalry and the Seventeenth Army Corps had swept like an avalanche along that road.

The temperature by this time had somewhat moderated, and Glazier and his companion, thinking it unlikely the road would be much used for a time, concluded that they might with safety lie down and obtain some necessary rest and sleep. In their exhausted condition, they slept through the day and the greater part of the following night, arousing themselves with difficulty for the work still before them.

Judging from the fact that many of the dead horses seen on the road bore the brand of the "United States," and from other indications, they arrived at the conclusion that the Union forces were not very distant, and that they themselves were now possibly in the wake of Sherman's army. This being the case, the hope revived in their breasts of soon joining their friends—unless they had the misfortune to be picked up by the enemy's scouts. Hence, having lost so much of the night, they decided to travel this time by day, and at once put their determination into practice. Glazier and his friend soon discovered, however, that they were not expedited in their journey to any great extent—the streams being greatly swollen from the recent rains, and forming a serious obstacle to their progress.

They also felt that traveling by daylight was attended with much hazard to their safety. One advantage of journeying through a part of the country lately traversed by an invading army, was found in the fact of there being much smouldering fire along their line of march, and thus our friends ran no risk of attracting attention by approaching these fires at their several halting-places. This circumstance afforded one element of comfort—*warmth*. But another, still more important, was lacking, namely—*food*.

They had traveled the entire day without meeting a single negro, and hence, their commissariat was *non est*, and gaunt hunger created in them a sense of desperation. In this state they reached, after sunset, a plantation, where no house appeared but a number of humble shanties; and, weary, starving and desperate, they boldly advanced to the door of the best-looking cabin, and knocked for admission.

"Who's thar?" was answered in a tone, common to the poor whites and blacks of that section, that afforded no indication of the color of the speaker. That, however, was the first thing to determine before proceeding further. So our hero replied, interrogatively: "Are you black or white in there?" "Thar aint no niggahs heah," was the response, and the indignant tone of its delivery placed it beyond doubt that they had fallen upon a family of "poor whites." Glazier thereupon changed his voice to that of the "high-toned" rebel, and asked why he kept an officer of the Confederate army waiting for admittance. The man reluctantly opened the door, and the *soi-disant* Confederate demanded in an imperious tone, "How long is it since our army passed here?"

"What army?" was the cautious query, before an answer was vouchsafed.

"Why the rebel army, of course!"

The man hereupon stated that Wheeler's cavalry had passed by a week before, following Sherman's rear guard.

"How far is it to General Wheeler's headquarters?" asked Lieutenant Glazier.

"I dun'no!" growled the other; "but I guess it's a right smart distance."

To other questions, as to the possibility of obtaining one or more horses and mules, and even a suggestion that something to eat would not be unwelcome, the fellow protested that the —— Yankees had stripped the country of everything, and left them neither horses, mules, nor anything to eat. Through the intervention of his wife, however, Glazier finally obtained some bread and sweet potatoes; and, delivering a lecture to him upon the gross ingratitude of treating in such a niggardly manner a soldier who had left a home of opulence and comfort, to battle for *his* rights and liberties, with much more of a similar audacious character, he left the house.

Time, however, was too precious to be wasted, and, at the conclusion of the meal, they hurriedly resumed their march.

A solitary planter passed them, returning their carefully-worded salutation, and, evidently mistaking them for Confederates, volunteered the information that "our cavalry"—meaning Wheeler's, had passed that point last Tuesday. He was barely out of view, when they overtook a couple of negroes going to their work; and of them Glazier inquired the distance to the nearest plantation, receiving for answer, "Jess a mile, massa." "Are there any white folks there?" asked our hero. "Narry one, massa," was the reply; adding, "Dat ar planter is what dey call a Beeswaxer"—meaning a Bushwacker, "and Massa Sherman took dem all orf." Not wishing to commit themselves by imprudently revealing their true character, Glazier asked them indifferently, if they had seen any of Wheeler's cavalry lately. To which one of them responded, "Dar's right smart of dem down at Mars' Brown's, free mile from de swamp, and dey's hazin' de country all 'round."

This intelligence was not encouraging, but our friends thought it the wiser course to proceed at once to the plantation the negro had described. They soon reached the place, and, finding that the dwelling of the owner was closed, they, without delay, advanced to the nearest of the smaller tenements, such as were usually occupied by slaves.

Glazier did not pause to knock at the door, but boldly raised the latch and entered. He expected to see the usual negro auntie with her brood of pickaninnies, or to meet the friendly glance of one of the males, and therefore walked in very confidently, and with a pleasant smile. This, however, soon changed to a look of amazement, when he found himself face to face with a Confederate officer in full uniform. Quick as lightning, our hero determined upon his course.

"Ah, sir!" he exclaimed, with all the coolness he could assume, "I perceive we are in the same service. I can only hope you have not been so unfortunate as myself."

"How unfortunate may you have been, sir?" the *vis à vis* inquired.

"Why, at the late cavalry fight at Waynesboro', I lost my horse, having him shot under me. I have not had the good fortune to obtain another, and the consequence is, that I have been compelled to walk the whole distance to this point."

"I reckon, then, stranger, our cases are not altogether dissimilar," the Confederate rejoined; "I had my horse killed there, too, but luckily got a mule."

A MUTUAL SURPRISE.

In anticipation of an inquiry which, if addressed to himself, might lead to unpleasant complications, Glazier now asked: "What command he was attached to?" "Forty-third Alabama Mounted Infantry," said the other; and then put a similar question. "Third South Carolina Cavalry," said Glazier, feeling that he would be more at home as a trooper than an infantry soldier. To carry out his assumed character, he added some remarks regarding Sherman's barbarities, and was just congratulating himself upon the gullibility of the Confederate, when his apprehensions were revived by a remark, that it was "strange a rebel officer should be dressed in a Federal uniform."

"Not at all, sir," was the quick response, "a poor fellow must wear what he can get in times like these. I have not had a full equipment since I entered the service, and hang me, if I ever expect to get one. In the fight at Waynesboro' we captured a few Yanks, and I just stripped one fellow after he died, and took his clothes."

This explanation appeared to satisfy the rebel officer, as he remarked, "that was a good idea, and I wish I had been as sensible myself." After inquiry about the probability of obtaining some "grub" from the auntie, whose hut he supposed the place to be, and receiving a discouraging reply, Glazier was advised to call upon a Mr. Brown. The property of this *loyal* gentleman had been protected from seizure by General Sherman, on account of his having claimed to be a "good Union man," and by General Wheeler, because he was a "good rebel," and his larder was described to be, in consequence, well stocked. Our hero prepared to depart, first earnestly inquiring the road to Mr. Brown's residence.

"About two sights and a jambye," said the Alabamian, which interpreted, meant, twice as far as they could see, and the width of a swamp.

Having obtained all the information he desired, without the remotest intention of availing himself of the "good Union man's" hospitality, Glazier said "good-day," and rejoined his friend. They made the best of their way along a path, until a turn carried them out of the rebel officer's sight, then wheeled suddenly round, and ran rapidly for a considerable distance in the opposite direction to Mr. Brown's.

CHAPTER XXIV.

TRIED AS A SPY.

Fugitive slaves.—A rebel planter.—The big Ebenezer.—A sound of oars.—A *ruse de guerre.*—Burial of a dead soldier.—A free ride.—Groping in the dark.—" Who goes there!"—Recaptured.—*Nil desperaudum.*—James Brooks.—Contraband of war.—Confederate murders.—In the saddle again.—A dash for freedom.—Again captured.—Tried as a spy.

OUR hero had been somewhat impressed with the subdued tone and manner of the Confederate officer with whom he had lately parted. To some extent he manifested a discouraged and cowed bearing, and this, taken with some other circumstances in their recent experience, led our friends to hope that the end was not very remote.

After bidding adieu to the Confederate, they walked about two miles before discovering a place of concealment in another swamp. Here they unexpectedly came upon a party of negroes sleeping around a large fire. They proved to be fugitive slaves, who had abandoned their homes in Burke County, Georgia, to follow in the rear of Sherman's army. They had formed part of a body of several hundred persons of all ages and both sexes, who had escaped and sought refuge upon an island in Big Ebenezer Creek, and had been inhumanly shelled out by the Confederates. Thence they had scattered over the country in small bands, and the present detached party were working their way back to their masters. Captain Glazier despatched one of them with a haversack in search of some food among the resident colored people, and the result was so far satisfactory that our friends were put in possession of a good supply of sweet potatoes.

After another march, and while still in the swamp, they heard wood-choppers, and Lemon started to reconnoitre. Guided by the sound of the axe, he approached a small clearing, and seeing a negro, as he had expected, wielding the axe, walked forward to him, but was suddenly startled by observing a burly white man sitting on a log, smoking and looking on. They eyed each other for a minute in silence, when presently the planter demanded in a blustering voice, "What are you doing here, in a blue uniform?" Lemon was not slow to answer in a corresponding tone, "I am serving my country, as every loyal man should do: what have *you* to say about it?"

"I believe you're a d—d Yankee," said the planter. "You're welcome to your opinion, old Blowhard," responded Lemon. "This is a free country; I *am* a Yankee—all but the d—d—and now what do you propose to do about it?" (All this in an assumed tone of bluster, as the best adapted to the situation.) "We'll see! we'll see!" rejoined the planter, and at once started in a direct line for his house. Lemon lost no time, but returned as quickly as possible to his comrade, and without any deliberation they evacuated the enemy's country with as much expedition as their tired legs were capable of exerting. Their ears were soon saluted with the music of a pack of hounds let loose on their track by the burly rebel, and the affair would have had a disastrous ending if they had not opportunely encountered a considerable stream, and by wading through it for nearly a mile, succeeded in cutting off the scent of the hounds.

The planter had raised a hue and cry for miles around, and our hunted friends, from their covert, saw mounted men patrolling the corduroy road through the swamp, seemingly under the belief that the "Yankees" would be driven to use this highway eventually, and thus fall an easy prey into their hands. The man-hunters, however, found themselves at fault, for our hero had learned, in the hard school of experience, to anticipate all such contingencies. He and Lemon therefore secreted themselves until late in the night, determined to rob them of their game.

It was approaching midnight, December fifteenth, when the fugitives crept cautiously to the margin of the swamp. A large fire denoted the position of the planter's picket. They ventured out through the mud and water with the purpose of flanking the enemy on their left—a hazardous proceeding, and attended with much suffering from the intense coldness of the water. In two hours, however, they had reached a point on the opposite side of the encampment, and fearing discovery and pursuit, soon placed two or three miles between themselves and the foe. Sometimes they were made cognizant of the nearness of the parties in search of them, by overhearing their conversation, which treated mainly of Sherman's march to the sea, how it would affect the Confederacy, and similar interesting topics.

Our friends passed the last picket at the edge of the swamp, but deeming it unwise to relax in speed or vigilance, pushed forward to the banks of the

"Big Ebenezer," which advanced them three miles further.

Here, upon the charred abutment of a burned bridge, Glazier and his friend paused, and with the dark river in their front, debated how they were to reach the other side. The dawn was just breaking, and through the rising mist they could discern the opposite shore, but no practicable mode of reaching it. They must not, however, remain here after daybreak, and therefore sought and found a place of concealment, again in the hateful swamp, but not far from the river's bank. They were soon enjoying the rest and sleep of the weary.

Lemon was startled from his slumber by a sound resembling that of oars. He awoke Glazier, and both listened intently, at a loss to understand the meaning of such a sound in such a place. In a few minutes the noise ceased, and looking cautiously from their hiding-place, they observed two men pass near them, having the appearance of messengers or couriers, with despatches, which they could plainly see in their hands. It at once occurred to our hero and his companion that the boat in which these men had rowed themselves up the river, could be made available for crossing to its opposite bank. They found it moored to a tree, and at once embarked and crossed the stream. To prevent pursuit they cast the boat adrift, and as speedily as possible left "Big Ebenezer" behind them.

At a short distance from the river side Lemon stumbled over the dead body of a soldier, which, upon examination, proved to be that of a Federal. Our friends having no means of placing the body underground, concluded to bury it in the river, and thus prevent to some extent its desecration by dogs or other carrion-seeking animals that might find it exposed. This was the best they could do under the circumstances, and thus the poor body found a sailor's, if not a soldier's grave.

They had advanced not many paces again when they discovered two horses tied to a tree, possibly the property of the two couriers whose boat they had previously utilized. These they looked upon as fair spoil in an enemy's country, and with little compunction and less ceremony mounted and started on their way. A few miles brought them to the verge of the wood, and the day was now breaking. They therefore reluctantly dismounted, turned their steeds adrift for fear of detection, and trudged forward on foot once more.

Soon they had reason to congratulate themselves on their prudence in dismounting. Another quarter of a mile brought within view a Confederate picket, but they were not themselves observed. They accordingly sought a hiding-place among the thick undergrowth, and were soon asleep, remaining so until midnight. They then turned the flank of the picket and proceeded on their journey.

Long immunity from the peril of recapture had now inspired Glazier and his friend with hope and full confidence in successfully attaining the end of their struggles. The swamp, the river, the alligator, the man-hunter, and worse than all, the blood-hound, had been met and successfully overcome or evaded; and after three long weeks of travel from the execrable and inhuman people, who had held them as prisoners of war, and treated them worse than dogs, they now found themselves within twenty miles of Savannah.

Resting himself upon a fallen tree, clad in rags, hungry and reduced almost to the proportions of a skeleton by long fasting, Glazier and his companion were able to congratulate themselves upon their wonderful preservation thus far. All seemed to foreshadow their final triumph, and their spirits were cheered, notwithstanding that food had not passed their lips for the past thirty-six hours, with the exception of a few grains of corn picked up by the way. Probably within the brief space of twenty-four hours they would be again free and under the protection of the glorious flag, in whose defence they had fought and suffered so much.

Flushed with their past success and elated with hope for the future they recommenced their march. They had no exact information as to the position of the Federal army, and were in fact groping their way in the dark—figuratively as well as literally—every sense on the alert to avoid the enemy's picket lines.

On reaching Little Ebenezer Creek about midnight they were chagrined to find the bridge destroyed, but after reconnoitring for a time, were satisfied that the coast was clear on the opposite side. Finding some broken planks they constructed a raft and paddled themselves across the stream.

They were now on the Savannah River Road, over which Kilpatrick's cavalry and the Fourteenth Army Corps had passed but a week before. Old camping-grounds were numerous along their way, and each was examined closely for any bread or other eatables they thought might have been left by the army.

They were closely engaged in this search, when "Who comes there?" was gruffly shouted by a voice near them.

RECAPTURED BY A CONFEDERATE OUTPOST.

"Friends," promptly answered Glazier.

"Advance one!" commanded the picket.

"I advanced promptly," writes Captain Glazier, in the history of his capture and imprisonment, "and arriving near my captors found them to be mounted infantry. They were sitting upon their horses in the shade of some cypress-trees. One asked, 'Who are you?' to which I replied, 'A scout to General Hardie, and must not be detained, as I have important information for the general.'

"The picket replied, 'I'm instructed to take every person to the officer of the picket that approaches this post after dark.'

"'I can't help it, sir. It is not customary to arrest scouts, and I must pass on.'

"'You cannot; I must obey orders. I do not doubt the truth of your assertion; but until you have seen the lieutenant, you will not be allowed to pass this post.'

"Finding that I had met a good soldier I saw that it was useless to trifle with him, and tried to console myself with the thought that I should be able to dupe the officer; and as we were hurried on towards the reserve of the picket my mind was occupied in arranging a plan for our defence, as spies to the great rebel chief. Arrived at the reserve we found nearly all asleep, in close proximity to a large rail-fire, including the lieutenant.

"A little rough shaking soon roused him up, and, rubbing his eyes, he asked, 'What's wanted?'

"I quickly answered, 'I'm surprised, sir, that scouts to our generals should be arrested by your picket.'

"He said, 'My instructions are positive, and no man can pass this post without examination.'

"'Very well, then,' I said, 'be good enough to examine us at once.'

"'Have you passes?'

"'No, sir; not at present. We had papers when we left the general's headquarters; but having been scouting in Northern Georgia, for the past two weeks, our papers are worn out and lost.'

"'You have some papers about you, I suppose?'

"Thinking that by answering in the affirmative, and producing quickly an old package of letters which had been received while in Libby Prison, that none of them would be examined, I hastily drew them from the side-pocket of my jacket and held them before me, saying, 'I hope here are enough, sir.'

"The lieutenant's curiosity led him to take one which had been received from Colonel Clarence Buel, of Troy, New York. He held it near the fire, and noticing the date, turned his eyes towards me and again to the letter; the second glance seemed to satisfy him that I was not a rebel, and he remarked very indignantly, 'Then you are scouting for General Hardie, are you? I believe you are a d—d Yankee spy! and if you were to get your deserts I should hang you to the first tree I come to.' Said I, 'Lieutenant, do not be too hasty. I can convince you that I have been a prisoner of war, and if you are a true soldier I shall be treated as such.'

"Becoming a little more mild he gave us to understand that we should start at ten o'clock the next morning for Springfield, the headquarters of General Wheeler.

"After detailing a special guard for the prisoners, and instructing them to be on the alert, the lieutenant laid himself down by the fire, leaving us to reflect upon the hardness of fate, and the uncertainties attending an effort to escape the clutches of a vigilant enemy."

Glazier did not despair, but at the first opportunity communicated to Lemon his determination to reach the Federal lines at all risks; he would never return to South Carolina a prisoner; the horrors of prison-life and the privations and sufferings they had already endured, should never be repeated in his case, but rather—welcome death! Their enemies—albeit fellow-countrymen and *Americans*—were inhuman and barbarous, and before putting himself in their hands again, he would submit to be hung by bushwhackers, or torn to pieces by blood-hounds. Their case was now desperate, and for his part he would take the first chance that offered of getting away. Our hero thought he could count on Lemon's concurrence and co-operation. The men of the picket told him they had been arrested at the outpost; and it was now clear that if the fugitives had been so fortunate as to pass this picket, they could have reached the Federal lines in less than an hour. Only a step intervened between captivity and freedom—the thought was very disheartening.

An instance of exceptional kindness on the part of a Confederate must not be omitted here. James Brooks, one of the picket, came to the prisoners and invited them to partake of some hoe-cake and bacon. He said he had been out foraging, and would share his plunder with them. Having been without food for forty-eight hours, save a few ears of corn, they eagerly embraced the generous offer. The hoe-cake was produced and partaken of ravenously and thankfully. The other men of the picket were disgusted at the liberality of their comrade, calling him a "blue belly," and a fool to give good bread to a couple of d—d Yanks. Like a true man, however, he made no reply to their brutal taunts, and gave the captives a most excellent breakfast.

Having finished their welcome meal, they asked permission to bathe themselves, under guard, in a little stream not many rods from the reserve, which request was granted. Here the prisoners in their desperation offered the guard one hundred dollars in Confederate scrip, which had been given them by their negro friends, to assist them in making their escape. The guards seemed to distrust each other, and declined the proposal. They, however, said they would be right glad to have the money, but feared to take it, as they were held responsible for the safe return of the prisoners. The offer of the bribe was reported to the lieutenant, who at once ordered the delinquents to be searched, and all the scrip found upon them was confiscated, as contraband of war, and appropriated to rebel uses, leaving our two unfortunate friends penniless. They were further threatened with condign punishment for offering to bribe the guard. One said "Shoot them;" another, "Let 'em stretch hemp;" several recommended that they be taken to the swamp and "sent after Sherman's raiders,"—referring, probably, to the manner in which they had disposed of some of the Federal sick, who had been left in the rear of the army. Of this incident Glazier writes: "I had been told by the negroes that fifteen of our sick,

THE ESCAPE AND PURSUIT.

who fell into the hands of the rebels but a few day before our recapture, were taken to a swamp, where their throats were cut, and their bodies thrown into a slough hole. I cannot vouch for the truth of this statement, but it came to me from many whose veracity I have no reason to doubt."

Let us in the name of humanity doubt it!

At ten o'clock A. M. a mounted guard, consisting of a corporal and two men, were detailed to march the prisoners to the headquarters of General Wheeler. They had not proceeded far when Glazier assumed to be footsore, and pleaded his utter inability to walk any further. Believing this, one of the guards dismounted and helped him into the saddle. Our hero was no sooner mounted than he decided that, come what would, he would make his escape. In a few moments the guard who was on foot espied a black squirrel darting across the road, and oblivious of his responsibility, gave chase to it, Glazier looking on and biding his time. The squirrel soon ran up a tree, and leaped from bough to bough with its usual agility. Suddenly it halted on a prominent branch, seeming to bid defiance to its pursuer. The carbine was instantly raised, and discharged. Without waiting to note the result, Glazier, feeling that *now* was his opportunity, dashed off at a gallop, urging his horse to the top of his speed. Before the squirrel-hunter could reload, he was many yards away. The corporal in charge fired his revolver, and at each discharge of the weapon, shouted to the fugitive to halt! but Glazier gave no heed to the summons, and might have succeeded in reaching the swamps and defied recapture, if he had not unfortunately galloped into a rebel camp! Baffled, he turned his horse, and endeavored to cross an open field, but the corporal continued to shout, "Halt that d—d Yankee!" when a body of Texan Rangers from General Iverson's cavalry division, some mounted and some dismounted, gave chase, hooting and yelping, and finally overtook and compelled him to surrender.

The guard whose horse Lieutenant Glazier had ridden came up and vented his rage at the escapade in no measured language. The Texans, however, enjoyed the fun of the thing, and laughed at, and ridiculed him. Said one, "You are a d—d smart soldier to let a blue-belly get away from you—and on your own horse too!" Another joined in with, "Say, Corporal, which of them nags can run fastest?" Nothing of course was said about the *squirrels!*

On Lemon and his guard coming up they resumed their march to headquarters—Glazier's lameness exciting no further sympathy, nor the offer of another mount.

The escort with their charge reached General Wheeler's headquarters in the afternoon, and the report handed in stated that, "the two prisoners had been captured while attempting to pass the out-post, under the pretence of being scouts to General Hardie."

Wheeler ordered them at once into his presence and questioned them closely.

Captain Glazier thus graphically relates the interview:

. "'Then you are scouting for Confederate generals?' said Wheeler.

"I replied, 'We would have rejoiced if we could have convinced your out-post that we were.'

"'None of your impudence, sir! Remember that you are a prisoner.'

"'Very true; but when you ask questions, you must expect answers.'

"'What are you doing with that gray jacket?'

"'I wear it, sir, to protect myself from the sun and storm.'

"'Where did you get it?'

"'One of the guards at Columbia was kind enough to give it to me, when he saw that I was suffering for the want of clothing to cover my nakedness.'

"'He could not have been a true rebel, to assist a Yankee in making his escape.'

"'He knew nothing of my intention to escape; and I believe he was at least a kind-hearted man.'

"'Why don't you wear the Federal uniform? Are the Yankees ashamed of it?'

"'By no means, sir! What few garments were spared me at the time of my capture were worn out during a long imprisonment, and the clothing which was sent on to Richmond by our Government during the winter of 1863 for distribution among the prisoners, was, for the most part, appropriated by your authorities.'

"'Like most of your contemptible Yankee crew, I believe you to be a lying scoundrel, and you shall answer to the charge of spy.'

"'Very well, sir, I am compelled to await your pleasure; but you have heard nothing but the truth.'

"'Guard! take the prisoners to the jail, place them in a cell, and keep them in close confinement until further orders.'"

The above colloquy between Wheeler and his prisoners reflects small credit upon him as a leader of "Southern Chivalry."

CHAPTER XXV.

FINAL ESCAPE FROM CAPTIVITY.

In jail.—White trash.—Yankees.—Off to Waynesboro.—No rations. Calling the roll.—Sylvania.—Plan for escape.—Lieutenant John W. Wright.—A desperate project.—Escaped!—Giving chase.—The pursuers baffled.—Old Richard.—" Pooty hard case, massa."—Rebel deserters.—The sound of cannon.—Personating a rebel officer.—Mrs. Keyton.—Renewed hope.—A Confederate outpost.—Bloodhounds.—Uncle Philip.—March Dasher.—Suspicion disarmed.—" Now I'ze ready, gemmen."—Stars and stripes.—Glorious freedom.—Home!

IN obedience to orders, Glazier and his comrade were at once marched off to the county jail at Springfield, Georgia, then in the hands of the military authorities. They were the only military prisoners confined there, and were allowed the privilege of leaving their cell and going into the yard for fresh air. They were not a little amused by the crowds of wondering citizens who visited the jail to view the "two live Yanks."

These worthy citizens were greatly exercised that the prisoners should be permitted to leave their cells, and called on the jailer to remove them from the yard or they would take the keys into their own hands; but the officer in command told them that he was personally responsible for their safe-custody, and refused to remove them. These white Georgians were a very primitive class of people. Utterly illiterate and uninformed, their mode of speech was as bad as that of the most ignorant slaves on the plantations. The term "white trash," whatever its origin, was a most appropriate designation. No care had been taken to educate them—no school-houses built; education being confined to the few whose wealth enabled them to send their children to Northern schools, or to engage a private tutor. Discovering that the prisoners were harmless, many of these people asked them questions of a curious and comical nature. They thought Yankees were imps of darkness, possessed of horns and hoof, and, seeing that the prisoners were formed not unlike themselves, were with difficulty persuaded that they were "Yankees." Their idea of the causes and character of the war was ludicrous in the extreme, and will hardly bear description—the negroes themselves being far better informed upon this, as they were upon most other subjects.

A very brief examination before a hastily convened board of officers resulted in a finding that the captives were "escaped prisoners of war," and not "spies." They were accordingly asked, where they were captured, where imprisoned, when they escaped, etc.; and then a strong guard from the Second Georgia Cavalry was detailed to convey them, with fifteen other prisoners from the Fourteenth Army Corps, to Waynesboro.

From the other prisoners Glazier gleaned much useful information concerning the situation of the Union lines, and also learned where the rebel troops were stationed in Sherman's rear. Should he attempt another escape, this knowledge would be valuable. The rebel escort cared very little for the wants of their prisoners, and issued no rations whatever to them— they themselves being entirely dependent on foraging for their own supplies. As the unfortunate prisoners could not forage for themselves they had to go without, a condition of things that spoke little for the soldierly feeling of the guard. All attempts to elude the vigilance of the latter during the day had failed, and as darkness drew on, Glazier and his friend felt in very low spirits. They came to a halt a few minutes before dark, and were quartered in an old building for the night.

In passing through a large swamp, just before halting, the water was so deep that each man had to wade through as he best could. The guard exerted themselves to their utmost to keep them together, but in spite of their efforts to do so, one of the prisoners fell out, and his absence was overlooked by the sergeant, although noticed by his fellow-prisoners, who succeeded in convincing the sergeant that all were present. The mode was this: Glazier found out the absent man's name, and then volunteered to call the roll from a list in the sergeant's possession. It being dark, a piece of pitch-pine was lighted, and the list handed to Glazier, who proceeded to call the names. All answered, except the absentee, when, according to previous arrangement, each affirmed that no such man had been among them. The sergeant sapiently concluded that the name had found its way upon the roster by some error, and nothing further was said about it. Had this little ruse not been resorted to, great efforts would have been made to recover the fugitive. Picked men would have been detailed, hounds called out from the nearest plantation, and a very short time would have convinced the unfortunate victim how little hope there was for him who sought to shun the horrors of prison-life by an escape.

THE ESCAPE FROM SYLVANIA, GEORGIA.

We do not propose entering into any detail of this march into captivity, more especially as our hero has himself fully and graphically described it in his "Capture, Prison-Pen and Escape," compiled from a diary kept during the whole period of his adventurous career, and published in 1865. We will merely state here that on Monday, December nineteenth, 1864, after a dreary march of twenty-five miles, the captives found themselves encamped for the night at the little village of Sylvania, Georgia; half-way between the point of their departure and that of their destination, Waynesboro.

Glazier's mind, during the whole of the day, had been preoccupied with but one subject—*how to escape!* —this problem excluding every other thought or consideration of himself or his surroundings.

Early in the evening the prisoners were stationed on the porch of a large unoccupied building, and here it was determined they should pass the night. The villagers of Sylvania knew little of the sad realities of war, having hitherto happily escaped the visits of the armed hosts. They surrounded the men of the escort, and plied them with many curious questions, which were good-naturedly answered with as much, or as little exaggeration as good soldiers usually indulge in when confronted with greenhorns. Their attention, thus agreeably occupied by the simple-minded villagers, was in some degree removed from their charge, and this little circumstance seemed propitious to Glazier, who was watching intently his opportunity.

The sergeant had notified the prisoners that his foragers had returned with a quantity of sweet potatoes and some corn-bread; that the former would be issued to the "Yanks," and the latter to the guard. Orders also were given to place all the food at one end of the porch, where a fire had been kindled of rail fence; and the potatoes were to be served to the prisoners from that point.

Glazier, under the pretence of desiring to use the fire for the purpose of roasting the potatoes, obtained leave for all to remain outside on the porch until after supper. This concession reluctantly granted, hope sprang in his breast that the opportunity he so ardently sought was now at hand. Quickly he determined upon his plan of operation, and seeing Lieutenant John W. Wright, of the Tenth Iowa Volunteers, near him, whispered in his ear an outline of his desperate project, and invited the latter to join in putting it into execution. To this proposition, without a moment's consideration, Wright consented.

The two candidates for freedom then sauntered towards the end of the porch, conversing loudly and cheerfully upon general topics, and thus excited no suspicion of their intentions. The hungry prisoners gathered around the ration-board, when Glazier, covertly signaling his companion, each suddenly clutched a good handful of the corn-bread. Under cover of the increasing darkness, and screened from observation by the men who stood between them and the guard, they quietly but rapidly, in a stooping position, stole away, making for the edge of a neighboring wood. Not a word was spoken, and in less time than it takes to record it, they were concealed among the foliage and undergrowth; and, befriended by the darkness, were completely masked from the observation of the enemy.

Fortunately their flight was unobserved until after the distribution of the rations, when the guard missed their corn-bread. This seemed to be felt more than the loss of their prisoners, the sergeant exclaiming, in euphemistic southern (according to Glazier), "By dog on't! the d—d Yankee officers have done gone and took all our corn-bread. I'll have them, if it costs me a horse!"

Calling out a corporal and four men, he quickly ordered them to go to the nearest plantation for hounds, and to " bring back the two Yanks dead or alive," adding that he "guessed they had taken the Springfield road," which was the nearest route to the Federal lines.

It happened, however, that the peremptory orders of the sergeant were overheard by Glazier and Wright, who were hidden not many yards away in the wood. Instead, therefore, of proceeding on the direct road by way of Springfield, they retraced their steps in the dark, and by this means baffled their pursuers. Having reached the Middle Ground Road, over which they had lately passed, they bounded over it to avoid leaving their foot-prints, and thus broke the trail. They were now in a large and densely-wooded swamp, and, effectually concealed by the umbrageous covering, sat down to a council of war.

We may here state that Lieutenant Lemon, the late faithful companion of our hero, had been prevented from participating in the plan of escape, and was eventually taken back to be re-tortured in his old quarters at Columbia. Wright was also an escaped prisoner from Columbia, whom Glazier had often met during his imprisonment there. He escaped from "Camp Sorghum" a few days after Lemon and Glazier, but unfortunately was recaptured just when he felt that he was about to bid adieu to his captivity.

Lieutenant Wright possessed one advantage for the dangerous and desperate enterprise they had now re-entered upon—he knew the country. By his advice, therefore, it was agreed to remain quietly concealed in the swamp until night, when he would lead the way to the hut of a negro who had befriended him during his previous attempt to escape.

About midnight he piloted Glazier to the hut of "Old Richard," a worthy and kind-hearted negro, who had supplied him with hoe-cake and bacon just before his recapture. Richard was in ecstasies on beholding his friend, Massa Wright, again, whom he knew to have been retaken, and with due formality, our hero was introduced. On being asked for some bacon and sweet potatoes to put with their corn-bread, he replied: "Pooty hard case, massa; but dis yer darkey 'll do de best he can. Can't get nuffin' on this plantation, but reckon I can buy some 'tatoes down at Massa Smith's, three miles from yer, and will go down thar after I finish my task to-morrer. As to meat," he said, "you know, massa, dat in the Souf de slave takes what de white folks frows away, and I reckon you all couldn't eat a tainted ham dat ole massa gib me t'other day; but if you can, God knows dis chile gibs it to you wid all his heart." Having become, from long fasting, almost entirely indifferent to the sense of taste, our friends gave Old Richard to understand that the ham would be welcome.

The important question of rations having been thus satisfactorily arranged, Richard was asked to guide the fugitives to some place of hiding, where no rebel could find them. Accordingly, they were conducted to a swamp, and soon discovered a secure place of concealment for the day. "The whippoorwill and turtle-dove," Captain Glazier writes, "enlivened the hours with their inspiring notes, and as night began to approach, the gloomy owl, from the tree-tops, uttered his solemn warning cry. The pine and cypress, swayed by the breeze, moaned a perpetual chorus, and under their teaching we learned, during the long, dreary hours, how much we were indebted to these dismal wilds, that concealed both friend and foe.

"Here the rebel deserter concealed himself from his pursuers. Here the loyalist found a hiding-place from the rebel conscripting officer. Here the trembling negro had his first taste of freedom. Here the escaped Union prisoner was enabled to baffle blood-hounds and human-hounds, and make his way to the Federal lines."

The day wore away at length, and as darkness was approaching, Old Richard, true to his promise, was on hand with the supplies. He gave the fugitives all he had been able to purchase with his small means, and they, after asking God to bless him for his kindness, departed. Our friends trudged away, rejoicing, notwithstanding their fatigue, and the bodily weakness of Glazier. For the latter had by this time been reduced in weight to not more than ninety pounds, his usual weight having been about one hundred and forty-five. He was still, however, filled with indomitable "pluck," and a determination to conquer the situation, with all its dread horrors, and return to his colors. Wright, on the other hand, had a splendid physique, and cared little for hardships that would have intimidated, or perhaps killed, an ordinary man. On several occasions he picked Glazier up and generously bore him upon his broad shoulders over the worst parts of the swamp, the latter being too weak to make his way alone without falling into the slough-holes.

They were startled, in the course of this night, on seeing two men, who, by their conversation, which was overheard, proved to be rebel deserters from Wheeler's command. Our friends deemed it the wisest plan to secrete themselves behind a log until the men had passed.

At break of day they again concealed themselves, and rested between the roots of an ancient cypress. Their ears were now greeted with the distant boom of heavy cannon, which came from the direction of Savannah. This helped in directing their course for the following night, and also announced to them in plain language that they were not very far from the friends they longed to meet.

Refreshed and recruited they started as the shades of evening fell, determined, if possible, to accomplish a good march before daylight.

They had not, however, proceeded far, when a large plantation became visible, the white mansion gleaming through the trees. Wright recognizing the place, suggested that Glazier might procure a good supper, and something for the haversack, if he would boldly call and personate a rebel officer, trusting to his face and ready wit to carry him through. He had heard from some negroes that the only occupant was a Mrs. Keyton and some young children, the wife and family of the planter, who was an officer in the rebel army; and further that there were no hounds about the place.

Glazier, with characteristic promptness, acquiesced;

and the following is a description of the interview, extracted from the diary, which amid all his wanderings and trials he never failed to keep regularly written up:

"After hearing Wright's description, and having agreed upon signals of danger, should any occur, I started on my foraging expedition, with a good degree of assurance.

"Stepping up to the door of the mansion, I rapped, and the lady soon made her appearance. She seemed both refined and intelligent. I asked, 'Can you give this rebel a supper?' She replied, 'You shall have the best the house affords,' and invited me to step in and take a seat by the fire. I did so, saying, as I took my seat, 'Madam, I am shocked at the dastardly conduct of General Sherman in his march through Georgia. It has been characterized by nothing but what should excite revenge, and move to action, every man possessing a true Southern spirit. Our aged citizens, who have banded together for mutual protection, have been treated as bushwackers—have been driven from their homes, and their property confiscated. Our hounds, always true to the interests of the South, have been shot down by the road-side for no other reason than that they were used in tracking escaped prisoners—'

"Interrupting me here, the lady remarked, much to my surprise, that she could not see that the Yankees were much worse than the Confederates, after all. She added: "'When the Yankee army passed through this State, they took from the rich the supplies necessary for their sustenance; and when our cavalry followed they took nearly all that was left, seeming to care but little for our wants, and often stripping defenceless women and children of their last morsel of bread.'

"'I regret, madam, that the conduct of our troops has been such as to give you reason for complaint.'

"'I, too, regret that our men have not proved themselves worthy of a cause which they appear so willing to defend.'

"'Remember,' I continued, 'that our commissary department has been completely wrecked, and that we are entirely dependent upon the people for the subsistence of a large army.'

"By the sad expression of her countenance, which accompanied and followed this remark, I saw clearly that she felt we had reached a crisis in the war, when Providence was turning the tables, and she accordingly interrogated:

"'And what do you think of present prospects?'

"I quickly responded, 'Our future looks dark—our cause appears almost hopeless, but the sacrifices of our gallant dead remain unavenged. Therefore, we must fight while there is a man left, and die in the last ditch.'

"'If there be no longer any hope of success, sir, I should say that it would be better to lay down our arms at once, and go back under the old flag.'

"'Madam, we must fight, we *must fight!*'

"'But it is wickedness and worse than madness to continue this awful massacre of human beings, without some prospect of ultimate success.'

"'Very true; but we have lost all in this struggle, and must sell our lives as dearly as possible.'

"By this time the good lady seemed to have waxed

enthusiastic, and warm as the fire over which the servant was preparing my supper, and she answered:

"'My husband is a captain in the Twenty-fifth Georgia Infantry. He is the father of these children, and is very dear to both them and me. Long have I prayed that he might be spared to return to his family, but fear that we shall never be permitted to see him again. When he entered the army, I admired his patriotism, and was glad to see him go in defence of what I supposed to be the true interests of the southern people; but *we have been deceived from the beginning by our military and political leaders*. It is time to open our eyes, and see what obstinacy has brought us. We are conquered. Let us return to the administration of the Federal government, ere we are ruined.'

"Madam, your sympathies appear to be largely with the Yankees.'

"'It is not strange, sir; I was born and educated in New England;—and your speech would indicate that you too are not a native of the South.'

"'You are right; I am a New Yorker by birth, but have been for a considerable time in South Carolina.'

"After partaking of the frugal meal set before me, which consisted of corn-bread and sweet potatoes, I thanked the lady for her kindness, and told her that I regretted very deeply that I was not in a situation to remunerate her for so much trouble. Noticing my blue pants as I arose from the table, she remarked:

"'It is impossible for me to know our men from the Yankees by the uniform; but a few days since, two soldiers asked me to get them some supper, claiming to be scouts to General Wheeler; they told many very plausible stories, and the next day, to my astonishment, I was charged with harboring Yankee spies.'

"'I do not wonder that you find it difficult to distinguish the Yankee from the Confederate soldier, for in these trying times a poor rebel is compelled to wear anything he can get. The dead are always stripped, and at this season of the year, we find the Federal uniform far more comfortable than our own.'

"'It must be an awful extremity that could tempt men to strip the dying and the dead!'

"'We have become so much accustomed to such practices, that we are unmoved by scenes which might appall and sicken those who have never served in our ranks.'

"'I sincerely hope that these murderous practices will soon be at an end.'

"Feeling that I had been absent from my comrade long enough, and that it was time to make my departure, I arose, saying,

"'I must go, madam; may I know to whom I am so much indebted for my supper and kind entertainment this evening?'

"'Mrs. James Keyton. And what may I call your name?'

"'Willard Glazier, Fifty-third Alabama Mounted Infantry.'

"'Should you chance to meet the Twenty-fifth Georgia, please inquire for Captain Keyton, and say to him that his wife and children are well, and send their love.'

"'He shall certainly have your message if it is my good fortune to meet him. Good-night.'"

Leaving Mrs. Keyton with her fears for the rebel cause in general, and her husband in particular, Glazier hurried out to find his friend Wright pacing up and down the road in a bad humor at having been kept so long waiting; but setting their faces in the direction of Springfield, they at once started on their march. They soon found themselves approaching the rebel forces in General Sherman's rear, and determined at all risks to obtain information of the two armies. They were at General Iverson's headquarters, and at one time were within fifteen paces of the house he occupied.

Cautiously concealing themselves behind trees they reached a spot within earshot of the provost-guard, and overheard their conversation. The prospects of the war were freely discussed, and the fall of Savannah. The conclusion forced on the minds of our friends was that the Confederate cause was losing ground, and its armies would soon be compelled to surrender to the Union force.

Glazier and his comrade left the spot inspired with renewed courage.

Six miles on their road to Springfield found daylight approaching, and the fugitives hurriedly secreted themselves among some tall swamp grass. They were suddenly aroused by the baying of a blood-hound, and immediately sprang to their feet.

"We are followed!" exclaimed Wright.

"What do you propose to do?" quickly asked Glazier.

"I am undecided," was the unsatisfactory reply.

"It is my opinion," said Glazier, promptly, "that if we are not off at once we shall be prisoners."

"Well, off it is!" spoke Wright; and both struck off in a southeasterly direction in double quick time. Fences and ditches were leaped, and streams forded, the hounds approaching so nearly that their baying could be distinctly heard by the fugitives; but fortunately, or providentially, they came to a large creek, and jumping in, waded along its course for a distance of some sixty rods, then emerging, pursued their journey in the direction they had intended. About one o'clock they concluded they had out-generaled the bushwhackers and their hounds. Elated by success they became less cautious and did not halt. About two o'clock Glazier was startled by seeing his companion drop suddenly and silently behind a tree. Glazier followed, watching the movements of Wright, and presently saw that they were within a few rods of a Confederate picket. Before they had time to move a cavalry patrol came up to the post with instructions, and, as soon as he had passed, our friends crawled upon their hands and knees into the friendly swamp, and thus screened themselves from their enemy.

The *hounds*, however, were a source of greater danger to the fugitives than the rebel pickets; the training and scent of the former having been so perfected and developed by long and cruel use in the recapture of fugitive slaves, that, to evade them, was almost an impossibility. Hence the sense of caution was strained to the utmost both by night and day on the part of our friends.

The use of blood-hounds in warfare is considered *barbarous* in every country pretending to civilization, even if they are employed against a foreign foe. How much more so, in a war waged between fellow-citizens of one blood, one history, one language, and in numerous instances, bearing domestic or family relations to each other; and this, in support of a cause, the righteousness of which was doubted by many who found themselves unwillingly compelled to give in their adherence at the dictation of a few ambitious men. For this sin a righteous God has judged them! A cause thus supported deserved defeat in the estimation of just men of every nation, apart from all political considerations.

Captain Glazier and his friend congratulated themselves on having so far eluded, by every expedient known to them, the sanguinary fangs of these barbarous instruments of warfare; and after nightfall continued their route, passing the picket in the darkness.

Soon after they encountered a colored friend, known among his people as "Uncle Philip." This good darkey informed them that the Federal forces had possession of Cherokee Hill, on the Savannah River Road, only eight miles distant—news which afforded them inexpressible joy! Uncle Philip was asked if he would guide them to the lines; and replied: "I'ze neber ben down dar, massa, sense Massa Sherman's company went to Savannah; but I reckon you-uns can git Massa Jones, a free cullered man, to take you ober. He's a mighty bright pusson, and understands de swamps jest like a book."

On reaching Jones' hut his wife informed them that her husband was out scouting, but was expected back about eleven o'clock. She urged our friends to enter and await his return, as he was always glad to do all in his power for the Yankees. Fearing the rebel scouts might discover them, they, at first, hesitated, but consented on Mrs. Jones promising to be on the alert. She accordingly volunteered her two boys, one of eight years and the other six, for out-post duty, charging them strictly to notify her immediately if they saw any one approaching, so that she might conceal the fugitives. Auntie then promptly placed before them a bountiful supply of hoe-cake and parched corn, the best her humble cot afforded, and most welcome to the famished men.

Jones returned at the appointed hour, but informed his guests that, while very willing to guide them, he was not sufficiently acquainted with the safest route to do so; and referred them to a friend of his, who would accompany them, and whom he could strongly recommend as a competent and safe guide. On visiting this man he also pleaded ignorance of any *safe* route; but mentioned the name of still another "friend of the Yankees," who, he said, had come up from the Union lines that morning and would willingly return with them. This friendly negro also was found. He was a genuine negro, as black as ebony and very devout in his mode of speech. His name was "March Dasher." "I'll do it, massa, if God be my helper!" he answered to their eager inquiry.

Glazier and his comrade were impatient to start at once, but upon this point Dasher was inexorable. "Dis chile knows whar de pickets is in de day-time," he emphatically declared, "but knows nuffin 'bout 'em arter dark;" and absolutely declined to take the risk of falling within the Confederate lines—an act of prudence and firmness for which he was to be much commended.

A fear of treachery was aroused when Dasher tried to induce them to remain in his hut till morning, but this was immediately and entirely removed when he and his household at a signal, fell on their knees, and joined in simple but fervent prayer to the Almighty, as a friend of the friendless—beseeching Him to protect and prosper them in their efforts to flee from their enemies; and much more of a nature to disarm any suspicion of their fidelity and good-will to the Union cause.

Our friends, however, declined to remain in the hut, fearing a surprise from the outpost; and at the conclusion of the prayer, betook themselves to a pine thicket with the joint resolution of giving their dark friend no peace until he started with them to the Federal lines.

About one o'clock in the morning, Wright, impatient of delay, proceeded to the hut, and arousing Dasher, told him that day had just begun to break. He came to the door, and pointing to the stars in the unclouded sky, remarked, with a good-tempered smile, " I reck'n it's good many hours yet till break ob day, massa. Yer can't fool March on de time; his clock neber breaks down. It's jest right ebery time." Wright returned to his lair in the thicket, remarking irritably, as he threw himself down, "Glazier, you might as well undertake to move a mountain, as to get the start of that colored individual!"

At the first peep of dawn, punctual to his promise, Dasher thrust his black, good-humored face into the thicket, and announced:

" Now I'ze ready, gemmen, to take you right plum into Mr. Sherman's company by 'sun-up;'" and as Sol began to gild the tree-tops and the distant eastern hills, the trio came within sight of the Federal camp, and witnessed the "Stars and Stripes," floating triumphantly in the breeze!

What pen can describe their emotions, when—after more than fourteen long months' suffering from imprisonment, starvation, nakedness, bodily and mental prostration, and every inhumanity short of being murdered, like many of their imprisoned comrades, in cold blood—they again hailed *friends* and found *freedom* at last within their grasp! Words would fail to tell their joy. Let us leave it to the reader to imagine.

On first approaching the camp they were supposed, by their motley attire, to be deserters from the enemy; and, as true soldiers and deserters never fraternize, no signal of welcome was offered by the "boys in blue." The suspicions of the latter, however, were allayed on seeing Glazier and his companion wave their caps: then they were beckoned to come forward. And when it was discovered that they were *escaped prisoners*, an enthusiastic grip was given to each by every soldier present, accompanied by cordial congratulations on their successful escape from the barbarous enemy who had had them in custody.

"Each man," writes Glazier, "took us by the hand, congratulating us on our eventful and successful escape, while *we* cheered the boys for the glorious work they had accomplished for the Union. Haversacks were opened and placed at our disposal. There was a great demand for hard-tack and coffee; but the beauty of it all was, Major Turner was not there, to say what he often repeated, 'Reduce their rations; I'll teach the d—d scoundrels not to attempt to escape!'

"I cannot forget," he adds, "the sea of emotion that well-nigh overwhelmed me, as soon as I could realize the fact that I was no longer a prisoner, and especially when I beheld the starry banner floating triumphantly over the invincibles who had followed their great General down to the sea."

Our hero and his friend became objects of much

curiosity, while their eventful escape was the subject of general conversation and comment by the brave boys who pressed around them, and who proved to be a detachment of the One Hundred and First Illinois Volunteers, Twentieth Army Corps. Their most intimate friends would have failed to recognize them. Glazier was clad in an old gray jacket and blue pants, with a venerable and dilapidated hat which had seen a prodigious amount of service of a nondescript kind; while a tattered gray blanket that had done duty for many a month as a bed by day and a cloak by night, and was now in the last stage of dissolution from age and general infirmity, completed his unmilitary and unpretentious toilet. Having at first no one to identify them, Glazier and his companion were as strangers among friends, and necessarily without official recognition. At length, however, after much searching, they found Lieutenant Wright's old company, and thus the refugees became officially identified and recognized as Federal officers.

In company with Lieutenant E. H. Fales, who had been his fellow-prisoner at Charleston, and effected his escape, Glazier proceeded on horseback to the headquarters of General Kilpatrick. The General, cordially welcoming and congratulating Glazier on his happy escape, at once furnished him with the documents necessary to secure his transportation to the North. His term of service having expired, he was anxious to revisit his family, who thought him dead, and bidding an affectionate adieu to his friend Wright, he and Lieutenant Fales embarked on a steamship on December twenty-ninth for home. After experiencing the effects of a severe storm at sea, the vessel arrived at the wharf of the metropolis, and our hero adds: "I awoke to the glorious realization that I was again breathing the air of my native State. There was an exhilarating rapture in the thought, which I can never repress, and that moment was fixed as a golden era in my memory. I hope never to become so hardened that that patriotic and Christian exultation will be an unpleasant recollection."

There have probably been few hearts that beat higher with martial ardor, than that of Willard Glazier; but at that moment the thought of "Battle's red carnival" was merged in the gentler recollection of kindred and friends, rest and home.

CHAPTER XXVI.

GLAZIER RE-ENTERS THE SERVICE.

Glazier's determination to re-enter the army.—Letter to Colonel Harhaus.—Testimonial from Colonel Clarence Buel.—Letter from Hon. Martin I. Townsend to governor of New York.—Letter from General Davies.—Letter from General Kilpatrick.—Application for new commission successful.—Home.—The mother fails to recognize her son.—Supposed to be dead.—Recognized by his sister Marjorie.—Filial and fraternal love.—Reports himself to his commanding officer for duty.—Close of the war and of Glazier's military career.—Seeks a new object in life.—An idea occurs to him.—Becomes an author, and finds a publisher.

HOME, with its rest, its peaceful enjoyments and endearments, was no abiding place for our young soldier while his bleeding country still battled for the right, and called upon her sons for self-denying service in her cause. He had registered a vow to remain in the army until relieved by death, or the termination of the war. His heart and soul were in the Union cause, and finding that at the expiration of his term of service he had been mustered out, he had determined before proceeding to his home to apply for another commission, and, if possible, resume his place at the front.

The following letter, which we think stamps his earnest loyalty to the cause he had espoused, and for which he had already suffered so much, was addressed to his friend and patron:

ASTOR HOUSE, NEW YORK, }
January 10*th*, 1865. }

COLONEL OTTO HARHAUS,
Late of the Harris Light Cavalry:

DEAR COLONEL: Having reached our lines, an escaped prisoner, on the twenty-third of last month, I at once took steps to ascertain my position in the old regiment, and regret to say, was informed at the war department that as my term of service expired during my imprisonment; and, as I had not remustered previous to capture, I am now regarded supernumerary. I wish to remain in the service until the close of the war, and so expressed myself before I fell into the hands of the enemy. Fourteen months in rebel prisons has not increased my respect for "Southern chivalry"—in short I have some old scores to settle.

I write, colonel, to ascertain if you will be kind enough to advise me as to what steps I had better take to secure a new commission in the Cavalry Corps, and to ask if you will favor me with a letter of recommendation to Governor Fenton. It was suggested to me at Washington that I should place my case before him, and if I conclude to do so, such a note from you will be of great value.

I learn through Captain Downing that I was commissioned a first lieutenant upon your recommendation soon after my capture. If so, I avail myself of this opportunity to acknowledge my deep appreciation of the favor, and to thank you very cordially for remembering me at a time when I was entirely dependent upon your impartial decisions for proper advancement in your command.

I made my escape from the rebel prison at Columbia, South Carolina, November twenty-sixth, 1864, was recaptured December fifteenth by a Confederate outpost near Springfield, Georgia; escaped a second time the following day and was retaken by a detachment of Texan cavalry under General Wheeler; was tried as a spy at Springfield; escaped a third time from Sylvania on the nineteenth of December, and reached the Federal lines near Savannah, four days later, and twenty-eight days after the escape from Columbia. I was at General Kilpatrick's headquarters on the Ogeechee, December twenty-sixth. The general was in the most exuberant spirits, and entertained me with stories of the great march from Atlanta to the sea. He desired to be remembered to all the officers and men of his old cavalry division in Virginia.

I expect to muster out of service to-day, and if so, shall start this evening for my home in Northern New York, which I have not visited since entering the army three years ago.

Soliciting a response at your earliest convenience,
I have the honor to remain, Colonel,
Very respectfully, your obedient servant,
WILLARD GLAZIER.

Impatient of delay in the gratification of his ardent and patriotic desire to rejoin the army, Glazier also addressed an earnest letter to Hon. M. I. Townsend, of his native State, accompanying it with the following glowing testimonial from his late superior officer and companion in arms, Colonel Clarence Buel:

SARATOGA SPRINGS, NEW YORK, }
February 14th, 1865.

HON. MARTIN I. TOWNSEND:

DEAR SIR: It is with great pleasure that I introduce to your acquaintance my friend Lieutenant Willard Glazier. He entered the service as a private in my company in the "Harris Light Cavalry," and was promoted for services in the field to his present rank. I considered him one of the very best and most promising young officers whom I knew, and his career has only strengthened my opinion of his merits. After a period of long and gallant service in the field he had the misfortune to be taken prisoner in a desperate cavalry fight, and he has but recently returned home after escaping from a terrible confinement of more than a year in the prison pens at Richmond, Danville, Macon, Savannah, Charleston, and Columbia. I wish you would take time to hear the modest recital which he makes of his experience in Southern prisons, and of his escape; and I feel sure you will agree with me, that he is worthy of any interest you may take in him.

He is desirous of re-entering the service as soon as he can procure a commission in any way equal to his deserts; and I told him that I knew of no one who could give him more valuable aid than yourself in his patriotic purpose. I do most cordially commend him to your consideration, and shall esteem anything you may do for him as a great personal favor. With very sincere regards,
I am, your obedient friend and servant,
CLARENCE BUEL.

Hon. Martin I. Townsend, on receipt of Colonel Buel's flattering introduction, at once interested himself in Glazier's behalf; and after fully investigating his previous record handed him the following to the Governor of New York State:

TROY, NEW YORK,
February 15th, 1865.

HIS EXCELLENCY R. E. FENTON, Governor of New York:

DEAR SIR: Willard Glazier, late of the "Harris Light Cavalry," and who served with honor as a lieutenant in that regiment, is a most excellent young patriot, and has many well-wishers in our city. He desires to enter the service again. I take the liberty to solicit for him a commission. No appointment would be more popular here, and I undertake to say, without hesitation, that I know of no more deserving young officer. His heart was always warm in the service, and he now has fifteen months of most barbarous cruelty, practised on him while a prisoner, to avenge.

Very respectfully yours,
MARTIN I. TOWNSEND.

His former commanders, Generals H. E. Davies and Judson Kilpatrick, also bore their willing testimony to the qualifications and merits of our young subaltern in the following handsome manner:

HEADQUARTERS, FIRST BRIGADE, CAVALRY DIVISION,
NEAR CULPEPPER, VA.,
February 16th, 1865.

To HIS EXCELLENCY HON. R. E. FENTON:

Lieutenant Willard Glazier, formerly of the Second New York Cavalry, served in the regiment under my immediate command, for more than two years, until his capture by the enemy.

He joined the regiment as an enlisted man, and served in that capacity with courage and ability, and for good conduct was recommended for and received a commission as second lieutenant. As an officer he did his duty well, and on several occasions behaved with great gallantry, and with good judgment. Owing to a long imprisonment, I learn he has been rendered supernumerary in his regiment, and mustered out of service. I can recommend him highly as an officer, and as well worthy to receive a commission.

Very respectfully,
H. E. DAVIES, JR.,
Brigadier-General U. S. Volunteers.

HEADQUARTERS CAVALRY COMMAND, M. D. M., }
NEAR SAVANNAH, GEORGIA, *December 27th*, 1864. }
LIEUTENANT WILLARD GLAZIER,
    Harris Light Cavalry :
    LIEUTENANT: I take great pleasure in expressing to you my high appreciation of your many soldierly qualities. I well remember the fact that you were once a private in the old regiment I had the honor to command; and that by attention to duty and good conduct *alone*, you received promotion. You have my best wishes for your future advancement, and may command my influence at all times.   Very respectfully and truly yours,
                                  JUDSON KILPATRICK,
                         Brigadier-General, U. S. Volunteers.

His application was crowned with success, and upon the twenty-fifth of February, 1865, he received his commission as First Lieutenant in the Twenty-sixth Regiment, New York Cavalry.

Not until this important matter was satisfactorily arranged would our young lieutenant turn his face towards home. He had been absent about three years, and a report had reached his family that he had died in prison at Columbia.

With his commission in his pocket, he now allowed thoughts of home to occupy his mind, and proceeded thither without the loss of a moment. On reaching the homestead which had been the scene of his birth, and of the adventures of his boyhood, he knocked and entered, and his mother met him at the threshold. Three years between the ages of sixteen and nineteen, especially after vicissitudes and sufferings such as he had endured, effect changes in the features and height and general appearance, much more pronounced than a similar interval would produce at a later or an earlier period of life. The mother did not recognize her son; and seeing this, he did not announce himself, but inquired if any news had recently been received of her son Willard, who, he said, was in the same regiment as himself. She answered that her son was *dead*—she had seen his name in the death-record of the prison of Columbia, and asked earnestly concerning him. By this time his sister Marjorie, with three years added to her stature, but still in her teens, entered the room, and, looking fixedly at the stranger's solemn countenance, exclaimed, with a thrilling outcry: " Why, that's Will!" The spell was broken, and mother and son, sister and brother, amid smiles and sobs, embraced, and the young soldier, "who was dead and is alive," was welcomed to the fond hearts of those who had grieved over his loss.

Filial and fraternal love was a trait in Glazier's character which claims a few words. A dutiful son and an affectionate brother, he had never neglected an opportunity of assisting and furthering the interests of his family. Before entering the army he had contributed of his scant earnings as a teacher towards the education of his three sisters, and during his service in the war had, from time to time, as he received his pay, made remittances home for the same unselfish purpose. On being mustered out of the army, the government had paid him the sum of $500, and this sum he now generously handed over to his parents to be also expended in perfecting the education of his sisters.

Lieutenant Glazier now hastened to report himself to the commanding officer of his regiment, and displayed all his wonted energy and devotion to the cause of the Union. He served faithfully and honorably until the mighty hosts of the Republican army melted back into quiet citizenship, with nothing to distinguish them from other citizens but their scars and the proud

A NEW CAREER.

consciousness of having SERVED AND SAVED THEIR COUNTRY.

This brief history of the military career of a remarkable man would not be complete without some account of his life subsequent to the dissolution of the great army of volunteers. Willard Glazier's conduct as a soldier formed an earnest of his future good citizenship—his devotion to duty at the front, a foreshadow of his enterprise and success in the business of life.

Having been honorably mustered out, he lost no time in looking about for an occupation. Joining the volunteer army when a mere youth, his opportunities of learning a profession had been very limited, and he consequently now found himself without any permanent means of support. His education had been necessarily interrupted by the breaking out of the war, and his chief anxiety, now that the struggle was over, was to enter college and complete his studies.

This desire was very intense in our young citizen-soldier, and absorbed all his thoughts; but where to find the means for its accomplishment he was at a loss to discover. In ponderings upon this subject from day to day, an idea suddenly occurred to him, which formed an epoch in his life, and the development of which has proved it to have been the basis of a successful and useful career. The *idea* that has borne fruit was this: During the period of his service in the war he had kept a diary. Herein he had recorded his experiences from day to day, adding such brief comments as the events called for, and time and opportunity permitted. This diary he always kept upon his person, and while on a long and hurried march, or in a battle with the enemy, his *vade mecum* would be, of necessity, occasionally neglected, no sooner did the opportunity offer than his mind wandered back over the few days' interval since the previous entry, and each event of interest was duly chronicled. Again during the period of his confinement in Southern prisons, sick, and subjected to most inhuman treatment and privation, and while escaping from his brutal captors, concealed in the swamps during the day, tired, hungry, and cold, his diary was never forgotten, albeit, the entries were frequently made under the greatest difficulties, such as to most men would have proved insurmountable.

This journal was now in his possession. He had stirred the souls of relatives and friends by reading from it accounts of bloody scenes through which he had passed; of cruelties practised upon him and his brother-patriots in Southern bastiles; of his various attempts to escape, and pursuit by blood-hounds and their barbarous masters. The story of his war experiences entranced hundreds of eager listeners around his home, and the idea that now occurred to him, while anxiously pondering the ways and means of paying his college fees, was, that his story might possibly, by the aid of his diary, be arranged in the form of a book, and if he were fortunate enough to find a sale for it, the profits would probably furnish the very thing he stood so much in need of.

Prompt in everything, the thought no sooner occurred to the young candidate for college honors than he proceeded to reduce it to action. He forthwith commenced arranging the facts and dates from the diary; constructed sentences in plain Saxon English; the work grew upon him; he "fought his battles o'er again;" was again captured, imprisoned and escaped; the work continued to grow, and at the end of six weeks' hard application, always keeping his *object* in view, Willard Glazier, the young cavalryman, found himself an author—*i. e.*, in manuscript.

Not a little surprised and gratified to discover that he possessed the gift of putting his thoughts in a readable form, he now felt hopeful that the day was not distant when the desire of his soul to enter college would be realized.

CHAPTER XXVII.

CAREER AS AN AUTHOR.

Glazier in search of a publisher for "Capture, Prison-Pen and Escape."—Spends his last dollar.—Lieutenant Richardson a friend in need.—Joel Munsell, of Albany, consents to publish.—The author solicits subscriptions for his work before publication.—Succeeds.—Captain Hampton.—R. H. Ferguson.—Captain F. C. Lord.—Publication and sale of first edition.—Great success.—Pays his publisher in full.—Still greater successes.—Finally attains an enormous sale.—Style of the work.—Extracts.—Opinions of the press.

STILL very young, and knowing nothing of the trade of the Publisher, Glazier found his way to the Empire City, and, manuscript in hand, presented himself before some of her leading publishers—among them, the Harpers, Appletons, Carleton, Sheldon and others.

To these gentlemen he showed his manuscript, and received courteous recognition from each; but the terms they offered were not of a character to tempt him. They would publish his book and pay him a small royalty on their sales. His faith in his manuscript led him to expect more substantial results. The subject of the work was one of absorbing interest at the time, and if he had handled it properly, he knew the book must meet with a commensurate sale. He therefore determined, if possible, to find a publisher willing to make it to his order, and leave him to manipulate the sale himself. He was already in possession of many unsolicited orders for it, and although knowing nothing of the subscription-book business, determined that, when printed, his book should be brought out by subscription.

Meanwhile, he was, unfortunately, like many incipient authors, without capital, and could not therefore remain longer in New York for lack of means, having literally nothing left wherewith to defray even his board or procure a lodging. He was, consequently, compelled to leave if he could obtain the means of doing so. He had arrived in New York with sanguine expectations of readily meeting with a publisher, but discovered, from bitter experience, as many others have done, that authors and publishers not unfrequently view their interests from divergent points. Courteous but cool, they offered the unknown author little encouragement, who, but for this, would have made the metropolis the starting-point in his successful literary career.

At this juncture he called on Lieutenant Arthur Richardson, an old comrade of the "Harris Light," who had also been his fellow-prisoner, and was then residing in New York. To him he confided his difficulty in finding a publisher for his book, and his extremely straitened circumstances, at the same time stating his strong wish to return, if possible, to Albany, where he was known. Without ceremony and without conditions Richardson generously handed him twenty dollars, and, with this godsend in hand, Glazier at once returned to Albany.

Arrived in the capital of his native State, he lost no time in calling on the bookmen of that city, and among them, fortunately, on Mr. Joel Munsell, of 82 State

Street. This gentleman, well known for his learning and probity throughout the State, and far beyond its limits, combined the profession of an author with the more lucrative one of publisher and bookseller, and was pre-eminently in good standing as a worthy citizen and man of business.

Glazier introduced himself, and once more produced his fateful manuscript for inspection. Mr. Munsell glanced at it through his glasses, and candidly admitted the subject to be one of great interest, adding that he also thought the manuscript was carefully written, and spoke in general complimentary terms of the author and his production.

Glazier, elated with this praise, at once asked to have the work stereotyped and made into a book of some four hundred pages, with ten illustrations. Mr. Munsell would be only too ready to fill the order, but politely suggested, as a preliminary condition, an advance of two hundred dollars! Our author modestly confessed, without hesitation, that he was not worth two hundred cents; had no means of obtaining such a sum, and could therefore advance nothing. The worthy old gentleman was startled, and answered that such was the custom of the trade. He then inquired if Glazier had any friends who would endorse a note for the amount at thirty days. The reply was that he had none; that he would exert himself to obtain a small sum from army friends, and if he succeeded, would hand it over to him; that his only capital at present was his conduct and character as a soldier, for testimony to which he would refer to his late commanding officer, "and," he added, "faith in the success of my book." He further offered to solicit subscriptions for the book himself before publication, and report the result to the publisher.

INTERVIEW WITH JOEL MUNSELL.

Mr. Munsell, pleased with his appearance and ingenuousness, hinted at the purchase of the manuscript, but the proposal being respectfully declined, inquired, if the writer undertook to sell the book himself, would he "stick to it." "Yes!" was the emphatic answer, "until everything is fully paid for."

The reply of Munsell was equally prompt and decisive: "I have never in all the years I have been in business published a work under such circumstances, *but I will get that book out for you.*" Glazier thanked the worthy man, and expressed a hope that he would never have occasion to regret his generous deed; he would place the manuscript in his hands forthwith.

He then set out to solicit subscriptions for his work, and without prospectus, circular, or any of the usual paraphernalia of a solicitor—with nothing but his own unsupported representations of the quality of his projected book, succeeded in obtaining a very considerable number of orders. These he hastened to hand over to Joel Munsell, who was now confirmed in his good opinion of the writer, and the promising character of the venture.

Thus our young soldier-author was fortunate enough to find a publisher and a friend in need. A contract was drawn up, and feeling that his prospects were now somewhat assured, he ventured to write to his comrade, and late fellow-prisoner, Captain Hampton, of Rochester, New York, for the loan of fifty dollars. This sum was promptly sent him, and he at once handed it over to his publisher. Mr. R. H. Ferguson, late of the "Harris Light," also generously came forward to the assistance of his former comrade and tent-mate, and advanced him one hundred dollars to help on the work.

It may be stated here, that the friendship of Ferguson and Glazier dated from before the war, while the latter, a mere youth, was teaching school near Troy, in Rensselaer County, New York: that together, on the summons to arms, they enlisted in the Harris Light Cavalry; together went to the seat of war; that both fell into the hands of the rebels and had experience of Southern prisons; and that both effected their escape after the endurance of much suffering. Finally, their friendship and common career resulted in a business connection which was attended with considerable success, Mr. Ferguson having become the publisher of some of Captain Glazier's subsequent writings. Captain Frederick C. Lord, of Naugatuck, Connecticut, also contributed to Glazier's need, and enabled him by the opportune loan of twenty-five dollars to defray his board bill while waiting anxiously upon Munsell in the reading of proofs, and soliciting subscriptions in advance.

To return to the first work of our young author, now in the hands of Joel Munsell, of Albany, which was entitled "The Capture, Prison-Pen and Escape;" the first edition consisted of five hundred copies, which Glazier by his energy disposed of in a few days, handing over the proceeds to the publisher. At the end of six months he had called for several editions of his book, and sold them all through the instrumentality of solicitors selected by himself, some of them maimed soldiers of the war, paid Mr. Munsell in full, and had himself three thousand dollars in hand. Success is the mother of success.

Having prospered thus far beyond his expectations, he was anxious to add to his store. Visions of large sales over other territory than his native State of New York presented themselves to his eager mind; the book was purchased by the public as soon as it was published; reviewers spoke in enthusiastic praise of its merits. It was not a pretentious work—the author was simply a young man and a patriot. But passages of great beauty and of painful interest pervaded it, alternated with vivid descriptions of battles in which the writer had himself shared. A veteran author need not have been ashamed of many of its glowing pages. Lofty patriotism, heroic fortitude, and moral purity, characterized it throughout.

The account given of the sufferings of our soldiers while in the prison-pens of the South, and of his own and his comrades' while effecting their escape to the Federal lines, are so vividly portrayed, that our feelings are intensely enlisted in their behalf, and our minds wander to their dreary abodes—in thought sharing their sufferings and their sorrows.

Encouraged by his success in this new vocation our young author resolved, for the present at least, to postpone going to college, and devote himself to the sale of his book, by the simple agency before mentioned. This resolution cannot be considered surprising when we reflect upon the great amount of prosperity he had met with, and the prospect before him of attaining still greater advantage from a business upon which he had, by the merest accident, ventured. The college scheme was at length finally abandoned as the business continued to increase. "The Capture, Prison-Pen and Escape" ultimately reached the enormous sale of over four hundred thousand copies; larger by many thousands than that most extensively circulated and deservedly popular book, "Uncle Tom's Cabin," had ever attained to, inclusive of its sale in Europe.

The first book written and published by Willard Glazier is of a character to surprise us, when we consider the antecedents of the writer up to the date of its publication, December, 1865. Enlisting in the ranks of a cavalry regiment at the age of eighteen, during the exciting period of the civil war; a participant in many of its sanguinary battles; captured by the enemy and imprisoned under circumstances of the greatest trial and discouragement, his position and surroundings were not a very promising school for the training of an author. The book he produced is, in our judgment, not unworthy of comparison with the immortal work of Defoe, with this qualification in our author's favor that "Robinson Crusoe" is a fiction, while Glazier's is a true story of real adventure undergone by the writer and his comrades of the Union army.

His style in narrating his adventures is admirably adapted to the subject; while the simple, unpretentious manner in which he describes the terrible scenes he witnessed, and passed through, enlists the reader's interest in the work, and sympathy for the modest writer himself. By the publication of this book, Glazier stamped his name upon his country's roll of honor, and at the same time laid the foundation of his fortune.

As a specimen of his easy flowing style we give part of the opening chapter of "Capture, Prison-Pen and Escape:"

"The first battle of Bull Run was fought July twenty-first, 1861, and the shock of arms was felt throughout the land, carrying triumph to the South, and to the North dismay. Our proud and confident advance into

'Dixie' was not only checked, but turned into a disastrous rout. The patriotic but unwarlike enthusiasm of the country, which had hoped to crush the rebellion with seventy-five thousand men, was temporarily stifled. But the chilling was only like that of the first stealthy drops of the thunder-gust upon a raging fire, which breaks out anew and with increased vigor when the tempest fans it with its fury, and now burns in spite of a deluge of rain. The chill had passed and the fever was raging. From the great centres of national life went forth warm currents of renovating public opinion, which reached the farthest hamlet on our frontiers. Every true man was grasping the stirring questions of the day, and was discussing them with his family at his own fireside, and the rebellion was just as surely doomed as when Grant received the surrender of Lee's army. In a deeper and broader sense than before, the country was rising to meet the emergency, and northern patriotism, now thoroughly aroused, was sweeping everything before it. Everywhere resounded the cry, 'To arms!' and thousands upon thousands were responding to the President's call.

"It was under these circumstances that I enlisted, as a private soldier, at Troy, New York, on the sixth day of August, in a company raised by Captain Clarence Buel, for the Second Regiment of New York Cavalry. It is needless to make elaborate mention of the motives which induced me to enter the service, or the emotions which then filled my breast; they can be readily conjectured by every loyal heart."

The Press, throughout the North (and West, as far as its circulation had reached), spoke very highly of the production and of its author, all bearing the same testimony to its excellence and truthfulness. The Albany *Evening Post* says:

"'The Capture, Prison-Pen and Escape' is the title of an intensely interesting work, giving a complete history of prison-life in the South. The book is at once accurate, graphic and admirably written. It is full of adventure, and quite as readable as a romance. A person who reads this volume will have a better idea of what it cost in the way of blood, suffering and courage, to preserve the Republic, than he can now possibly entertain."

The Cleveland *Daily Leader* writes:

"We have had the pleasure of reading this book. It describes, in the most graphic and interesting style, the prison-life of Union soldiers in the South, their plans of escape, and their various trials and hardships there. The history contained in the book is very valuable. The Press, all over the land, speaks very highly of it, and we can do naught but add our commendations to the rest."

The New York *Reformer* exclaims:

"From the title-page to its close, the volume is full of fresh incidents, attracting the reader on, from page to page, with unbroken, though at times with melancholy, at others indignant, and at others wrathful, interest."

CAVALRY FORAGING PARTY RETURNING TO CAMP.

CHAPTER XXVIII.

"THREE YEARS IN THE FEDERAL CAVALRY."

Another work by Captain Glazier.—"Three Years in the Federal Cavalry."—Daring deeds of the Light Dragoons.—Extracts from the work.—Night attack on Falmouth Heights.—Kilpatrick's stratagem.—Flight of the enemy.—Capture of Falmouth.—Burial of Lieutenant Decker.—Incidents at "Brandy Station."—"Harris Light" and "Tenth New York."—"Men of Maine, you must save the day!"—Position won.—Some Press reviews of the work.

THE combined industry and intellect of our soldier-author had, in the meantime, produced another book of equal merit with his first. This he named, "Three Years in the Federal Cavalry." It is a work of thrilling interest, and contains much of history relating to the Civil War, and more especially to the cavalry service. It was the opinion of Captain Glazier that the Union cavalry had never been properly appreciated, and for this reason he took up his pen in its defense. He narrates the daring deeds of our Light Dragoons, their brilliant achievements during the first three eventful years of the war; and his own personal experiences are pictured with a vividness of color and an enthusiasm of manner which carry the reader straight to the field of action.

We quote the following brief but graphic description of the opening of the great Rebellion, as a specimen of the style of this second product of his intellect:

"The eleventh of April, 1861, revealed the real intention of the Southern people in their unprovoked assault upon Fort Sumpter. The thunder of rebel cannon shook the air not only around Charleston, but sent its thrilling vibrations to the remotest sections of the country, and was the precursor of a storm whose wrath no one anticipated. This shock of arms was like a fire-alarm in our great cities, and the North arose in its might with a grand unanimity which the South did not expect. The spirit and principle of rebellion were so uncaused and unprovoked, that scarcely could any one be found at home or abroad to justify them.

"President Lincoln thereupon issued a call for seventy-five thousand men to uphold and vindicate the authority of the government, and to prove, if possible, that secession was not only a heresy in doctrine, but an impracticability in the American Republic. The response to this call was much more general than the most sanguine had any reason to look for. The enthusiasm of the people was quite unbounded. Individuals encouraged individuals; families aroused families; communities vied with communities, and States strove with States. Who could be the first and do the most, was the noble contention which everywhere prevailed. All political party lines seemed to be obliterated. Under this renovating and inspiring spirit the work of raising the nucleus of the grandest army that ever swept a continent went bravely on. Regiments were rapidly organized, and as rapidly as possible sent forward to the seat of government; and so vast was the number that presented themselves for their country's defence, that the original call was soon more than filled, and the authorities found themselves unable to accept many organizations which were eager to press into the fray.

"Meanwhile the great leaders of the rebellion were marshalling the hordes of treason, and assembling them on the plains of Manassas, with the undoubted intention of moving upon the national capital. This point determined the principal theatre of the opening contest, and around it on every side, and particularly southward, was to be the aceldama of America, the dreadful 'field of blood.'

"The first great impulse of the authorities was in the direction of self-defence, and Washington was fortified and garrisoned. This done, it was believed that the accumulating forces of the Union, which had become thoroughly equipped and somewhat disciplined, ought to advance into the revolted Territory, scatter the defiant hosts of the enemy, and put a speedy end to the slave-holders' rebellion."

Again we quote a description of an incident of the cavalry fight at Brandy Station:

"At a critical moment, when the formidable and ever increasing hosts of the enemy were driving our forces from a desirable position we sought to gain, and when it seemed as though disaster to our arms would be fatal, Kilpatrick's battle-flag was seen advancing, followed by the tried squadrons of the 'Harris Light,' the 'Tenth New York,' and the 'First Maine.' In echelons of squadrons his brigade was quickly formed, and he advanced, like a storm-cloud, upon the rebel cavalry, which filled the field before him. The 'Tenth New York' received the first shock of the rebel charge, but was hurled back, though not in confusion. The

'Harris Light' met with no better success, and, notwithstanding their prestige and power, they were repulsed under the very eye of their chief, whose excitement at the scene was well-nigh uncontrollable. His flashing eye now turned to the 'First Maine,' a regiment composed mostly of heavy, sturdy men, who had not been engaged as yet during the day; and, riding to the head of the column, he shouted, 'Men of Maine, you must save the day! Follow me!' With one simultaneous war-cry these giants of the North moved forward in one solid mass upon the flank of the rebel columns. The shock was overwhelming, and the opposing lines crumbled like a 'bowing wall' before this wild rush of prancing horses, gleaming sabres, and rattling balls.

"On rode Kilpatrick, with the 'men of Maine,' and, on meeting the two regiments of his brigade, which had been repulsed, and were returning from the front, the General's voice rang out like trumpet notes, above the din of battle, 'Back, the "Harris Light!" Back, the "Tenth New York!" Reform your squadrons and charge!' With magical alacrity the order was obeyed, and the two regiments, which had been so humbled by their first reverse, now rushed into the fight with a spirit and success which redeemed them from censure, and accounted them worthy of their gallant leader. The commanding position was won; a battery, lost in a previous charge, was re-captured, and an effectual blow was given to the enemy, which greatly facilitated the movements which followed."

From numerous press notices, eulogistic of this work, which appeared shortly after its publication, we select the following from the Chicago *Times:*

"For the thousands of warriors who entered upon life too late to participate in the war of the rebellion; for the thousands who entered upon life too soon to be permitted a sight of its glorious and hideous scenes; for the thousands who snuffed the smoke of battle from afar; no better book could have been produced than this 'Three Years in the Federal Cavalry.' . . . It tells them in thrilling and glowing language of the most exciting phases of the contests. . . . It is a book that will thrill the heart of every old soldier who reads its historic pages. . . . The author carries his readers into every scene which he depicts. Throughout the book one is impressed with the idea that he saw all that he describes. . . . The triumphs, the despondencies, the sufferings, the joys of the troops, are feelingly and vigorously painted. . . . His book is a noble tribute to the gallant horsemen, who have too often been overlooked."

The Syracuse *Herald* remarks:

"Among the newest, and we may truly say the best of the books on the civil war, is a work by the widely-known author, Captain Willard Glazier, entitled 'Three Years in the Federal Cavalry.' . . . Its pages teem with word-painting of hair-breadth escapes, of marches, of countermarches, bivouacs and battles without number. Stirring memories of Brandy Station, Chantilly, Antietam, Fredericksburg, Yorktown, Falmouth and Gettysburg, are roused by the masterly *raconteur*, until in October, 1864, just beyond New Baltimore, the gallant captain was captured, and for a year languished in 'durance vile.' The interest in the narrative never flags, but rather increases with each succeeding page. For those who love to fight their battles o'er again, or those who love to read of war's alarms, this volume will prove most welcome."

The New York *Tribune* is

"Sure that 'Three Years in the Federal Cavalry' will meet with the same generous reception from the reading public that has been given to the former works of this talented young author. The fact that Captain Glazier was an eye-witness and participant in the thrilling scenes of which he writes, lends additional interest to the work."

The Boston *Post* proclaims that

"Captain Glazier is one of the most pleasing writers who has added a contribution to our war literature. He takes you, through the vividness of his description, into the very scenes which he portrays. 'Three Years in the Federal Cavalry' cannot fail to interest every reader, and we predict for it a sale unprecedented in the book trade."

The Scranton *Times* observes:

"The cavalry arm of the service is a most romantic one, and the author of this book has painted its scenes with the hand of an artist as well as with the eye of a participator. He rises above the conventional 'war writer's' idioms, and gives his descriptions a place in literature and history. Here is found the stern actuality of war's fearful tug; here the beautiful pathos of pure manly sentiment flowing from the heart of many a burly form on the battle's eve; here the scenes of sad and solemn burial, where warriors weep. The din of battle on one page, and the jest at peril past upon the next—the life-test and the comedy of camp—these, alternating, checker the work over, and give the reader a truer insight into the peril and the fun of our brave defenders than any work we have read."

From the New York *Telegram* we extract:

"The success which has attended the previous works of Captain Glazier has induced him to add another book to the array of our war literature. Leaving the old and well-trodden path he has cut a new road for himself, in giving a history of the campaigns of the Union cavalry attached to the army of the Potomac. It supplies facts not to be found in official reports—facts, doubtless, held trivial at the moment, but which are to-day recognized as having borne an important part in the contest, contributing to victory, or precipitating defeat. Aside from its historical value, 'Three Years in the Federal Cavalry' will be found decidedly entertaining to the ordinary reader. The greater portion is written in the form of a diary, in which the author records all that transpired during his three years' campaign. Battles, victories and defeats, heroic deeds and daring exploits, are recounted briefly and concisely, though always with spirit and animation. No attempt is made to enter into the minute details of engagements and marches. Captain Glazier has contented himself with giving us sketches of the cavalry operations in Virginia, and his pictures are all agreeably drawn. We recommend the book as something really readable and very interesting."

The New York *Star* says:

"'Three Years in the Federal Cavalry' brings to light many daring deeds upon the part of the Union heroes, that have never yet been recorded, and gives an insight into the conduct of the war which historians, who write but do not fight, could not possibly give. It is full of incident, and one of the most interesting books upon the war that we have read."

From the New York *Globe* we cull the following:

"To a returned soldier nothing is more welcome than conversation touching his experience 'in the field' with his companions, and next to this a good book written by one who has known 'how it is himself,' and who recounts vividly the scenes of strife through which he has passed. Such a work is 'Three Years in the Federal Cavalry.' Captain Glazier's experiences are portrayed in a manner at once interesting to the veteran, and instructive and entertaining to those who have but snuffed the battle from afar. An old soldier will never drop this book for an instant, if he once begins it, until every word has been read. There is an air of truth pervading every page which chains the veteran to it until he is stared in the face with 'Finis.' The details and influences of camp-life, the preparations for active duty, the weary marches to the battle-field, the bivouac at night, the fierce hand-to-hand strife, the hospital, the dying volunteer, the dead one—buried in his blanket by the pale light of the moon, far, far away from those he loves—the defeat and victory—every scene, in fact, familiar to the eye and ear of the 'boy in blue,' is here most truthfully and clearly photographed, and the soldier is once more transported back to the days of the rebellion. Captain Glazier's style is easy and explicit. He makes no endeavor to be poetic or eloquent, but tells his story in a straightforward manner, occasionally, however, approaching eloquence in spite of himself. We cheerfully and earnestly commend 'Three Years in the Federal Cavalry' to the public as a most readable, entertaining and instructive volume."

Among the manifold testimonials we have seen to the merits of this work, the following from the poetic pen of Mrs. Maud Louise Brainerd, of Elmira, New York, is at once beautiful and eloquent of praise, and must not therefore be omitted from the chaplet we are weaving for the brow of the 'soldier-author:'

> 'Have you heard of our Union Cavalry,
>   As Glazier tells the story?
> Of the dashing boys of the 'Cavalry Corps,'
>   And their daring deeds of glory?
>
> "This modest volume holds it all,
>   Their brave exploits revealing,
> Told as a comrade tells the tale,
>   With all a comrade's feeling.
>
> "The Union camp-fires blaze anew,
>   Upon these faithful pages,
> Anew we tremble while we read
>   How hot the warfare rages.
>
> "We hear again the shock of arms,
>   The cannon's direful thunder,
> And feel once more the wild suspense
>   That then our hearts throbbed under.
>
> "The deeds of heroes live again
>   Amid the battle crashes,
> As, Phœnix-like, the dead take form
>   And rise from out their ashes.
>
> "Where darkest hangs the cloud and smoke,
>   Where weaker men might falter,
> The brave Phil Kearney lays his life
>   Upon his country's altar.
>
> "Kilpatrick's legions thunder by,
>   With furious clang and clatter,
> Rushing where duty sternly leads,
>   To life or death—no matter!
>
> "Oh, hero-warriors, patriots true!
>   Within your graves now lying,
> How bright on History's page to-day
>   Shines out your fame undying!

A CAVALRY BIVOUAC.

"THREE YEARS IN THE CAVALRY."

"The pomp and panoply of war
   Have vanished; all the glitter
Of charging columns, marching hosts
   And battles long and bitter,

"Recede with the receding years,
   Wrapped in old Time's dim shadow;
Where once the soil drank patriot gore,
   Green, now, grow field and meadow.

"But here the written record stands
   Of all that time of glory,
And bright through every age shall live
   These names in song and story.

"Willard Glazier wrote his name
   First in war's deeds, then slipping
His fingers off the sword, he found
   The mightier pen more fitting.

"Read but the book—'twill summon back
   The spirits now immortal,
Who bravely died for fatherland
   And passed the heavenly portal!"

Such was the demand for the work that one hundred and seventy-five thousand copies of it were sold, and we may safely predicate that in the homes of thousands of veterans scattered all over the land, the book has been a source of profound interest in the help it has afforded them in recounting to family and friends the thrilling events of their war experience.

CHAPTER XXIX.

"BATTLES FOR THE UNION."

"Battles for the Union."—Extracts.—Bull Run.—Brandy Station.—Manassas.—Gettysburg.—Pittsburg Landing.—Surrender of General Lee.—Opinions of the press.—Philadelphia "North American."—Pittsburg "Commercial."—Chicago "Inter-Ocean."—Scranton "Republican."—Wilkes-Barre "Record of the Times."—Reading "Eagle."—Albany "Evening Journal."

"BATTLES FOR THE UNION," (published by Dustin Gilman and Company, Hartford, Connecticut) was the next work that emanated from our soldier's prolific pen. The most stubbornly contested battles of the great Rebellion herein find forcible and picturesque description. "I have endeavored," Glazier writes in his preface to this interesting work, "in 'Battles for the Union' to present, in the most concise and simple form, the great contests in the war for the preservation of the Republic of the United States;" and as evidence of the manner in which this task was undertaken, we shall again present to the reader some passages from the work itself.

As an illustration of descriptive clearness and force, combined with conciseness and simplicity of narrative, we present the opening of the chapter on Bull Run:

"The field of Bull Run and the plains of Manassas will never lose their interest for the imaginative young or the patriotic old; for on this field and over these plains are scattered the bones of more than forty thousand brave men of both North and South, who have met in mortal combat and laid down their lives in defence of their principles.

"On the twenty-first of July, 1861, was fought the battle of Bull Run, the first of a long series of engagements on these historic plains. The battles of Bristoe, Groveton, Manassas, Centreville, and Chantilly succeeded in 1862, and in the summer and autumn of 1863 followed the cavalry actions at Aldie, Middleburg, Upperville, and New Baltimore.

"No battle-ground on the continent of America can present to the generations yet to come such a gigantic Roll of Honor. Here also was displayed the best military talent, the keenest strategy, and the highest engineering skill of our civil war. Here were assembled the great representative leaders of slavery and freedom. Here Scott, McDowell, Pope, and Meade on the Federal side, and Beauregard, Johnson, and Lee on the Confederate side, have in turn held the reins of battle and shared both victory and defeat.

"The action which resulted in the fall of Fort Sumter developed extraordinary talent in the rebel General P. G. T. Beauregard, and brought him conspicuously before the Confederate government. Called for by the unanimous voice of the Southern people, he was now ordered to take command of the main portion of the Confederate army in northern Virginia. He selected Manassas Junction as his base of operations, and established his outposts near Fairfax Court-House, seventeen miles from Washington.

"General Beauregard's forces, on the line of Bull Run, numbered on the sixteenth of July nearly forty thousand men, and sixty-four pieces of artillery, together with a considerable body of cavalry. The threatening attitude of this force, almost within sight of the National capital, led General Scott to concentrate the Union forces in that quarter with a view to meeting the Confederates in battle, and, if possible, giving a death-blow to the rebellion.

"Ludicrous, indeed, in the light of subsequent events, was the general conviction of the hostile sections, that a single decisive engagement would terminate the war. Little did the Unionists then know of the ambitious designs of the pro-slavery leaders, and still less did the uneducated, misguided masses of the South know of the patriotism, resources, and invincible determination of the North. On both sides there was great popular anxiety for a general battle to determine the question of relative manhood: and especially on the side of the South, from an impression that one distinct and large combat resulting in its favor, and showing conspicuously its superior valor, would alarm the North sufficiently to lead it to abandon the war. The New York *Tribune*, which was supposed at that time to be a faithful representative of the sentiment and temper of the North, said, on the nineteenth of July, 1861: 'We have been most anxious that this struggle should be submitted at the earliest moment to the ordeal of a fair, decisive battle. Give the Unionists a fair field, equal weapons and equal numbers, and we ask no more. Should the rebel forces at all justify the vaunts of their journalistic trumpeters, we shall candidly admit the fact. If they can beat double the number of Unionists, they can end the struggle on their own terms.'

"A field for the grand combat was soon found, but its results were destined to disappoint both the victors and the vanquished. The South had looked forward to this field for an acknowledgment of its independence; the North for a downfall of the rebellion."

The chapter on "Brandy Station" affords several illustrations of our author's glowing descriptive power, thus:

"The words Brandy Station will ever excite a multitude of thrilling memories in the minds of all cavalrymen who saw service in Virginia, for this was the grand cavalry battle-ground of the war.

"On these historic plains our Bayard, Stoneman, and Pleasanton have successively led their gallant troopers against the commands of Stuart, Lee, and Hampton. The twentieth of August, 1862, the ninth of June, twelfth of September, and eleventh of October, 1863, are days which cannot soon be forgotten by the 'Boys in Blue' who crossed sabres with the Confederates at Brandy Station.

"Converging and diverging roads at this point quite naturally brought the cavalry of the contending armies together whenever we advanced to, or retired from, the Rapidan. Being both the advance and rear-guard of the opposing forces, our horsemen always found themselves face to face with the foe on this field; in fact, most of our cavalrymen were so confident of a fight here, that as soon as we discovered that we were approaching the station we prepared for action by tightening our saddle-girths and inspecting our arms.

"Upon the withdrawal of the Army of the Potomac from the Peninsula, General Lee, contemplating the invasion of Maryland and Pennsylvania, started his army northward with the view, no doubt, of driving Pope from northern Virginia, and carrying the Confederate standard into the loyal States. The battle of Cedar Mountain temporarily checked his forward movement and compelled him to retire to the south bank of the Rapidan. The reappearance of rebel skirmishers at the various fords of the river on the morning of August the eighteenth, 1862, was an evidence to our pickets that the enemy was about to resume hostilities.

"General Pope at once ordered his artillery and infantry to retire beyond the Rappahannock, while General Bayard, commanding the cavalry, was charged with covering the rear of the retiring army. We disputed the advance of the rebels so stubbornly that they found no opportunity to interfere with the retreat of the main column. The morning of the twentieth found the 'Harris Light,' Tenth New York, First Pennsylvania, First Maine, First Rhode Island, and First New Jersey Cavalry, bivouacked at Brandy Station.

"The engagement opened at six o'clock by an attack of Stuart's cavalry upon the Harris Light, acting as rear-guard of Bayard's brigade.

"This preliminary onset was speedily repulsed by the Harris Light, which regiment kept the enemy in check until General Bayard had gained sufficient time to enable him to form his command at a more favorable point, two miles north of the station, on the direct road to the Rappahannock. Here the Harris Light, led by Colonel Kilpatrick and Major Davies, again charged the advanced regiments of the Confederate column, thus opening the series of memorable conflicts at Brandy Station, and adding fresh laurels to its already famous record. A deep cut in a hill, through which the Orange and Alexandria Railroad passes, checked our pursuit, else we should have captured many prisoners. The First New Jersey and First Pennsylvania coming to our relief enabled us to reform our broken squadrons, and, as Pope had instructed General Bayard not to bring on a general engagement, the cavalry now crossed the Rappahannock and awaited the orders of the general-in-chief."

The following description of "Manassas or Second Bull Run" shows great mastery of his subject, and the possession of a facile and impartial pen:

"On the twenty-ninth of August, 1862, the storm of battle again broke over the plains of Manassas, and surged furiously along the borders of Bull Run creek and down the Warrenton pike. The figure of General Franz Sigel stands out in bold relief against the background of battle, the first actor appearing on the scene in this drama of war and death.

"The time is daybreak, and the rosy light of early dawn, so peaceful and so pure, flushes the sky in painful contrast to the scenes of strife and bloodshed below.

"At noon on the day previous, General Pope had ordered Reno, Kearney and Hooker to follow Jackson, who, through the miscarriage of well-laid plans, had been allowed to escape in the direction of Centreville. McDowell's command, then on the way to Manassas, was ordered to march to Centreville, while Porter was directed to come forward to Manassas Junction. The orders were promptly executed by the various commands, excepting that of Fitz-John Porter, who unaccountably on loyal principles, remained inactive during the ensuing contest. Kearney drove the enemy out of Centreville, and in their retreat along the Warrenton Road they encountered the division of King, McDowell's advance, marching eastward to intercept them.

"A sharp fight took place, terminating to the advantage of neither, and at night the contestants bivouacked near the battle-field.

"On the night of the twenty-eighth, Pope's forces were so disposed that twenty-five thousand men under McDowell, Sigel and Reynolds, were ready to attack Jackson from the south and west, and the corps of Reno, Heintzelman, and Porter, consisting of an equal number of troops, were to complete the attack from the east. Lee was pushing forward his forces to support Jackson at Thoroughfare Gap, and it was necessary for the Union army to use all possible celerity of movement, in order to make the attack before the main movement of the Confederate army under Lee could come up. But this combination failed like many another, and during the night King's division fell back towards Manassas Junction, at which place Porter's Corps had recently arrived, and the road to Gainsville and Thoroughfare Gap was thus left open to Jackson. A new arrangement of troops became therefore necessary." . . . .

There are several fine passages in the description of the battle of Gettysburg which show graphic power, and penetration into the motives of the leaders. The story of this sanguinary struggle for victory is well told throughout. We extract the following:

"Night came on to close the dreadful day. Thus far the battle had been mostly to the advantage of the rebels. They held the ground where Reynolds had fallen, also Seminary Ridge, and the elevation whence the Eleventh Corps had been driven. They also occupied the ridge on which Sickles had commenced to fight. Sickles himself was *hors de combat* with a shattered leg, which had to be amputated, and not far from twenty thousand of our men had been killed, wounded, and captured. The rebels had also lost heavily in killed and wounded, but having gained several important positions, were deluded with the idea that they had gained a victory.

. . . . . .

"During these days of deadly strife and of unprecedented slaughter, our cavalry was by no means idle. On the morning of the first, Kilpatrick advanced his victorious squadrons to the vicinity of Abbottstown, where they struck a force of rebel cavalry, which they scattered, capturing several prisoners, and then rested. To the ears of the alert cavalry chieftain came the sound of battle at Gettysburg, accompanied with the intelligence from prisoners mostly, that Stuart's main force was bent on doing mischief on the right of our infantry lines, which were not far from the night's bivouac.

"He appeared instinctively to know where he was most needed; so, in the absence of orders, early the next morning he advanced on Hunterstown. At this point were the extreme wings of the infantry lines, and as Kilpatrick expected, he encountered the rebel cavalry, commanded by his old antagonists, Stuart, Lee and Hampton. The early part of the day was spent mostly in reconnoitring, but all the latter part of the day was occupied in hard, bold, and bloody work. Charges and counter-charges were made; the carbine, pistol and sabre were used by turns, and the artillery thundered long after the infantry around Gettysburg had sunk to rest, well-nigh exhausted with the bloody carnage of the weary day. But Stuart, who had hoped to break in upon our flank and rear, and to pounce upon our trains, was not only foiled in his endeavor by the gallant Kilpatrick, but also driven back upon his infantry supports and badly beaten.

"In the night, Kilpatrick, after leaving a sufficient force to prevent Stuart from doing any special damage on our right, swung around with the remainder of his division to the left of our line, near Round Top, and was there prepared for any work which might be assigned him.

"Friday, July third, the sun rose bright and warm upon the blackened forms of the dead which were strewn over the bloody earth; upon the wounded, who had not been cared for, and upon long glistening lines of armed men, ready to renew the conflict. Each antagonist, rousing every slumbering element of power, seemed to be resolved upon victory or death.

"The fight commenced early, by an attack of General Slocum's men, who, determined to regain the rifle-pits they had lost the evening before, descended like an avalanche upon the foe. The attack met with a prompt response from General Ewell. But after several hours of desperate fighting, victory perched upon the Union banners, and with great loss and slaughter, the rebels were driven out of the breast-works, and fell back upon their main lines near Benner's Hill.

"This successful move upon the part of our boys in blue was followed by an ominous lull or quiet, which continued about three hours. Meanwhile the silence was fitfully broken by an occasional spit of fire, while every preparation was being made for a last, supreme effort, which it was expected would decide the mighty contest. The scales were being poised for the last time, and upon the one side or the other was soon to be recorded a glorious victory or a disastrous defeat. Hearts either trembled, or waxed strong in the awful presence of this responsibility.

"At length one o'clock arrived, a signal-gun was fired, and then at least one hundred and twenty-five guns from Hill and Longstreet concentrated and crossed their fires upon Cemetery Hill, the centre and key of our position. Just behind this crest, though much exposed, were General Meade's headquarters. For nearly two hours this hill was plowed and torn by solid shot and bursting shell, while about one hundred guns on our side, mainly from this crest and Round Top, made sharp response. The earth and the air shook for miles around with the terrific concussion, which came no longer in volleys, but in a continual roar. So long and fearful a cannonade was never before witnessed on this continent. As the range was short and the aim accurate, the destruction was terrible.

. . . . . .

"Gradually the fire on our side began to slacken, and General Meade, learning that our guns were becoming hot, gave orders to cease firing and to let the guns cool, though the rebel balls were making fearful havoc among our gunners, while our infantry sought poor shelter behind every projection, anxiously awaiting the expected charge. At length the enemy, supposing that our guns were silenced, deemed that the moment for an irresistible attack had come. Accordingly, as a lion emerges from his lair, he sallied forth, when strong lines of infantry, nearly three miles in length, with double lines of skirmishers in front, and heavy reserves in rear, advanced with desperation to the final effort. They moved with steady, measured tread over the plain below, and began the ascent of the hills occupied by our forces, concentrating somewhat upon General Hancock, though stretching across our entire front.

. . . .

"General Picket's division was nearly annihilated. One of his officers recounted that, as they were charging over the grassy plain, he threw himself down before a murderous discharge of grape and canister, which mowed the grass and men *all 'around him'* as though a scythe had been swung just above his prostrate form.

"During the terrific cannonade and subsequent charges, our ammunition and other trains had been parked in rear of Round Top, which gave them splendid shelter. Partly to possess this train, but mainly to secure this commanding position, General Longstreet sent two strong divisions of infantry, with heavy artillery, to turn our flank, and drive us from this ground. Kilpatrick, with his division, which had been strengthened by Merritt's regulars, was watching this point and waiting for an opportunity to strike the foe. It came at last. Emerging from the woods in front of him came a strong battle-line, followed by others.

"To the young Farnsworth was committed the task of meeting infantry with cavalry in an open field. Placing the Fifth New York in support of Elder's battery, which was exposed to a galling fire, but made

BATTLE OF GETTYSBURG.

reply with characteristic rapidity, precision and slaughter, Farnsworth quickly ordered the First Virginia, the First Vermont, and Eighteenth Pennsylvania in line of battle, and galloped away and charged upon the flank of the advancing columns. The attack was sharp, brief and successful, though attended with great slaughter. But the rebels were driven upon their main lines, and the flank movement was prevented. Thus the cavalry added another dearly earned laurel to its chaplet of honor—*dearly earned*, because many of their bravest champions fell upon that bloody field.

. . . . . .

"Thus ended the battle of Gettysburg—the bloody turning-point of the rebellion—the bloody baptism of the redeemed republic. Nearly twenty thousand men from the Union ranks had been killed and wounded, and a larger number of the rebels, making the enormous aggregate of at least forty thousand, whose blood was shed to fertilize the Tree of Liberty."

The following peroration to the glowing account of the battle of Pittsburg Landing, we quote as an illustration of the vein of poetry that pervades his writings:

"Thus another field of renown was added to the list, so rapidly increased during these years; where valor won deathless laurels, and principle was reckoned weightier than life.

"Peacefully the Tennessee flows between its banks onward to the ocean, nor tells aught of the bloody struggle on its shore. Quietly the golden grain ripens in the sun, and the red furrow of war is supplanted by the plowshares of peace. To the child born within the shadow of this battle-field, who listens wonderingly to a recital of the deeds of this day, the heroes of Shiloh will, mayhap, appear like the dim phantoms of a dream, shadowy and unreal, but the results they helped to bring about are the tissue of a people's life; the dust he treads is the sacred soil from which sprang the flowers of freedom, and the institutions for which these men died, make his roof safe over his head."

We conclude our extracts from the volume with a part of the chapter on "The Surrender." The story is told without flourish of trumpets, and in a manner to give no offense to the vanquished, while its strict and impartial adherence to truth must recommend it to all readers:

"The last act in the great drama of the war took place without dramatic accessory. There was no startling tableau, with the chief actors grouped in effective attitudes, surrounded by their attendants. No spreading tree lent its romance to the occasion, as some artists have fondly supposed.

"A plain farm-house between the lines was selected by General Lee for the surrender, and the ceremony of that act was short and simple. The noble victor did not complete the humiliation of the brave vanquished by any triumphal display or blare of trumpets. In his magnanimity he even omitted the customary usage of allowing the victorious troops to pass through the enemy's lines and witness their surrender. The two great commanders met with courteous salutation, General Lee being attended by only one of his aides. General Grant sat down at a table in the barely furnished room and wrote in lead-pencil the terms of capitulation, to which Lee dictated an agreement in writing. His secretary, Colonel Marshall, and Colonel

Baden, the secretary of General Grant, made copies of the agreement from the same bottle of ink.

. . . . .

"The final situation of the Confederate army before its surrender was indeed desperate—its environments hopeless. Hemmed in at Appomattox Court House, on a strip of land between the Appomattox and James rivers, the Union army nearly surrounded it on all sides. Sheridan was in front, Meade in the rear, and Ord south of the Court House. Lee had no alternative other than the wholesale slaughter of his reduced army, or its surrender to Federal authority. He wisely chose the latter.

"The decisive battle of Five Forks had put his army to rout, and sent it in rapid retreat towards the junction of the Southside and Danville railroads at Burkesville. The Union troops pressed forward in pursuit, and it became a vital question which would reach the junction first. Between Petersburg, their point of starting, and their destination, at Burkesville, the distance was fifty-three miles. The roads were bad, and the troops tired with two days' fighting; but they pushed on with determination in this race which was destined to decide the fate of two armies.

. . . . . .

"It was Palm Sunday, April the ninth, 1865, when the capitulation was signed, in the plain frame dwelling near Appomattox Court House.

"One is often struck with the curious coincidences —the apparent sympathy between nature and important human events. The dying hours of Cromwell and Napoleon were marked by violent storms. Omens in earth and sky were the precursors of the death of

Julius Cæsar and King Duncan. A great comet heralded the opening of the war, and Palm Sunday—the day which commemorates the victorious entry of Christ into Jerusalem, ushered in the welcome reign of peace. The time was auspicious; the elements were rocked to sleep in a kind of Sunday repose. The two armies, so long in deadly hostility, were now facing each other with guns strangely hushed. An expectant silence pervaded the air. Every heart was anxiously awaiting the result of the conference in the historic farm-house.

"When at last the news of the surrender flashed along the lines, deafening cheers rose and fell for more than half an hour, over the victorious Union army. Other than this, there was no undue triumphal display of the victors over the conquered foe. . . . The shout of joy which was sent up that day from Appomattox Court House echoed through the entire North. Cannons boomed forth their iron pæans of victory; the glad clash of bells was heard ringing 'peace and freedom in,' and bonfires flamed high their attestation of the unbounded delight everywhere exhibited. The day of jubilee seemed to have come, and rejoicing was the order of the hour. The storm of war which had rocked the country for four long years, was now rolling away, and the sunlight of peace fell athwart the national horizon. The country for which Washington fought and Warren fell was once more safe from treason's hands, and liberty was again the heritage of the people."

The Northern and Western press, as heretofore, again bore its flattering testimony to our author's diligence, truthfulness and loyalty to his colors; and to the surprising facility with which a soldier could sheathe his sword and wield a pen, charming alike the veteran by his details of valor, and the mother, wife and sister by his stories of pathos from the battle-field.

The following is from the Philadelphia *North American:*

"'Battles for the Union.'—Thoroughly representative of the courage and ability shown on either side in the great struggle that lasted from the close of 1860 to April, 1865. It is not the purpose of the author to present a standard and critical work like the works of Jomini, Napier and Allison; nor to include a discussion of political questions. His aim is rather to furnish a vivid and correct account of the principal battles in such simple and intelligible terms that every reader may gain a precise idea of each. His style is rather graphic and vigorous than ornate. He introduces effective details and personal episodes. His facts are gleaned from a variety of sources as well as from personal knowledge; and though proud of his own cause and of his companions, he does not belittle their renown by decrying the valor or the intelligence of his opponents. The conflicts themselves will never be forgotten. It is desirable that they shall be kept vivid and clear in the minds of the rising generation, to cultivate a correct idea of the necessity of personal valor and of military preparation and capacity, as well as impress a serious idea of the momentous importance of political issues. Captain Glazier's volume is excellently fitted to instruct and interest everywhere."

The Pittsburg *Commercial* says:

"Commencing with the siege and final surrender of Fort Sumter, the author traces the progress of the Union armies through all the chief battles of the war, giving vivid and glowing descriptions of the struggles at Big Bethel, Bull Run, Wilson's Creek, Ball's Bluff, Mill Spring, Pea Ridge, the fight between the 'Merrimac' and 'Monitor,' Newbern, Falmouth Heights, Pittsburg Landing, Williamsburg, Seven Pines, Fair Oaks, Malvern Hill, Cedar Mountain, Brandy Station, Manassas or Second Bull Run, Chantilly, Antietam, Corinth, Fredericksburg, Stone River, Chancellorsville, Aldie, Upperville, Gettysburg, Vicksburg, Port Hudson, Falling Waters, Chickamauga, Bristoe, New Baltimore, Fort Fisher, Olustee, Fort Pillow, Cold Harbor, Fort Wagner, Cedar Creek, Waynesboro,

Bentonville, Five Forks, and down to the surrender of Lee. Captain Glazier has evidently had access to the official records of the war, and his narrative of the great events are therefore accurate. The book is one the reading of which will make the blood tingle in the veins of every soldier who took part in the late war, while it will deeply interest every lover of his country. As a book for boys, it has few, if any, superiors."

The Chicago *Inter-Ocean* writes:

"'Battles for the Union' is such a history as every soldier and every man who has a pride in his country, should wish to possess. Captain Glazier was no carpet knight. He shared the glories of the Harris Light Cavalry in camp and field, earning his promotion from the non-commissioned ranks to the command for which he was so admirably fitted. There is the scent of powder in what he writes, the vivid reality of sight and understanding. We are particularly charmed with his style, which is plain, blunt, direct, and free from strain or affectation. He describes the fights as they were fought; individual deeds of bravery as they were performed; the march and its trials; the defeat and its causes; the victory and its effects. With the ardor of a young patriot, and the generous admiration of a good soldier, he feels as great a pride in the successes of a rival corps as in his own. Nor is this an unworthy feature of his work, because the army was full of little, and sometimes not particularly friendly, rivalries. Willard Glazier's chapters, in which every battle may be regarded as a separate picture, read like a grand panoramic view of gallant deeds and warlike pageantries. If the author occasionally covers up a clear defeat, excusing it with graceful art; if he feels disposed to over-estimate a slight advantage, and to claim a victory where the battle was evidently drawn, he errs upon the side of love for the Boys in Blue, and pride in the flag under which he fought. The work is divided into forty-four chapters, each containing a different battle. We confidently recommend these graphic and life-like pictures to the notice of our readers. They are thrilling as the sound of the trumpet, and soul-inspiring as the songs of Ossian. We call the reader's attention to the description of the combat between the 'Merrimac' and 'Monitor' in chapter eight. It is something which will fill with pride the sailor's heart."

The Scranton *Republican* observes:

"The author, Captain Willard Glazier, has given his attention, in forty-four chapters, to that number of the most important and exciting conflicts of the war, including some that are memorable, and will always remain so; for their magnitude—Antietam, Fredericksburg, Gettysburg and Vicksburg, and others that are notable for some of their accompanying circumstances, such as Olustee, where the colored boys in blue poured out their blood; Bull Run, whose disasters gave an awakening shock to the nation; Big Bethel, Ball's Bluff, Wilson's Creek, and Chantilly, on whose sad fields successively fell the brilliant Winthrop, the heroic Baker, the intrepid Lyon, and the chivalrous Kearney. The descriptions throughout the volume are spirited and highly interesting, and the book will no doubt have a large sale."

From the Wilkes-Barre *Record of the Times* we take the following:

"'Battles for the Union' is the title of a new volume by Captain Willard Glazier, the author of several popular works descriptive of military life in all its lights and shades. His preceding works have gained him a wide fame, and in the present volume he has certainly lost none of the vigor, strength and power which characterized his former writings. His style is easy and natural, and yet thrilling and graphic in the extreme. As he writes he sees again the scenes through which he passed during the rebellion, and his facile pen at once, and with peculiar fidelity, transfers the mental picture to the page before him. It is a wonderful power, and one which few men possess, to be able to carry with them through life the scenes of former years, and reproduce them at will for the pleasure of their readers. Captain Glazier demonstrates this fine gift with admirable force, and the fascinating pages before us are a moving, breathing panorama of the battles for the Union."

The *Utica Observer* states:

"A very handsome volume, bearing the title 'Battles for the Union,' is before us. It is by Captain Willard Glazier, and like his 'Capture, Prison-Pen and Escape,' and 'Three Years in the Federal Cavalry,' is exceedingly interesting, and will no doubt meet with that success to which it is justly entitled. The author is an easy and graceful writer, and holds the attention of the reader throughout the entire work; depicting the scenes of the battle-field with such earnestness and force, as to lead one in imagination into the midst of the fiercest battles, where such exhibitions of patriotism and bravery were enacted as thrill the very soul. The work will doubtless be read by every old soldier in the land, as it should be, as many of the incidents of the late war are brought so vividly before them, as to cause them to imagine that they are once more participating in the battles for the Union."

The Reading *Eagle* says:

"Captain Glazier was an eye-witness of, and actor in, many of the stirring incidents he relates, with a vivacity and freshness of style which proves him as ready in the effective use of his pen, as he was gallant in wielding the sword. The volume before us, 'Battles for the Union,' while strictly adhering to the facts of history, is invested with all the charm of the most thrilling romance, and will well repay perusal."

From the Albany *Evening Journal* we extract:

"In this volume the story of the great combats and the lesser skirmishes is told in simple, direct and intelligent terms, with sufficient detail to bring out the points of interest, but not so minute as to be wearisome or to blur the leading features. The strategy and tactics on both sides are clearly indicated, and the various movements and demonstrations succinctly delineated. Most of the conspicuous battles are depicted—indeed, we might say, most that are worthy of special note, for forty-six distinct combats are described. To very many of our Union heroes and heroines it will prove an acceptable volume."

CHAPTER XXX.

"HEROES OF THREE WARS."

Literary zeal.—" Heroes of Three Wars "—Extract from preface.—Sale of the work.—Extracts: Washington.—Winfield Scott.—Zachary Taylor. — Grant. — Sheridan. — Kilpatrick. — Press reviews, a few out of many: Boston " Transcript."—Chicago " Inter-Ocean."—Baltimore " Sun."—Philadelphia " Times."—Cincinnati " Enquirer."—Worcester "Spy."—Pittsburg "Gazette."

BY this time our soldier-author found himself not only famous, but, through the enormous sale of his books, in comparatively affluent circumstances. His literary zeal, however, was not yet spent, and work succeeded work with a rapidity almost without parallel, while the extent of their sale exceeded anything hitherto known in the literary world.

"Heroes of Three Wars," issued by Hubbard Brothers, Philadelphia, the latest production of his pen which he has as yet published, comprises original and life-like sketches of the brave soldiers of the Revolutionary, Mexican and Civil Wars; and the stories are told in a way that is not easily forgotten. In the wide field presented by these three important epochs in the history of our country, Glazier has labored to inculcate in the minds of young Americans the virtues of gallantry, true worth, and patriotism; and his work is valuable as presenting to the student in a small compass, so much of interest in biography and history.

In the preface to the work he observes: "Washington, Scott and Grant are names that will live forever in our history; not because they were the subjects of a blind adulation, but because their worth was properly estimated, and their deeds truthfully recorded. The time for deifying men has long since passed; we prefer to see them as they are—though great, still human, and surrounded with human infirmities; worthy of immortal renown, not because they are unlike us, but because they excel us and have performed a work which entitles them to the lasting gratitude of their countrymen. Another object of this book is to group around these three generals, those officers and men who climbed to immortality by their side, shared their fortunes, helped to win their victories, and remained with them to the end." Again: "Biographies possess but little value unless they give living portraits, so that each man stands out clear and distinct in his true character and proportions."

Several thousand copies of this valuable work have already been called for by the public, and it bids fair to equal its predecessors in amount of circulation. As a specimen of its style, we present to the reader the following extract from the biographical sketch of Washington:—"There is a singular unanimity of opinion in ascribing to George Washington an exceptional character. It was certainly one of peculiar symmetry, in which a happy combination of qualities, moral, social and intellectual, were guided to appropriate action by a remarkable power of clear judgment. It was just the combination calculated to lead a spirited and brave people through such a trying crisis as the American Revolution. His star was not dark and bright by turns—did not reveal itself in uncertain and fitful glimmerings—but shone with a full and steady luminosity across the troubled night of a nation's beginning. Under these broad and beneficent rays the Ship of State was guided, through a sea of chaos, to safe anchorage. The voyage across those seven eventful years was one that tried men's souls. Often, appalling dangers threatened. Wreck on the rocks of Disunion, engulfment in the mountain waves of opposition, starvation and doubt and mutiny on shipboard—these were a few of the perils which beset their course. But a royal-souled Commander stood at the helm, and discerned, afar-off, the green shores of liberty. On this land the sunshine fell with fruitful power. The air was sweet with the songs of birds. Contentment, peace, prosperity, reigned. Great possibilities were shadowed forth within its boundaries, and a young nation, growing rapidly towards a splendid era of enlightenment, was foreseen as a product of the near future. It took a man with deep faith in the ultimate rule of right and in humanity, to occupy that position; a man with large heart, with unselfish aims, with prophetic instincts, with clear and equalized brain. George Washington possessed all these qualities—and more!"

The following is from the admirably graphic sketch of the sturdy soldier, Winfield Scott: "On the twenty-fifth of the same month (July, 1814), a little below that sublime spot where the wide waste of waters which rush over the Falls of Niagara roar and thunder into the gulf below, and where Lundy's Lane meets the rapid river at right angles, was enacted the scene of conflict which took its name from the locality, and is variously called the battle of 'Lundy's Lane,' or

'Niagara.' The action began forty minutes before sunset, and it is recorded that the head of the American column, as it advanced, was encircled by a rainbow—one which is often seen there, formed from the rising spray. The happy omen faithfully prefigured the result; for when, under the cloudy sky of midnight the battle at length terminated, the Americans were in possession of the field, and also the enemy's cannon, which had rained such deadly death into their ranks. In this action General Scott had two horses killed under him, and about eleven o'clock at night he was disabled by a musket-ball wound through the left shoulder. He had previously been wounded, and at this juncture was borne from the fray. He had piloted Miller's regiment through the darkness to the height on Lundy's Lane, where the enemy's batteries were posted, and upon which the grand charge was made that decided the battle. Throughout the action he was the leading spirit of the occasion, giving personal direction to the movements of his men, and lending the inspiration of his presence to all parts of the field."

Of Zachary Taylor, our author writes, in his masterly way: "The blaze of glory which is concentrated upon the name and life of Zachary Taylor, reveals a hero as true in metal, as sterling in virtue, as intrepid in action, and tender of heart, as ever lifted sword in the cause of honor or country. On him has fallen that most sacred mantle of renown, woven from the fabric of a people's confidence, and lovingly bestowed—not as upon a being of superior race to be worshipped, but because he was a leader from among themselves—truly of the people. He was honored with their fullest trust in his integrity, and with their largest faith in his uprightness as a man. As Daniel Webster truly said, the best days of the Roman republic afforded no brighter example of a man, who, receiving the plaudits of a grateful nation, and clothed in the highest authority of state, reached that pinnacle by more honest means; who could not be accused of the smallest intrigue or of pursuing any devious ways to political advancement in order to gratify personal ambition. All the circumstances of his rise and popularity, from the beginning of his career, when, amid blood and smoke, he made the heroic defence of Fort Harrison, to the wonderful battles of Palo Alto, Resaca, and Buena Vista, and at last the attainment of the Presidential chair—all repel the slightest suspicion of sinister motive, or a wish for individual aggrandizement. The unwavering rule of his life—his guide in every action—was the simple watchword, 'duty.'

"As to his qualities of leadership, they shone out in high relief, from first to last. In the war of 1812, he was only a captain, yet at Fort Harrison he inspired the scanty garrison with a belief in his power, and they gave him their devoted support. In the Florida campaign he commanded only a brigade, yet he seemed to infuse into every soldier the most courageous bravery. In the beginning of the war with Mexico, he marched into action at the head of a single division, and when this force afterwards swelled into an army, it did not prove too much for the resources of its commanding general. The frowning heights and barricaded streets of Monterey, bristling with ten thousand Mexicans, did not daunt him. What though he had only six thousand men with which to hold them in siege? The assault was fearlessly made, the streets were stormed, the heights were carried, the city was won — and kept!

"The brilliant victory of Buena Vista, where five thousand Americans hurled back and repulsed a tumultuous Mexican horde of twenty thousand, only reiterates the same marvelous story of superior leadership."

. . . . . .

"Fresh from these splendid achievements, he received the nomination for President over the names of Henry Clay, Daniel Webster, and General Scott. It was a spontaneous expression of the people's confidence, unheralded and unsought. And when he was triumphantly elected over the Democratic and Free-soil candidates—General Cass, Martin Van Buren, and Charles Francis Adams—he accepted the high office in a spirit of humility and simple compliance with duty."

In the sketch of General U. S. Grant's life, our author has written with a masterly hand the outlines of the grand career of his favorite general, the salient points of which are given with a soldierly energy and dash befitting the theme. Thus the chapter commences:

"The occasion often creates the man, but the man who *masters* the occasion is born, not made. Many are pushed to the surface, momentarily, by the pressure of events, and then subside into common levels; but he is the true commander during a crisis, who can wield the waves of difficulty to advantage, and be a sure pilot amid the on-rush of events when they thicken and deepen into a prolonged struggle.

"When, during the late war, our country needed a leader to face and quell the threatened danger of disunion, and conduct her armies to successful issues; and when Government entrusted those momentous issues to Ulysses S. Grant, 'the man and the moment had met,'—the occasion had found its master.

"Napoleon said that the most desirable quality of a good general was that his judgment should be in equilibrium with his courage. To no commander of modern times could this rule apply with more force than to Grant. A man of no outward clamor of character, no hint of bluster or dash, quiet-voiced, self-controlled, but not self-asserting, he yet displayed vast power as an organizer, as a tactician, and in masterly combinations of large forces so as to produce the most telling effects. It has been truly said of him that no general ever stamped his own peculiar character upon an army more emphatically than did Grant upon the Army of the Tennessee. It was the only large organization which, as a whole, never suffered a defeat during the war. It was noted for its marvelous persistence—its determined fighting qualities—and had the reputation of being sure to win any battle that lasted over a day, no matter what the odds against it. It was at Grant's recommendation that a united command was concentrated in the Mississippi Valley—which concentration has since been acknowledged to be the basis of all our subsequent victories.

"Generosity, mildness and kind-heartedness, shone as conspicuously in Grant's character as his firmness and great generalship. Simplicity of manner and kindness of heart are always characteristic of the true hero.
> 'The bravest are the tenderest,
> The loving are the daring.'

The rapid and bold descent upon Fort Donelson, the unconquerable determination exhibited at Shiloh,

the brilliant capture of Vicksburg, and the high military science displayed at Chattanooga Valley, Lookout Mountain, and Missionary Ridge—these have never been surpassed in military history, in splendor of execution, or judiciousness of combination.". . .
For brevity and comprehensiveness we commend the following unique paragraph on the genealogy of his subject:

"The great-grandfather of Ulysses was Captain Noah Grant, who was killed at the battle of White Plains, during the French and Indian wars, in 1776. His grandfather, Noah Grant, Jr., fought at Lexington as lieutenant of militia, and afterwards, during the Revolution. His father, Jesse, emigrated from Pennsylvania to Ohio, and was married at Point Pleasant, Ohio, June, 1821, to Hannah Simpson, whose father was also from the Keystone State. Ulysses was born the following year, April twenty-seventh, 1822."

We quote again from the sketch of Grant:

"On the sixth of February the brilliant reduction of Fort Henry, on the Tennessee, was accomplished by Foote, and Fort Donelson, twelve miles distant, was next in line. Grant and Foote were co-operating by land and water; but Foote did not meet here with the same success that attended him at Fort Henry. It was the fifteenth of February, and Grant had spent two or three days in making an investment of the high and wooded bluff from which frowned the guns of Donelson. Before daybreak, on the fifteenth, he had gone on board the flag-ship of Foote, in consultation as to the time and manner of attack, when the enemy swept from their works and fell upon the Union lines with tremendous force. The fighting became furious at once, and for some time the battle-line swayed to and fro, between victory and defeat. It was desperate work; brigades and regiments were repulsed and by turns advanced—the brave commands disputing every inch of the rocky and difficult battle-field. When Grant reached the scene it was 'to find his right thrown back, ammunition exhausted, and the ranks in confusion.' With quick inspiration he took in the situation at a glance, comprehended that the enemy had exhausted his greatest strength, and ordered an immediate attack by the left on the Confederate works in front. General Smith was in command of this portion of the army, and had not actively participated in the conflict. He therefore brought fresh troops to the assault. McClernand was also ordered to reform his shattered ranks and advance. The combined forces charged with splendid valor up the rocky steeps, in the blaze of a withering fire poured down upon them from the fort. They did not falter for a single instant, but reaching the summit, swept over and into the Confederate works with ringing cheers. On the next morning a white flag was seen flying from the fort, and under its protection, proposals for an armistice were sent in. Grant replied that unconditional surrender, and that immediately, must be made, or he would move on their works at once. Thereupon, Buckner, who was in command, surrendered the fort with its thirteen thousand men. This splendid victory blazoned the name of Grant all over the country, and he immediately became the people's hero."

. . . . . .

" His next achievement, the capture of Vicksburg, was wonderful indeed. Its natural strength of position on a high bluff, one hundred feet above the water level, added to the formidable array of defences which bristled defiance to all foes, made Vicksburg a very citadel of power, and the fifty thousand men stationed there under Pemberton and Price did not lessen the difficulties to be overcome. A fort, mounting eight guns, sentineled the approach to the city from beneath, while the heights above were guarded by a three-banked battery. Eight miles of batteries lined the shore above and below Vicksburg. Grant made several fruitless attempts to get to the rear of the city by digging canals across the strip of land on which it stood, and making an inland route; but each one, after herculean labor, had been abandoned. He now decided on the bold enterprise of running the gauntlet of these batteries with his transports. This desperate feat was successfully accomplished; but before he could land his troops at Grand Gulf, which he had selected as his starting-point, it was necessary to run its batteries as he had those of Vicksburg, land his troops farther down the river, and capture the place by hard fighting. He waited for nothing. Hurrying forward the moment he touched land, his object was to take Grand Gulf before the enemy could reinforce it. . . . After conquering Grand Gulf, where he expected Banks to join him, he was confronted with the refusal of that general to co-operate with him. In this dilemma nothing but a master-stroke of genius could wring success from the materials of defeat. He saw what was before him, and with true inspiration became the master of circumstances. At the head of his brave command he pushed inland, aiming to crush the enemy 'in detail before he could concentrate his forces.' By a rapid series of brilliant marches, battles and victories, Grant had, at last, on the nineteenth of May, succeeded in completely investing Vicksburg. The whole plan from its outset was brilliant to an extraordinary degree, and the tireless persistence and energy shown in its accomplishment, stamped this man as a very Gibraltar of military genius.

"An assault on the enemy's works at first, had proven a failure, and now the wonderful siege began. For forty-six days the digging and mining went patiently forward, while screaming shells and booming shot produced a reign of terror in the city, until at last, Pemberton could hold out no longer and surrendered his starving garrison to the superior prowess and strategy of Grant. It was the morning of the fourth of July when our troops took possession of Vicksburg, and ran up the stars and stripes from the top of the court-house. The soldiers, standing beneath it, sang 'Rally round the Flag,' and Grant became more than ever the popular hero. On the thirteenth of July, Lincoln wrote him a letter of 'grateful acknowledgment for the almost inestimable service' he had rendered the country. In September he was placed in command of the 'Departments of the Ohio, of the Cumberland, and of the Tennessee, constituting the Military Division of the Mississippi.'

. . . . . .

"Grant assumed the duties of his high office [the lieutenant-generalship of the army] without flourish of any sort, and proceeded to inaugurate the successive steps of his last great campaign. The military resources which centered in his hand were stupendous, but had they fallen under the control of a man less great than he, their very immensity would have rendered them powerless. The splendid army of the Potomac was on the move by May third, and the last march to Richmond had begun. Then came the three-days' battle of the Wilderness, on the south bank of the Rapidan, bloody and terrible and strange, during which some of our troops were fighting continuously for forty-eight hours; and following close after came also Spottsylvania, which was the result of an endeavor to cut off Lee's retreat. This, too, was a desperate conflict, where precious blood flowed in rivers. Then followed the race between the two opposing armies, for the North Anna. After crossing this river, and finding the Confederates occupying a fortified position on the South Anna, Grant 'swung his army around to the Pamunky, and pitched his head-quarters at Hanover Court House.' These masterly flank movements, in which he manœuvred his vast army with such ease, exhibited his marvelous genius in stronger light than ever before. From the Pamunky he advanced to the Chickahominy, and, after the battle of Cold Harbor, made a rapid but quiet change of front on the night of the twelfth of June, and two days afterwards crossed the James and advanced against Petersburg and Richmond. The attack, at first a success, failed through a blunder, not Grant's; and then began the long siege which ended at last in the evacuation of Petersburg and Richmond. Nowhere was the joy more heartfelt over these results than among the released captives of Libby Prison.

"Lee made a desperate endeavor to escape the 'manifest destiny' that pursued him, and led his army a 'race for life.' But Grant, close on his track, environed him on all sides, and the surrender at Appomattox became inevitable. When, at the final scene, Lee presented his sword to Grant, the great general handed it back to him, saying, 'it could not be worn by a braver man.'"

. . . . . .

We present the reader with the following extracts from the sketch of General Sheridan. It will be observed that the author is extremely happy in the selection of his subjects, his aim evidently being to include those only whose reputation for heroism is unquestioned and national.

"Sheridan is probably the most intense type of 'soldiership' brought to light by the last war. Nor can any other war furnish an individual example that will surpass him in fiery concentration. In battle he is the very soul of vehement action—the incarnate wrath of the storm. No historian can ever portray the man so truly as did the remarkable victory of Cedar Creek— a result solely of his extraordinary power. The marvelous will-force with which he could hurl himself in the front of battle, and infuse his own spirit of unconquerable daring into the ranks, is phenomenal, to say the least."

. . . . . .

"When Grant became Lieutenant-General, Sheridan was given the command of the cavalry of the army of the Potomac, and all his subsequent movements evinced wonderful daring, skill and energy. No trust committed to his charge was ever misplaced, no matter what its magnitude or importance.

"When the Confederate Generals Ewell and Early were sent into the Shenandoah Valley, and went so far north as to threaten Washington, Grant consolidated the four military divisions of the Susquehanna, Washington, Monongahela and West Virginia, into the 'army of the Shenandoah,' and placed Sheridan in command. He defeated Early at Opequan, September nineteenth—for which he was made brigadier-general of the United States army; defeated him again at Fisher's Hill on the twenty-second, and on October the nineteenth occurred the battle of Cedar Creek.

"The position of Sheridan's army at this time was along the crest of three hills, 'each one a little back of the other.' The army of West Virginia, under Crook, held the first hill; the second was occupied by the Nineteenth Corps, under Emory, and the Sixth Corps, with Torbet's cavalry covering its right flank, held the third elevation. Early, marching his army in five columns, crossed the mountains and forded the north branch of the Shenandoah River, at midnight, on the eighteenth. He knew that Sheridan had gone up to Washington, and wanted to take advantage of his absence to surprise the unsuspecting camp. The march was conducted so noiselessly that, though he skirted the borders of our position for miles, nothing came to the ears of our pickets, save in a few instances where a heavy muffled tramp was heard, but disregarded as of no consequence.

"The gray gloom of early morning hovered over the camp, when a reconnoitring force from Crook's army was preparing to go out. Suddenly, a wild yell burst through the fog which hid from view the Confederate army. A withering musketry fire and the clash of arms quickly followed. Before our surprised and panic-stricken troops could be formed in battle-array, the enemy were upon them, and after a short and sharp encounter, the army of Western Virginia was thrown into utter rout—a mass of fugitives flying before the pursuing foe back towards the second hill where the Nineteenth Corps was encamped.

. . . . . .

"The Nineteenth Corps attempted to arrest the Confederate advance, but the enemy getting in our rear and enfilading us with our captured batteries, the troops broke ranks and fell back in confusion towards the encampment of the Sixth Corps, on the third hill in the rear.

. . . . . .

"Sheridan, meantime, was at Winchester, where he had arrived the night before, intending to go on to Cedar Creek the next morning. As he sipped his coffee at breakfast he did not for an instant dream of the terrible rout and disaster hovering at that moment over his army. When he rode out of Winchester the vibrations of the ground under the heavy discharges of artillery in the distance gave the first intimations of danger. But he was not yet alarmed, knowing the security of his position. As he went onward, however, the thunder of the cannon deepened, and then the terrible truth flashed upon him. He dashed spurs into his horse and was soon tearing madly along the road, far ahead of his escort.

"For five anxious hours the desperate struggle had gone on, when Sheridan arrived on the field, encountering first the stream of fugitives surging northward. They turned about as they saw their invincible leader flying towards the front, and even the wounded along the roadside cheered him as he passed. Swinging his cap over his head, he shouted: 'Face the other way, boys!—face the other way! We are going back to our camps! We are going to lick them out of their boots!'

"It was about ten o'clock when, with his horse covered with foam, he galloped up to the front. Immediately, under his quick commands, the broken ranks were reformed, and when the Confederates made their next grand charge across the fields the terrific repulse that met and hurled them back showed the turn of the tide, and compelled them to relinquish the offensive. For two hours Sheridan rode back and forth along the line, seeming to be everywhere at once, infusing into the men his own daring courage and enthusiasm. Shouts and cheers followed him; and though the tired soldiers had been fighting for five long hours and had eaten nothing since the night before, his presence was both food and inspiration, and everything seemed to be forgotten in an all-controlling impulse to follow their glorious leader to victory.

"Early retired his troops a short distance after their repulse, and began throwing up breastworks. But the intrepid Sheridan had no notion of allowing him to retain that position. He meant to regain Cedar Creek and rout the enemy. At half-past three a bold charge was made. An awful musketry and artillery fire was poured into the advancing Union columns, and, at first, the lines broke and fell back; but Sheridan rose at once to the needs of the crisis, and with superhuman efforts restored order and resumed the advance. Then came 'the long-drawn yell of our charge,' and 'everything on the first line, the stone walls, the tangled wood, the advanced crest, and half-finished breastworks, had been carried.'

"The panic-stricken enemy was sent flying in utter rout through Middletown, through Strasburg, through Fisher's Hill, and to Woodstock, sixteen miles beyond. Early was thus effectually driven out of the Shenandoah Valley, and permanently crippled.

"This wonderful victory, due to Sheridan's personal presence alone, put a crown on his head which few warriors could pluck from the heights of Fame."

. . . . . .

"On March the fourth, 1869, he received the promotion of lieutenant-general, and was appointed to the command of the Division of the Missouri, of the Platte, and of Texas, with head-quarters at Chicago."

. . . . . .

The name of Kilpatrick kindles enthusiasm in the breast of every cavalryman of the late war, and our author, having served under him, has sketched his life, con amore, in vivid and thrilling language, and with a keen appreciation of his great merits as a cavalry leader. The following extract will confirm our view:

"Like the French Murat, Kilpatrick seems to have been born to become a very demi-god of cavalry. Daringly heroic on the field, he displayed a supreme genius for war, especially for that department of the service whose alarum cry is, 'To horse!' and whose sweeping squadrons, with wild clatter of hoofs, seem to the fervid imagination to be making a race for glory, even though it be through the gates of death.

"It is quite in keeping with everything about Kilpatrick that he should choose the cavalry as a vehicle for his high ambition and noble patriotism. Such energies as his could scarcely be content with less dash or less brilliance of action. The beginning of his war career was one of romance, and his previous life indicated an unusual range of abilities. He first figures as the boy-orator, speaking in favor of a Congressional candidate, with all the fresh warmth and enthusiasm of his young nature. Then we see him as cadet at West Point, from which he graduates fifteenth in his class and is given the honor of valedictorian. The day of graduation is hastened a few months by the startling guns of Sumter, which proclaim treason rampant, and fire all loyal breasts with a desire to rush to the rescue of their country's beloved flag. The impatience and enthusiasm of Kilpatrick could not be restrained, and through his influence a petition was signed by thirty-seven of his class to be allowed to graduate at once and go to the front. The request was granted, and that day was one of especial significance at West Point. It was also one of equal significance in his life; for the little chapel, where had rung out the words of his farewell address, also witnessed the sacred ceremony of his marriage with the lady of his love, and on that evening the young soldier and his bride took the train for Washington and the front. We know little of the bride except that she was enshrined in her husband's heart, and that her name—'Alice'—was inscribed on the silken banner under which he fought, and so gloriously led his troopers to victory and renown. No one can tell how much that name may have had to do with his future marvelous success. To natures like his, the magic of a name thus loved, fluttering aloft in the smoke of battle, becomes talismanic, and inspires almost superhuman heroism."

. . . .

"When McDowell marched to Falmouth, he was once more at the front, and, in conjunction with Colonel Bayard and the First Pennsylvania Cavalry, made a brilliant night-attack on Falmouth Heights, routing Lee's cavalry and capturing the place. For this dashing achievement Kilpatrick received the thanks of the commanding general. Afterwards, under Pope's command, he made his first famous raid in breaking up 'Stonewall' Jackson's line of communication with Richmond from Gordonsville in the Shenandoah Valley, over the Virginia Central Railway. At Beaver Dam, Frederick's Hall, and Hanover Junction, he burned the stations, destroyed the tracks, and daringly attacked the enemy wherever he could find him. These events took place during July and August, 1862, and the boldness of the operations, in the very heart of the enemy's country, filled the North with Kilpatrick's fame. . . . . .

"When Hooker was placed at the head of the Army of the Potomac, the cavalry was reorganized under Stoneman as chief, and that general, in the following campaign, assigned to Kilpatrick the work of destroying the railroad and bridges over the Chickahominy. Four hundred and fifty men were given him for the work; but with this small force he brought to the difficult mission his usual skill, and, avoiding large forces of the enemy, raided to within two miles of Richmond, where he captured 'Lieutenant Brown, aide-de-camp to General Winder, and eleven men within the fortifications.' He says: 'I then passed down to the left to the Meadow Bridge on the Chickahominy, which I burned, ran a train of cars into the river, retired to Hanover-town on the Peninsula, crossed just in time to check the advance of a pursuing cavalry force, burned a train of thirty wagons loaded with bacon, captured thirteen prisoners, and encamped for the night five miles from the river.' This was the manner of his conquering quest, until on the seventh he again struck the Union lines at Gloucester Point, having made a march of about 'two hundred miles in less than five days, and captured and paroled over eight hundred prisoners.' In the accomplishment of this splendid feat he lost only one officer and thirty-seven men.

"At Chancellorsville, when Lee came into Maryland and massed his cavalry at Beverly Ford, Pleasonton was sent forward on a reconnoissance, and met the enemy in battle at Brandy Station. This is renowned as the greatest cavalry battle of the war. General Gregg arrived upon the field at half-past ten in the morning, and though his noble squadrons fought well and bravely, these columns were rolled back, and for a moment, all seemed lost, and overwhelmed by the superior numbers of the foe. But at this crisis, Kilpatrick, posted on a slight rise of ground, unrolled his battle-flag to the breeze, and his bugles sounded the charge. He had under his command, the Harris Light, Tenth New York, and First Maine. The formation for an onset was quickly made, and the disciplined squadrons of these three regiments were hurled upon the enemy. But the Tenth New York recoiled before the murderous fire of the enemy's carbines. So did the Harris Light. Kilpatrick was maddened at the sight. He rushed to the head of the First Maine regiment, shouting, 'Men of Maine, you must save the day!' Under the impulse of this enthusiasm, they became altogether resistless, and in conjunction with the reformed squadrons of the two other regiments, swept the enemy before them, and plucked victory, with glorious valor, from the very jaws of defeat. On the next day Kilpatrick was made brigadier-general."

. . . .

Having presented extracts from "Heroes of Three Wars," and ventured to express, incidentally and briefly our own humble opinion of the merits of this work, we will now, in confirmation of our judgment, give some reviews of the Press—a few out of many. Throughout the North the work was hailed with not a little enthusiasm, by soldiers and civilians alike—as a work of decided literary merit, and one written in a fair, truthful, and loyal spirit, replete with much valuable historical information of a character not otherwise easily attainable, and calculated to accomplish much good among the rising generation.

The Boston *Transcript* says:

"The bivouac, the march, the hand-to-hand conflict with bristling steel, the head-long charge, the ignominious retreat, and the battle-field after the bloody assault, with its dead and wounded heroes, are all excellently portrayed, and with an ease and vigor of style that lend a peculiar charm to the book, and rivet the attention of the reader from cover to cover. It is really refreshing to meet with such a work as this in these degenerate days of namby-pamby novels, so enervating to mind and morals. Captain Glazier's work elevates the ideas, and infuses a spirit of commendable patriotism into the young mind, by showing the youth of the country how nobly men could die for the principles they cherished and the land they loved."

The Chicago *Inter-Ocean* writes as follows:

"It is correct in facts, graphic in its delineations, and in all its makeup is a most admirable volume. It will do the young men, and even those older, good to glance at these pages and read anew the perils and hardships and sacrifices which have been made by the loyal men who met and overthrew in battle the nation's enemies.

The book is of absorbing interest as a record of brave deeds by as brave and heroic men as ever answered a bugle's call. The author writes no fancy sketch. He has the smoke and scars of battle in every sentence. He answered roll-call and mingled amid the exciting events he relates. No writer, even the most praised correspondents of the foreign journals, have given more vivid descriptions soul-stirring in their simple truthfulness, than Captain Glazier in his 'Heroes of Three Wars.'"

The Baltimore *Sun* writes:

"'Heroes of Three Wars' is written by the masterly hand of one who has evidently enjoyed a personal acquaintance with many of the subjects introduced, and is not only thoroughly imbued with the spirit of his work, but as thoroughly inspires his readers. Captain Glazier has familiarized himself with all of the details of interest in the lives of a grand galaxy of heroes, and has put on paper, in a condensed and graphic form, a clear picture of what he has treasured up in his own mind. We know of no book that contains so faithful a presentation of our brave defenders in so condensed and satisfactory a form."

The Philadelphia *Times* observes:

"The soldier-author does his work in an artless, patriotic, beautiful style, and gives to his readers a real and not an imaginary idea of army life in all its lights and shades. Captain Glazier has laid his countrymen under lasting obligations to him, especially in this new book, Heroes of Three Wars.'"

The Cincinnati *Enquirer* remarks:

"Captain Glazier rises above the conventional war-writers' idioms, and gives his work a place in literature and history. Here is found the stern actuality of war's fearful tug; here the beautiful pathos of pure manly sentiment flowing from the heart of many a brave soul on the battle's eve; here the scenes of sad and solemn burial where warriors weep. The din of battle on one page, and the jest at the peril past on the next—the life-test and the comedy of camp—these alternatingly checker the work over, and give the reader a truer insight into the perils and privations of our brave defenders than any book we have read."

From the Worcester *Spy* we quote:

"'Heroes of Three Wars' is a graphically written volume by no new candidate for public favor, but one who has already won the appreciative admiration of thousands of readers. An air of truth, which is of romantic interest, pervades the work, in the depiction of the terribly interesting events in the lives of his famous subjects. Captain Glazier was an active participant in the war for the Union, and followed the lead of Bayard, Stoneman, Pleasanton, Gregg, Custer and Kilpatrick. He portrays the daring deeds and glorious achievements of his heroes with an enthusiasm which fairly enchains the reader, and makes him feel for the time that he is either fighting his battles over again, or standing an awe-bound spectator of the clash of arms and fall of noble steeds and their brave riders."

The Pittsburg *Gazette* says:

"The nature of this book is very forcibly expressed in the title page. The writer wields a graphic pen. In the statement of facts he is painstaking and conscientious. Commencing with Washington, forty subjects are presented. The writer has the vivacity which is so essential in the composition of a work of this character. One is often thrilled as the panorama of war passes before his mind."

CHAPTER XXXI.

OCEAN TO OCEAN ON HORSEBACK.

From Boston to San Francisco.—An unparalleled ride.—Object of the journey.—Novel lecture tour.—Captain Frank M. Clark.—"Echoes from the Revolution."—Lecture at Tremont Temple.—Captain Theodore L. Kelly.—A success.—Proceeds of lecture.—Edward F. Rollins.—Extracts from first lecture.—Press notices.

THE story of the career of Willard Glazier will not be complete without some description of his novel and adventurous feat of riding on horseback across the continent of North America—literally from ocean to ocean, or from Boston to San Francisco. This unparalleled ride was satisfactorily accomplished by him in 1876—the Centennial year. It was a long and trying journey, extending over a period of two hundred days, and a distance of four thousand one hundred and thirty-three miles, but at the same time a journey of great interest. His object was to study, at comparative leisure, the line of country through which he would pass, and to note the habits and condition of the people he came in contact with. The knowledge thus laboriously acquired he purposed placing before the public in book form.

While thus in the commendable pursuit of knowledge, he also contemplated making some practical return for the many kindnesses and courtesies he had received at the hands of soldiers since the disbandment of the volunteer army, and the wide circulation

CAPTAIN GLAZIER AT TREMONT TEMPLE, BOSTON.

of the first product of his pen, "The Capture, Prison-Pen and Escape;" and it had occurred to him that to accomplish this he might turn his journey to beneficial account by lecturing at the various towns he visited, and handing over the proceeds to the widows' and orphans' fund of the "Grand Army of the Republic," of which patriotic society he was a member; or to some other benevolent military organization.

The thought no sooner entered his mind than, with his usual promptitude, the resolution was formed, and, with the following letter of introduction from Captain Frank M. Clark, of New York, he at once proceeded to Boston:

4 IRVING PLACE,
NEW YORK, *April* 20, 1876.

To COMRADES OF THE G. A. R.:

I have been intimately acquainted with Captain Willard Glazier, a comrade in good standing of Post No. 29, Department of New York, "Grand Army of the Republic," for the past eight years, and know him to be worthy the confidence of every loyal man. He is an intelligent and courteous gentleman, an author of good repute, a soldier whose record is without a stain, and a true comrade of the "Grand Army." I bespeak for him the earnest and cordial support of all comrades of the Order.

Yours very truly in F., C. and L.,
FRANK M. CLARK,
Late A. A. G. Department of New York, G. A. R.

On the evening of the eighth of May, 1876, our hero delivered a lecture at Tremont Temple, Boston, *apropos* of the Centennial year, entitled "Echoes from the Revolution." This was the first occasion of any importance on which he had ever appeared on the rostrum. It may here be mentioned that his friends strongly recommended him to deliver the first lecture before a smaller and less critical audience than he would be likely to confront in Boston, and thus prepare himself for a later appearance in the literary capital; but our soldier reasoned that as lecturing was a new experience to him, his military education dictated that, if he could carry the strongest works the weaker along the line would fall, as a matter of course; and so resolved to deliver his first lecture in Tremont Temple. The lecture, as we have said, had been prepared with a view to its delivery at various towns and cities on the route he contemplated traveling. He was introduced to his Boston audience by Captain Theodore L. Kelly, Commander of Post 15, Grand Army of the Republic, and was honored by the presence on the platform of representatives from nearly all the Posts of Boston. Captain Kelly introduced his comrade in the following complimentary manner:

"LADIES AND GENTLEMEN: It gives me pleasure to have the honor of introducing to you one who, by his services in the field and by the works of his pen, is entitled to your consideration, and the confidence of the comrades of the 'Grand Army of the Republic.' I desire to say that he comes well accredited, furnished with the proper vouchers and documents, and highly endorsed and recommended by the officers of the Department of the State of New York. Though young in years, his life has been one of varied and exciting experience. Born in the wilds of St. Lawrence county, New York, his education was drawn from the great book of nature; and from his surroundings he early imbibed a love of liberty. His early associations naturally invested him with a love of adventure and excitement, and when the call of war was heard he at once responded, and enlisted in the Harris Light Cavalry, with which corps he passed through many exciting scenes of march and fray. His experience amid the various vicissitudes of the war, in camp and field and prison, have been vividly portrayed by his pen in his various publications. Still inspired by this love of adventure, he proposes to undertake the novelty of a journey across the continent in the saddle. His objects are manifold. While visiting scenes and becoming more familiar with his own country, he will collect facts and information for a new book, and at his various stopping-places he will lecture under the auspices and for the benefit of the 'Grand Army of the Republic,' to whose fraternal regard he is most warmly commended. Allow me then, ladies and gentlemen, without further ceremony, to present to you the soldier-author, and our comrade, Willard Glazier."

The lecture proved a success both financially and in the marked pleasure with which it was received by a very select audience. In fulfilment of his generous purpose in the application of the proceeds, Glazier on the succeeding morning addressed a letter to the Assistant Adjutant-General, Department of Massachusetts, Grand Army of the Republic, in the following words:

REVERE HOUSE, BOSTON, MASS.,
May 9th, 1876.

CAPTAIN CHARLES W. THOMPSON,
    A. A. G. Department of Massachusetts, G. A. R.

COMRADE: I take pleasure in handing you the net proceeds of my lecture delivered at Tremont Temple last night, which I desire to be divided equally between Posts 7 and 15, G. A. R., of Boston, for the benefit of our disabled comrades, and the needy and destitute wards of the "Grand Army." Gratefully acknowledging many favors and courtesies extended to me in your patriotic city,

        I am yours in F., C. and L.,
            WILLARD GLAZIER.

To this the following response was received:

> HEADQUARTERS, ENCAMPMENT JOHN A. ANDREW,
> POST 15, DEPT. OF MASS., G. A. R.,
> BOSTON, *May 12th*, 1876.
>
> CAPTAIN WILLARD GLAZIER:
>
> COMRADE: In obedience to a vote of this Post, I am pleased to transmit to you a vote of thanks for the money generously donated by you, through our Commander, as our quota of the proceeds of your lecture in this city; and also the best wishes of the comrades of this Post for you personally, and for the success of your lecture tour from sea to sea. Yours in F., C. and L.,
>
> EDWARD F. ROLLINS,
> Adjutant of Post.

We have said the lecture was a success, and as an evidence of the appreciation by the audience of its subject, and the manner of its delivery, together with the friendly feeling manifested towards the lecturer, we adduce the following:

> DEPARTMENT OF MASS.,
> "Grand Army of the Republic."
> BOSTON, *June 16th*, 1876.
>
> *To Captain Willard Glazier:*
>
> DEAR SIR AND COMRADE:
>
> The undersigned comrades of "John A. Andrew" Encampment, Post 15, Department of Massachusetts, G. A. R., desire to testify to the pleasure afforded them by your lecture delivered at Tremont Temple on May 8th; also, to return their thanks for the liberal donation presented to this Post; and at the same time to express the hope that you may be successful in your object and journey.
>
> [Signed.]
>
> THEODORE L. KELLY, *Commander.* THOMAS LANGHAM.
> EDWARD F. ROLLINS, *Adjutant.* J. HENRY BROWN.
> W. BROOKS FROTHINGHAM. GEORGE W. POWERS, *Chaplain.*
> JAMES T. PRICE. ROBERT W. STORER, *Q. M. S.*
> FRANK BOWMAN. OLIVER DOWNING.
> THEODORE L. BAKER. JAMES MCLEAN.
> WILLIAM S. WALLINGFORD.

Before proceeding with our account of the journey, let us dwell for a moment upon the features of the lecture prepared by Willard Glazier for delivery at Boston. As might have been expected, it was a military-historical lecture, adapted to the understanding and taste of a mixed and educated audience, and was written in the same earnest, original, patriotic and rousing style that characterizes his writings throughout. Some parts of this lecture, in our opinion, are worthy of comparison with the oratorical deliverances of eminent and practised lecturers, and that the reader may judge for himself if the "Echoes of the Revolution" lose aught of their sonorousness at this distant date, when the reverberation reaches them through a lecture, we here present an abstract of the opening:

INTRODUCTORY.

"The year 1876 re-echoes the scenes and events of a hundred years ago. In imagination we make a pilgrimage back to the Revolution. We visit the fields whereon our ancestors fought for liberty and a Republic. We follow patriots from Lexington to Yorktown. I see them walking through a baptism of blood and of fire; their only purpose liberty; their only incentive duty; their only pride their country; and their only ambition victory. I see them with Warren and Prescott at Bunker Hill; I see them with Washington at Valley Forge, hatless, without shoes, half-clad, and often without food; encamped in fields of snow; patiently enduring the rigors of a northern winter. I see them pushing their way through the ice of the Delaware. I see them at Saratoga, at Bennington, at Princeton, and at Monmouth. I follow Marion and his daring troopers through the swamps of Georgia and the Carolinas. And, finally, we come to that immortal day at Yorktown, when Cornwallis surrendered his sword and command to George Washington.

"All the world is familiar with the causes which led to the struggle for independence in America. We all know the spirit which animated the people of the Colonies, from the seizure of Sir Edmond Andross in 1688 to the destruction of the tea in Boston harbor in 1774. No American is ignorant of the efforts of John Hancock, Samuel Adams, Joseph Warren, Patrick Henry, Alexander Hamilton, Paul Revere, and others, at clubs, in newspapers, in pulpits, in the streets, and in coffee-houses, to guide and prepare the people for the approaching crisis. All the facts from the beginning to the close of that memorable conflict are given in school-books, as well as in more pretentious history. But the immediate cause of the march of the English troops from Boston to Concord seems to be necessary to a comprehensive view of the subject.

. . . . . .

"On the nineteenth of April, 1775, a handful of the yeomanry of Massachusetts, obeying a common impulse, came hurriedly together, confronted a force of English regulars outnumbering them ten to one, received their fire, were repulsed, and left eighteen of their number dead and wounded on the green in front of Lexington. On the same day, at Concord, less than four hundred undisciplined militia met a regiment of the enemy, fired upon them, put them to flight, and compelled them to retire to their intrenchments at Boston. It was the first step in that war which gave us a Republic, and may be classed in history as one of the decisive conflicts of modern times.

"Lexington and Concord were not the great battles

of the Revolution; they were, in fact, only skirmishes as compared with the more sanguinary actions; but I dwell upon them as the opening scenes, the starting-points, where the first shots were fired in an eight years' war against British rule and British oppression in America. . . . . .

JOHN STARK.

"Despair was turned into joy by the telling victories of the Americans at Trenton and Princeton, and the country began to see that her precious blood had not been spilled in vain. Just at this juncture of affairs, when it was necessary to follow up the tide of victory with vigorous work, the term of enlistment of most of the men expired, and the personal popularity and influence of the leaders was thus put to the test. Would the men go, or could they be induced to stay through another term of enlistment before seeking the respite they desired at their homes? At this critical period, John Stark made an earnest appeal to his regiment, and every man without exception re-enlisted for six weeks under the banner of their beloved leader. Then Stark went to New Hampshire for recruits, and hundreds flocked around his standard.

. . . . . .

"Soon after the surrender of Cornwallis, General Stark returned once more to his home and farm. He had served his country long and faithfully, and retired from his protracted period of active service beloved by the people and full of honors. He lived to be ninety-four years old, and consequently witnessed the war of 1812.

"He sleeps on the banks of the Merrimac, nor heeds the noisy rush of the river as it speeds on its mission to the sea. No clash of musketry, no roar of cannon will ever waken him more from his last deep repose. Men call it death, but if it be death, it is that of the body only, for his *memory* still lives and speaks to us across the years. It bids us be noble and unselfish, and high of purpose, and grand of aim. Will the oncoming generations who con the story of the life of John Stark listen to the preaching of such an example in vain? . . . . .

PERORATION.

"The surrender of Cornwallis may be considered the closing scene in the war of the Revolution. The grim spectre of British rule over the American Colonies vanished like the smoke of battle, while hirelings were trembling and the patriot was prince. That was indeed a day of triumph—a day of rejoicing. It was to the patriots the crown of all their efforts. A long, loud, thrilling shout of joy arose from the victorious band of Washington, and as the tidings of actual surrender were borne throughout the country, the people everywhere broke forth in wild huzzahs that echoed and re-echoed along the plains and among the hills, from the lakes to the gulf, and from the Atlantic to the mountains. There was joy because there was to be no more needless sacrifice of life; because the soldier could now exchange the camp for his home; the implements of war for the implements of industry; the carnage of battle for the amenities of peace.

"The work for which they buckled on the armor was accomplished. They did not rush to arms for the love of glory, nor to ward off an imaginary foe. They came at their country's call, and having achieved her independence, they were now ready for the pursuits of peace. They even longed for the coveted seclusion of their homes, and the sweet security of their firesides. I see them now marshaled for the last time to receive an honorable discharge from a long campaign, the ensigns of victory everywhere above them, the air vocal with the benedictions of a grateful people. But on that great day of final discharge, at the last roll-call, the heroes were not all there to answer to their names; there were vacant places in the ranks. In the marching and counter-marching, in the assault and in the defence; in the swamp and in the prison, mid the fever and the pestilence, the patriots faltered not, but fell as falls the hero, nobly daring, bravely dying; and though dead they are not forgotten: their works do follow, and will forever live, after them. . . . .

"Justice to our heroic ancestors does not forbid reference to the equally gallant 'Boys in Blue,' who by their invincible valor on the battle-fields of the Rebellion preserved the unity of the Republic.

"'The fight is done, and away in the far horizon the glorious days are waxing dim. Even now, it is the bearded men who speak of Gettysburg; and children clasp the knees that marched to Corinth and Chickamauga. Year after year our soldiers meet to talk of glory; and year by year their ranks grow thinner, older, grayer; and, by and by, the last survivors of the war for the Union will sleep with their brothers who fell at Bunker Hill."

The press of Boston were highly commendatory in their notices of the lecture and its delivery, as will be seen by the following extract from the *Globe:*

"A very fair audience, considering the unfair condition of the elements, was gathered in Tremont Temple last night, to hear Captain

Glazier's lecture upon 'Echoes from the Revolution.' The frequent applause of the audience evinced not only a sympathy with the subject, but an evident liking of the manner in which it was delivered. The lecture itself was a retrospective view of the leading incidents of the Revolution. It would have been unfair to expect to hear anything very new upon a subject with which the veriest school-boy is familiar; but Captain Glazier wove the events together in a manner which freed the lecture from that most unpardonable of all faults, which can be committed upon the platform—dulness. He passed over, in his consideration of the Revolution, the old scenes up to the time when Cornwallis surrendered up his sword and command to George Washington. 'The year 1876,' said Captain Glazier, 're-echoes the scenes and events of a hundred years ago. In imagination we make a pilgrimage back to the Revolution. We visit the fields whereon our ancestors fought for liberty and a republic. We follow patriots from Lexington to Yorktown. I see them pushing their way through the ice of the Delaware—I see them at Saratoga, at Bennington, at Princeton, and at Monmouth. I follow Marion and his daring troopers through the swamps of Georgia and the Carolinas;' and in following them up, the lecturer interspersed his exciting narrative with sundry droll episodes. Treating of the battles of Trenton and Princeton, he expatiated upon the devoted heroism of John Stark, and briefly traced his career until, at Bennington, Burgoyne's victor announced to his comrades, 'We must conquer to-day, my boys, or to-night Molly Stark's a widow.' One battle after another was handled by the lecturer in a pleasing manner, showing that he was thoroughly familiar with the subject he had chosen for his theme. After speaking in a most zealous manner of the troops on land, Captain Glazier remarked: 'Our victories on the ocean during the war of the Revolution were not less decisive and glorious than those achieved on land. John Paul Jones and the gallant tars who, under his leadership, braved the dangers of the deep, and wrested from proud Britain, once queen of the sea, that illustrious motto which may be seen high on our banner beside the stars and stripes.'

"Captain Glazier made special mention of the naval engagement between the Bon Homme Richard and the British man-of-war Serapis, which took place in September, 1789. He described in glowing words the fierce nature of that memorable contest, until the captain of the Serapis, with his own hand, struck the flag of England to the free stars and stripes of young America. Captain Glazier has elements in him which, carefully matured and nurtured, will make him successful on the platform, as he has already proved himself in the fields of literature. He has a strong and melodious voice, a gentlemanly address, and unassuming confidence. He was presented to the audience by Commandant Kelly, of Post 15, 'Grand Army of the Republic,' in a brief but eloquent speech. Captain Glazier will start on his long ride to San Francisco, from the Revere House, this morning, at 9.30, and will be accompanied to Bunker Hill and thence to Brighton, by several distinguished members of the 'Grand Army,' and other gentlemen, who wish the captain success on his long journey."

The Boston *Post* said:

"The lecturer spoke with a soldier's enthusiasm of those stirring times. In a very eloquent manner he traced the movements of the Revolutionary heroes from that day in April, 1775, when the undisciplined militia at Concord put the red-coats to flight and forced them to retire to their entrenchments at Boston, onward through the various battles to the surrender of Cornwallis. The different acts passed in rapid succession before the audience, and were enlivened with interesting details. In touching upon the different battles, the lecturer descanted upon the more eminent individuals whom the fate of war and opportunity brought to the front, and enshrined forever in the gallery of patriots. Bunker Hill came in for especial notice, where 'many brave and noble men gave up their lives.'. . . .

"Captain Glazier was frequently and loudly applauded during the delivery of his lecture. His voice is rich and powerful, his intonation accurate, and his general manner could not help imparting interest to the stirring deeds which he so graphically delineated."

CHAPTER XXXII.

FROM BOSTON TO CHICAGO.

In the saddle.—Bunker Hill.—Arrives in Albany.—Reminiscences.—The Soldiers' Home.—Contributions for erecting Soldiers' Home.—Reception at Rochester.—Buffalo.—Dunkirk.—Swanville.—Cleveland.—Massacre of General Custer.—Monroe.—Lectures for Custer Monument.—Father of General Custer.—Detroit.—Kalamazoo.—An adventure.—Gives "Paul Revere" a rest.—Decatur.—Niles.—Michigan City.—Chicago.

FROM a journal kept by Captain Glazier during his horseback ride from ocean to ocean, we shall gather most of the incidents of his journey—a journey, so far as we are aware, without any precedent, and having for its sole object the acquirement of knowledge. His intention was to lecture in the leading cities and villages through which he passed, in the interest of the relief fund of the "Grand Army of the Republic," to which order he was greatly attached.

The Boston *Globe* of May ninth, 1876, contained the following brief notice:

"BOSTON TO SAN FRANCISCO.—Captain Willard Glazier started from the Revere House this morning at eleven o'clock, on horseback, for San Francisco. Quite a gathering of his friends and comrades of the 'Grand Army' were present to wish him God-speed. He was escorted by Colonel John F. Finley and E. A. Williston, who were mounted; and Adjutant-General Charles W. Thompson, Department of Massachusetts, 'G. A. R.;' Commander Theo. L. Kelly, of Post 15; Adjutant Grafton Fenno, of Post 7, and many others in carriages, who will accompany him to Bunker Hill and thence to Brighton."

BOSTON TO BRIGHTON—FIRST DAY OF THE JOURNEY.

The Captain's horse, which he had named "Paul Revere," was a noble creature, black as jet, of good pedigree, and possessing, in no slight measure, the sterling qualities of endurance, pace, and fidelity, albeit occasionally somewhat restive and wilful.

On leaving the "Revere," the party referred to in the above notice proceeded to Bunker Hill, gazed reverentially at the monument commemorating the famous battle, and then headed for Brighton. The short journey had been rendered comfortless by a continuous downfall of rain, and when the friends halted at the Cattle-Fair Hotel for dinner, they were all more or less drenched to the skin.

Much cordial interest was manifested in the work the captain had undertaken and the motives that actuated him; and at length, taking leave of his friendly escort, he pushed forward through Worcester, Springfield, Pittsfield, Nassau, and on to Albany, covering a distance of two hundred miles. At Beckett he found "Paul's" back becoming sore, and as a good rider is always humane to his horse, he removed the saddle, washed the abrasion with cold water, and before resuming his journey put a blanket under the saddle-cloth, which kindly care afforded "Paul" considerable relief. At Pittsfield, Glazier delivered his fourth lecture in the Academy of Music, being introduced to his audience by Captain Brewster, Commander of the Pittsfield Post,"Grand Army of the Republic."

His journey from Pittsfield was by the Boston and Albany Turnpike, over the Pittsfield Mountain, passing the residence of Honorable Samuel J. Tilden, then Governor of New York, and a candidate for the Presidency. Starting from Nassau at eleven o'clock, he reached the old Barringer Homestead soon after. It was with this family that he had spent his first night in Rensselaer County, sixteen years before, when looking for a school to teach, and he could not resist the temptation to stop a few minutes at Brockway's, where he had boarded the first week after entering the school at Schodack Centre as a teacher. At the hotel he found Mrs. Lewis, the landlady, awaiting his approach, as she had been told he would pass that way. He also halted for a moment at his old school-house, where he found Miss Libby Brockway, one of the youngest of his old scholars, teaching the school. "Thoughts of Rip Van Winkle," he says, "flitted across my imagination as I contrasted the past with the present."

On the eighteenth of May Captain Glazier reached the fine old city of Albany, capital of his native State, and in the evening of the same day delivered his fifth lecture at Tweddle Hall.

Thrilling memories awaited him in Albany. Here, in 1859, he entered the State Normal School. It was here his patriotism was aroused by intelligence of the firing upon Fort Sumter, and he at once formed the resolution to enter the army in defence of the Union; and it was in Albany that the first edition of his first book saw the light through the press of Joel Munsell, in the autumn of 1865. Here, it may be said, his career in life commenced, when, leaving his country home in Northern New York, he entered the Normal School.

The erection of a Soldiers' Home having been recently projected, Glazier called on the adjutant-general at the State House, in relation to his lecturing in the interest of the fund for that purpose. Colonel Taylor, assistant adjutant-general, whom he had known for some years, presented him to General Townsend, and he was recommended to see and consult with Captain John Palmer, Past Grand Commander of the State, G. A. R.

Nothing can better prove the disinterested motives and objects of Willard Glazier in undertaking his long and tedious journey on horseback, than the numerous voluntary offerings he made to certain military organizations whose claims so forcibly presented themselves to him. This was simply characteristic of him. He has never valued money but for the practical uses to which it may be applied in the amelioration of the condition of others. Simple in his habits, and unostentatious in his mode of life—indulging in no luxuries—he has managed by sheer hard work to accumulate a fair fortune, which is of value to him only so far as he can do good with it—first to those having the strongest domestic claims upon him, and secondly, to his comrades of the camp and the battle-field.

The following letters will explain themselves:

ALBANY, NEW YORK,
May 28th, 1876.

CAPTAIN JOHN PALMER, Past Grand Commander,
Department of New York, G. A. R.

DEAR SIR AND COMRADE: I feel great pleasure in handing you herewith, forty dollars, which I wish to be applied to the fund for the erection of a Soldiers' Home, as lately proposed by our comrades at Brooklyn. Should it be your pleasure to endorse my lecture tour across the State, I feel confident that I could raise from five hundred to a thousand dollars for this most worthy object. Pledging my best efforts in the work, which I hope I need scarcely add, enlists my warmest sympathies, I have the honor to remain,

Yours in F., C. and L.,
WILLARD GLAZIER.

Captain Palmer, in acknowledging the donation, wrote as follows:

> HEADQUARTERS DEPARTMENT OF NEW YORK,
> "Grand Army of the Republic,"
> ALBANY, *May* 31*st*, 1876.
>
> CAPTAIN WILLARD GLAZIER:
>
> COMRADE: Your gift of forty dollars to the fund for the erection of the "Soldiers' Home" is duly received, and the same has been forwarded to Captain E. O. Parkinson, Chairman Soldiers' Home Committee, Brooklyn, New York, for which accept my thanks.
>
> Very truly yours, in F., C. and L.,
>
> JOHN PALMER,
> Department Commander.

On the twenty-second of May, "'Paul' being in good condition and the best of spirits," our soldier-author started for Schenectady, paying his respects to Captain Palmer on his way up Washington Avenue. Schenectady was reached at four o'clock P. M. through frequent showers of rain. Putting up at Gwinn's Hotel, he delivered his lecture at Union Hall at the usual hour in the evening, to a fair audience, notwithstanding the rain.

The Schenectady *Union* had heralded his approach by the following notice:

> "CAPTAIN GLAZIER.—This noted soldier, author, rider, and raider, who raided during the war with General Kilpatrick, will advance upon this place next Monday, and in the evening lecture upon 'Echoes from the Revolution.' Captain Glazier is a member of the 'Grand Army' in good standing, and will be assisted here by the members of Post 14, with whom he will divide the profits of the lecture. The Captain was an inmate of Libby Prison at one time during the war, and finally made his escape to the Union lines. The book entitled 'Capture, Prison-Pen and Escape,' and several other war books, were produced by him."

Reaching Fonda, May twenty-sixth, we find the following entry in the Journal: "Scenery charming. I saw nothing in Massachusetts equal to the Valley of the Mohawk, and am surprised that novelist and poet have not found more material here for legendary romance."

Passing through St. Johnsville, Little Falls, Utica, and Rome—where he met a large number of his "Grand Army" comrades, and was introduced to Hon. H. J. Coggleshall, Colonel G. A. Cantine, Hon. W. T. Bliss, and many others—he arrived in Syracuse June second, registered at the Vanderbilt House, and lectured at Shakespere Hall in the evening. Rochester was reached on the eighth, where the tenth lecture was delivered to an appreciative audience in Corinthian Hall—the introduction being made by Colonel Reynolds. The Rochester *Democrat* noticed the lecture in the following paragraph:

"A very large audience assembled at Corinthian Hall last evening to listen to Captain Willard Glazier's lecture on 'Echoes from the Revolution.' The lecture was a very interesting one, and the audience were agreeably entertained. Captain Glazier proposes to go to Batavia, and from thence to Buffalo. He is meeting with deserved success in his journey on horseback from ocean to ocean, which increases as he becomes better known."

It may here be remarked that during Captain Glazier's stay in Rochester, an exception was made to the usually courteous reception given him by the local press. One of the papers threw doubts on the genuineness of his credentials and the rectitude of his motives. This, however, had little effect on him. He was conscious of his own integrity of purpose, and of being guided by a desire to do good while seeking knowledge and recreation in his own way, and the only notice we find of the circumstance in his Journal is in a few words under date of June eleventh: "Was pleased with an article in the *Express*, contradicting falsehoods in the *Union*."

The following is the article referred to:

"On Friday our evening cotemporary took occasion to treat Captain Willard Glazier, who lectured in Corinthian Hall the night previous, with a degree of contempt and misrepresentation suggestive of Confederate sympathies on the part of the writer. As to the methods of Captain Glazier's business we have nothing to do. As a man and a soldier, he is above reproach. We have examined the original documentary testimonials to his military character, and no man could be better endorsed. That he has devoted himself since the war to illustrate the war of the rebellion in books and upon the rostrum is to his credit, and certainly to the benefit of the people whose patriotism he keeps alive by his appeals with pen and tongue. Doubt was cast upon his services on account of his youth. But the fact stands that Willard Glazier was a captain of cavalry at the age of eighteen, certainly a higher record than that of a stay-at-home Copperhead. He performed his duty, was honorably discharged, and is a member in good standing of that noble organization of veterans, the 'Grand Army of the Republic.' We trust that when Captain Glazier comes again to Rochester, he will have better treatment and a still better audience. His trip across the continent will result in the public's having a record of observations which cannot fail to be valuable and entertaining."

Batavia, Croft's Station, Crittenden and Lancaster were passed through, the usual courtesies tendered and accepted, lectures delivered with unvarying success, and the city of Buffalo reached on the morning of the nineteenth of June.

With a soldier's instinct, Glazier halted here at the parade-ground, and witnessed the drill of the militia. He then located himself at No. 34 Oak Street, where he was visited by many comrades of the "Grand Army" and other prominent citizens of Buffalo. Arrangements having been made, he lectured to a full house at St. James Hall, being introduced to the audience by Major John M. Farquhar. The following endorsement had appeared in the Buffalo *Express* the day preceding his arrival in the city, signed by prominent members of the "Grand Army of the Republic:"

BUFFALO, NEW YORK,
June 18*th*, 1876.

Captain Willard Glazier served his country with great credit in the Harris Light Cavalry. He was a brave soldier and has a splendid army record. His numerous works upon army life, recording his personal experiences on the battle-field, in camp and in prison, are exceedingly interesting and of a highly patriotic character; they are universally commended by the press and by men of army experience.

He is highly endorsed as a member in good standing of the "Grand Army of the Republic," and as a lecturer.

The object of his lectures being to add to the fund for a Soldiers' Home in this State, we most cheerfully commend him to the people of this city, and earnestly hope he will receive a liberal patronage, and have a full house at St. James Hall on Monday evening, the nineteenth of June.

[Signed]

GEORGE N. BROWN,	WILLIAM F. ROGERS,
GEORGE W. FLYNN,	G. L. REMINGTON,
JOHN B. WEBER,	JOHN M. FARQUHAR,
JAMES N. MCARTHUR,	CHARLES B. DUNNING,
G. A. SCROGGS,	ALFRED LYTLE,
P. J. RIPONT,	JOHN A. FRANKE,

RICHARD FLASH.

The lecture was a success, and the usual offering of the proceeds made to the fund of the Soldiers' Home.

"Paul" was ordered at eight o'clock the following morning, and, again in the saddle, Glazier proceeded at a walk to North Evans, distant from Buffalo fifteen miles. His road laid along the banks of Lake Erie, a circumstance which he notes in his diary as one of the events of his journey, the beauty of the scenery, and fresh, cool air from the lake being exceedingly pleasant and grateful on a hot day in June. He rode "Paul" down to the beach and into the water up to his girths.

June twenty-fourth, we find the following entry:

"My journey from North Evans to Angola has been unusually pleasant. I could see the lake, and feel its cool refreshing influence nearly the whole distance."

Angola is situated on the Lake Shore Railroad, about three-quarters of a mile from Lake Erie. Here Mr. J. S. Parker, formerly of Malone, New York, called upon him on business connected with the lecture, and in the course of conversation, Captain Glazier discovered that his visitor knew many of his old neighbors and acquaintances in Northern New York. The events of his early years along the banks of the Oswegatchie were discussed with much interest, and it doubtless formed a pleasing episode of his journey. The lecture was delivered with satisfactory results, at the regular hour, in a building that had once been a church, but was now used as the Town Hall, and the introduction made by Leroy S. Oatman.

Dunkirk was reached June twenty-fifth, by way of the Buffalo Road. The beautiful lake, which had been very near the road from Buffalo to Angola, was now seldom seen, but the haying season had commenced, and the captain's love of nature was now gratified by the lively spectacle of the mowers and hay-makers— men, women and children at work in the fields as he rode past. Putting up at the Eastern Hotel, he was ready to deliver his lecture in the evening, and at Columbus Hall was introduced to a respectable audience by the Rev. J. A. Kummer, pastor of the Methodist church of Dunkirk. The following day being Sunday, he attended divine service at the Rev. Mr. Kummer's church.

Before leaving Dunkirk the following testimonial was handed him:

DUNKIRK, NEW YORK,
June 25th, 1876.

CAPTAIN GLAZIER:

We desire to express to you our warm appreciation of your highly instructive and most entertaining lecture delivered here this evening. We trust success beyond your most sanguine expectations will attend you in your journey; and we cheerfully recommend you and your lecture to any and all whom our endorsement might influence.

[Signed]   J. M. McWHARF, M. D.,
J. A. KUMMER, *Pastor*,
P. B. MORRELL.

Dunkirk, with its pleasant associations, was left June twenty-seventh, and, continuing along the Buffalo Road, our cavalier stopped for dinner at Silver Creek. Here he found the farmers of Chautauqua County largely engaged in the cultivation of fruit and grain. The flourishing vineyards near Fredonia had also arrested his attention, giving promise of the extensive cultivation of the grape which has since marked this locality. At Westfield he lectured in the Metropolitan Hall, being introduced by George Wilson, Esq., and on the following day passed through a fine fruit and grain region, stopping at a village named State Line for dinner. Here he had some trouble in finding the landlord of the caravansary, who, combining the business of "mine host" with that of a farmer, was at the time some distance away, industriously employed at hoeing corn.

At five o'clock P. M., Captain Glazier reached the flourishing little town of North East, where he found a large crowd of people in front of the Haynes House awaiting his arrival. He was taken by surprise when told that he had been announced to deliver a lecture there that evening. The band of the place escorted him to the "Hall," and, taking position in front of the audience, played "Hail Columbia" before, and "The Sword of Bunker Hill" after the lecture. This was a voluntary and quite an unexpected compliment to Captain Glazier, who was sensibly affected by it. The "Hall" was so crowded that many were compelled to stand throughout the lecture, and if applause is any evidence of the satisfaction of the applauders, he might fairly consider his effort to entertain the "North Easters" a decided success. Captain Bronson Orton introduced him to this audience, a gentleman who, although now in the peaceful practice of the law, had been with Sherman's army in its memorable march through Georgia.

Arrived at Erie, Pennsylvania, June twenty-ninth, Captain Glazier was cordially welcomed by Colonel F. H. Ellsworth, proprietor of the Reed House, who showed him many attentions while his guest. The lecture was delivered to a full house at the Academy of Music, the introduction being made by Hon. C. B. Carter.

At Swanville he became the guest of John Jacob Swan, an old and worthy resident, after whom the village had been named. Everything was done for his comfort by the Swan family, of which we find some pleasant reminiscences noted in the Journal. Mr. Swan's son, Andrew, was a lieutenant-colonel of cavalry during the civil war, and the patriarch himself had participated in the war of 1812. "Mr. Swan was one of the first settlers in Erie County," Captain Glazier notes, "and although more than half a century has passed, this old veteran still remembers distinctly, and describes minutely the scenes and events of his former life. He saw the first steamer launched on Lake Erie, and says it was regarded by the Indians as an evil omen: they styled it 'the devil's canoe,' were greatly frightened, and ran from the lake. . . . Took a stroll with Mr. Swan over his farm. He found great pleasure in showing me the wonderful changes which a half century has wrought upon his estate."

Taking leave of this amiable family, he left for Girard, and found Mr. Farrington, his advance agent, awaiting him at the Central House. At the lecture in the evening he was introduced by Jacob Bender, Esq., a brass band adding to the entertainment, and afterwards serenading him at his hotel. The Girard *Cosmopolite* came out on the next morning with the following notice of the lecture:

"Captain Willard Glazier, the soldier-author and lecturer, now on a journey on horseback from Boston to San Francisco, reached this place on Saturday evening, and delivered his lecture, 'Echoes from the Revolution,' to a highly respectable audience, at Philharmonic Hall. He speaks with a soldier's enthusiasm of those stirring times when our forefathers ' walked through a baptism of blood and of fire, their only purpose liberty; their only incentive duty; their only pride their country; and their only ambition victory.' He traces, in a very eloquent manner, the movements of the Revolutionary heroes from that day in April, 1775, when the undisciplined militia at Concord put the red-coats to flight and forced them to retire to their intrenchments at Boston, onward to the surrender of Cornwallis to Washington. . . . We are credibly informed that one of the chief objects of Captain Glazier's journey is to make observations and collect material for another book, which will no doubt be a very interesting one to read, and will add still greater honors to one who, though still a young man, has already acquired an enviable reputation as an author. After a very cordial shake of the hand from some comrades and citizens, the captain left the Central Hotel on his fine black horse, 'Paul Revere,' which has brought him safely thus far from Boston since the ninth of May, and which he proposes to ride to the Golden Gate by the first of December next."

July third found Captain Glazier at Ashtabula, Ohio. The people everywhere, during his ride from Girard, were engaged in preparations for the celebration on the following day of the glorious Centennial Fourth. It was his intention to have lectured at Ashtabula, but he was counselled not to do so, as almost every man and woman in the place was upon some committee preparing for the next day's festivities, and he would consequently get but a scant audience. He therefore concluded not to deliver his lecture here, but to push forward on his journey.

Under date July fourth, he writes:

"Mounted 'Paul' at nine o'clock this morning in front of the Fisk House, Ashtabula. Thousands upon thousands of country people were pouring into the town as I rode out. The booming of cannon, blowing of engine whistles, ringing of bells, and the discharge of fire-arms of every variety and calibre, welcomed the dawn of the One Hundredth anniversary of American Independence."

Willard Glazier suffered no occasion to pass that presented a chance of picking up useful information on topics connected with the localities he rode through —their population, industries, features of the country, prominent men, etc., his capacity for absorbing such knowledge being large, and the intention of utilizing it in the interest of the public having been his chief motive in undertaking the adventurous journey. The large amount of information thus collected has been reduced to system, and will, we trust, be shortly in the hands of the publisher.

Cleveland—the " Forest City "—was his next destination, and on July sixth he registered at the Forest City House, and delivered his lecture in the evening at Garrett's Hall. He was introduced by Major E. M. Hessler, of the "Grand Army of the Republic," who, in the name of many citizens and in testimony of their respect for the soldier, author, and lecturer, proposed a banquet on the following day. This, however, was modestly and respectfully declined. The result of the lecture is shown in the following letter:

NATIONAL SOLDIERS' HOME,
DAYTON, OHIO, *July 27th,* 1876.

CAPTAIN WILLARD GLAZIER:

My dear Comrade: We have received through Major E. M. Hessler your generous donation to aid in erecting the Soldiers' Monument at the "Home." You have the hearty thanks of three thousand disabled veterans now on our rolls; and a cordial invitation to visit us when it is your pleasure to do so. Again we thank you. Please find receipt from our treasurer,

Very respectfully,
WILLIAM EARNSHAW,
President, Historical and Monumental Society.

While in Cleveland the terrible news of the massacre of General Custer by the Indians reached Captain Glazier, who, as a cavalry officer, had seen service with him in the late war, and felt for him that respect and love which only a true soldier knows for a brave leader. The stunning intelligence left a deep impression, and in due time he showed his respect for the dead general by substantial aid rendered in the erection of a monument to his memory.

The following letter was received before leaving the Forest City:

HEADQUARTERS, POST No. 1,
"GRAND ARMY OF THE REPUBLIC," DEPARTMENT OF OHIO,
CLEVELAND, O., *July* 12*th*, 1876.

COMRADE: Through your unsolicited generosity I have the pleasure to acknowledge the receipt of the net proceeds of your lecture on "Echoes from the Revolution," delivered in our city July sixth, 1876, and by your direction have forwarded the amount to Chaplain William Earnshaw, President of the "Soldiers' Home Monumental Fund," at Dayton, to assist in erecting a monument to the memory of the veterans, who by the fortunes of war await the long roll at the National Military Home: and may your reward be no less than the love and gratitude of our unfortunate comrades.

By order of

GENERAL JAMES BARNETT, Commanding.

E. M. HESSLER, Q. M.

Leaving Cleveland and the many friends who had flocked around him in that hospitable city, offering encouragement in his undertaking, Glazier proceeded on his route, accompanied a short distance on horseback by an old scholar named Alexander Wilsey, whose affection for his teacher had not diminished by years of separation. Keeping along the lake-shore all day, and not a little tormented by the shoals of mosquitoes as the evening advanced, he rode into Sandusky City, July thirteenth, and delivered his lecture the same evening to a fair audience. He was introduced in a humorous and effective speech by Captain Culver, Judge of the Probate Court.

Fremont, the pleasant home of President Hayes, was visited, and then on through Elmore to the flourishing city of Toledo, where he registered at the Boody House, July seventeenth. Introduced by Dr. J. T. Woods, G. A. R., he lectured at Lyceum Hall, to an interested audience, who frequently signified their approval by applause.

Passing through Erie, Michigan, Captain Glazier reached Monroe, July twenty-fourth, the committee of the Custer Monument Association receiving him at the City Hall. Arrangements were made for the delivery of a lecture in the interest of the fund for the erection of the monument. This was of course most congenial to Glazier's feelings, Custer being his *beau ideal* of a soldier, and he therefore at once placed himself in the hands of the committee, offering them the entire proceeds of the lecture. The Monroe *Monitor*, of July twenty-sixth, noticed the proposal thus:

"The lecture announced to be given for the benefit of the Custer Monument Fund, on Monday evening at the City Hall, was postponed for various reasons until Thursday evening at the same place. On Monday evening several members of the association met Captain Glazier, and were most favorably impressed with him. They are convinced that he is thoroughly in earnest, and his proposition is a most liberal one. He offers to give the entire proceeds of his lectures to the association; and not only in this city but throughout the State, he generously offers to do the same thing. This is certainly deserving of the warm recognition of our own people at least, and we hope on Thursday evening to see the City Hall filled. Captain Glazier comes with the strongest endorsements from well-known gentlemen in the East, both as to his character as a gentleman and a soldier, and his ability as a speaker and writer. The captain served under the late General Custer in the cavalry, and has something to say regarding his personal knowledge of the dead hero...."

The lecture was duly delivered, and the following certificate placed in his hands:

> HEADQUARTERS,
> CUSTER NATIONAL MONUMENT ASSOCIATION,
> MONROE, MICH., *July 28th*, 1876.
>
> This is to certify that the proceeds of the lecture by Captain Willard Glazier in this city on Thursday evening, July 27th, 1876, have been paid into the treasury of this association; for which the members hereby tender him their sincere thanks.
>
> T. E. WING,
> Treasurer.

The following also is evidence of the benevolent aims of Captain Glazier during his journey in the saddle:

> HEADQUARTERS,
> CUSTER NATIONAL MONUMENT ASSOCIATION,
> MONROE, MICH., *July 28th*, 1876.
>
> *To Auxiliary Societies and Associations of the Custer Monument Association:*
>
> Captain Willard Glazier having kindly and generously volunteered to devote the proceeds of his lectures through Michigan to the fund being raised by this Association for the erection of a monument to the memory of the late General George A. Custer, he has made arrangements to remit to our treasurer here the money derived from such lectures, and we bespeak for him your earnest endeavors in aid of our common, glorious cause. Respectfully,
>
> J. M. BULKLEY,
> Secretary.

Before leaving Monroe, Glazier called upon Mr. E. J. Custer, the father of the deceased general, whom he represents as nearly crushed by the melancholy news of his son's tragic death. The worthy old gentleman was very courteous, and showed him some photographs and an oil-portrait of the late general, together with some relics from the Indian country which the general had sent him at different times. Mr. Custer seemed greatly interested in the journey on horseback, and asked the captain many questions concerning his plans for crossing the plains. Finally, he accompanied Captain Glazier as far as Strong's Hotel, and witnessed his start from Monroe. During his stay in Monroe our soldier-author was introduced to several prominent gentlemen of the place, and plans were discussed for availing themselves of his proffered services in behalf of the monument. The lecture was a financial success, and the whole of the proceeds were turned over to the Treasurer, Judge T. E. Wing. "I gave them all, although they generously offered to divide with me," is the simple entry in his journal under date July twenty-eighth.

Passing through Rockwood, Trenton, Wyandotte, and Ecorse, all in the State of Michigan, he reached Detroit on the thirty-first of July, and was met by General William A. Throop at the Russell House, as one of a committee appointed to confer with him on the subject of his lecture. At the usual hour the lecture was delivered to a full house at Saint Andrew's Hall, General L. S. Trowbridge introducing the lecturer to the audience in very complimentary terms.

The next morning the proceeds were turned over to the monument fund as indicated in the following letter to the treasurer, and its acknowledgment by the local committee.

DETROIT, MICHIGAN,
August 1st, 1876.

T. E. WING, ESQ., Treasurer,
Custer National Monument Association:

DEAR SIR: I send you through General L. S. Trowbridge of this city the net proceeds of my lecture delived at St. Andrew's Hall last night, the same to be applied to the fund of the Custer National Monument Association, for the erection of a monument to the memory of the late General Custer at Monroe. I hope and expect to be able to send you much larger contributions as soon as the lecture season is fairly open. My horse is still in excellent condition, and I shall anticipate a delightful and successful ride across the Peninsular State. Promising to write you again from Ypsilanti, I am

Ever truly yours,
WILLARD GLAZIER.

DETROIT, MICHIGAN,
August 1*st*, 1876.

Received of Captain Willard Glazier, forty dollars, for the benefit of the Custer Monument Association, as the proceeds of his lecture at Detroit on the evening of July 31st, 1876, in aid of such association. [Signed] L. S. TROWBRIDGE,
WILLIAM A. THROOP,
Committee.

While in Detroit, Captain Glazier visited all the public buildings and places of note, enjoying the courtesies and hospitality of many of its leading citizens; and, encouraged by the success he had met with so far in contributing to the Custer Monument Fund, he determined to devote the net proceeds of all his lectures delivered between Detroit and Chicago to the same object.

Leaving Detroit and passing through Inkster, he reached Ypsilanti through torrents of rain, and the same evening—August fifth—received calls at the Hawkins House from a large number of patriotic gentlemen interested in the Custer monument. The lecture was duly delivered in Union Hall and the proceeds handed over to the fund.

Arrived at Jackson, "a most enterprising little city," as Captain Glazier notes, August ninth, and delivered his lecture in the evening at Bronson Hall, to a very full house. The Jackson *Citizen* said on the following morning:

"Captain Willard Glazier lectured last evening in the interest of the Custer Monument Fund. His lecture was a good historical review delivered with graceful rhetoric and at times real eloquence. The captain is still in the city giving his horse—a noble Kentucky Black Hawk, whom he has ridden all the way from Boston, and whom he expects to carry him to San Francisco—a rest. He starts to-morrow morning for Battle-Creek, where he lectures on Saturday evening."

Through Parma, Albion, and on to Battle-Creek, which was reached August twelfth. Lieutenant Eugene T. Freeman here took the rôle of host and welcomed Captain Glazier to the city, introducing him to many admirers and friends of the late General Custer. Arrangements were completed for the lecture, which took place at the usual hour in Stuart's Hall before a numerous and attentive audience—the introduction being made by Lieutenant Freeman, and the proceeds applied to the monument fund. The following day being Sunday the lieutenant's invitation was accepted to accompany him to church, where an introduction to the pastor, Rev. Mr. Palmer, and others, took place. In the afternoon Captain Glazier was agreeably surprised by an invitation from Lieutenant Freeman to ride with him in his carriage to the delightful summer resort of that region—Goguac Lake; and in many other ways Lieutenant Freeman manifested a very friendly and cordial feeling for him.

Contrary to Captain Glazier's intention on setting out from Boston he yielded to invitations to lecture at Albion and Marshall, and, in the interest of the Custer Monument, also determined to visit South Bend, Indiana; and Grand Rapids, Michigan; which cities were not included in the route he had originally marked out for himself.

At Kalamazoo he delivered his lecture to a crowded house, being introduced by Major Judson, late of General Custer's staff. Nearing Comstock, Captain Glazier met with a serious adventure. His horse "Paul" becoming frightened by the approach of a train on the Michigan Central Railway, dashed over the embankment into the Kalamazoo River—a fall of nearly forty feet, and the captain came very near losing his life. No bones were broken, however, the result being happily confined to a considerable ducking and a no less considerable scare; "Paul" having fared as ill as his master.

The following letters and press notices will show the nature of the reception our soldier-author met with in Kalamazoo, Grand Rapids and South Bend, respectively:

KALAMAZOO, MICHIGAN,
August 18th, 1876.

J. M. BULKLEY, ESQ.,
Secretary C. N. M. Association,
MONROE, MICHIGAN.

DEAR SIR:—I have the pleasure of transmitting to Judge Wing, through Major R. F. Judson, the net proceeds of my lecture delivered in this place on the evening of the sixteenth instant. I desire to accompany my gift with an acknowledgment of many courtesies extended by the press and band of this patriotic village. I resume my journey this afternoon and shall speak at Niles, South Bend, and Laporte before the close of the present week. Hoping that your brightest anticipations for the "Monument" may be most fully realized, I remain,

Always sincerely yours,
WILLARD GLAZIER.

KALAMAZOO, MICHIGAN,
August 19th, 1876.

Received of Captain Willard Glazier the net proceeds of his lecture at this place, which sum is to be applied to the fund for the erection of a monument to the memory of the late General Custer, at Monroe City, Michigan.

We take great pleasure in speaking of Captain Glazier in the highest terms, not only on account of the self-devotion he has manifested in a noble cause, but of his indomitable perseverance and energy. We trust he will, wherever he goes, receive the unanimous support of the citizens whom he addresses.

F. W. CURTENIUS,
Late Colonel U. S. Volunteers.

I take great pleasure in fully endorsing the above and recommending to public confidence and support, Captain Willard Glazier, in his efforts in behalf of the Custer Monument Association.

R. F. JUDSON,
Late aide to General Custer.

From the South Bend *Herald:*

"As heretofore announced in these columns, Captain Glazier delivered his lecture ' Echoes from the Revolution ' at the Academy of Music last evening. Promptly at eight o'clock, the lecturer, with Mr. J. F. Creed, appeared on the platform. Mr. Creed, in introducing the lecturer, stated the object of the lecture to be in aid of the Custer Monument Association of Monroe, Michigan. He also read several letters introducing Captain Glazier to the public, from well-known citizens of Michigan, and acknowledging receipts of the proceeds of the lectures delivered in Detroit and Kalamazoo. The theme of the lecture afforded a fine field for the display of Captain Glazier's talents as a speaker. Possessing a fine imagination, good descriptive powers, and the real qualities of an orator, he could not fail to please the really intelligent audience which greeted him last evening. Probably one hour and a half were consumed in its delivery, but the interest and attention of the audience did not flag nor tire, and when the speaker took leave of his audience, he was greeted with several rounds of applause."

About this time his Boston friends were notified of his progress toward the setting sun in the following paragraph of the Boston *Inquirer:*

" Captain Willard Glazier, who undertook in May last to ride from this city to the Golden Gate on horseback, has reached Michigan, and has discoursed to large audiences at the various points along his route. The profits of his lecture at Cleveland, Ohio, were donated to the fund at Dayton, to assist in erecting a monument to the memory of the veterans who by the fortunes of war are destined to await the long roll-call at the National Military Home."

To return to his present point of departure, South Bend, Captain Glazier finding his horse " Paul " suffering from the accident previously recorded, and also from sore-back, left him with a veterinary surgeon for treatment, and sped on his way by rail to Grand Rapids. Here he lectured with favorable results, having been introduced by General Innes.

Said the Grand Rapids *Eagle:*

"A very large audience gathered at Luce's Hall last night to hear Captain Willard Glazier. The speaker was earnest and impassioned, his lecture was delivered with a force and eloquence that pleased his hearers, and all who were in the hall went away glad that they had been there, and ready to add to the praises that have been bestowed on Captain Glazier as a soldier, author, and orator."

Decatur, Dowagiac, Paw-Paw, Niles, and Buchanan, were all reached by railway, for the purpose of giving "Paul" a rest and an opportunity of recovering from his sore back. At Decatur, Glazier met an old comrade of the "Harris Light," named George L. Darby, with whom a pleasant exchange of reminiscences took place, and a cordial intercourse was renewed. "Thirteen years," says Captain Glazier in his Journal, "have slipped away, since the day of our capture at New Baltimore, which led him to Belle Isle, and me to Libby Prison. . . Darby called this afternoon with fishing tackle, and proposed that we should go out to 'Lake of the Woods,' a small lake not far from the village, and try our luck with hook and line. We went, and a delightful boat-ride followed, but in the matter of the fish which we tried to lure with tempting pieces of fresh meat, they are still enjoying their native freedom." We suspect the friends were too intent on fighting their battles o'er again to give due attention to their occupation.

The lecture here was delivered September fourth to a crowded house, over two hundred persons being compelled to stand for want of room to seat them. Captain Glazier was accompanied to the platform by several leading citizens, among whom were Hon. Ransom Nutting, Rev. Mr. Hoyt, Professor S. G. Burked and Albert W. Rogers, Esq., Mr. Nutting presenting him to the audience. The following will show the opinion entertained of the lecturer:

DECATUR, MICHIGAN,
September 4th, 1876.

CAPTAIN WILLARD GLAZIER,

MY DEAR SIR:—We take this means of expressing to you our appreciation of the highly instructive and very entertaining lecture delivered by you at Union Hall this evening.

Truly we admire your plan, and your generosity in giving the entire proceeds to the Custer Monument Fund. Our endorsement is the expression of our village people generally. You have made many friends here.

May success attend you throughout your journey.

Very respectfully,
S. GORDON BURKED,
RANSOM NUTTING,
ALBERT W. ROGERS.

Having lectured successfully at the several intermediate towns before mentioned, Captain Glazier with "Paul" now directed his course to Rolling Prairie, Indiana (a place romantic only in name), and thence to Michigan City. From the latter point he journeyed by railway to Chicago, arrangements having been made for the delivery of his lecture in that city for the benefit of the monument fund. A very full house greeted him at Farwell Hall. Major E. S. Weedon in introducing the lecturer alluded in an eloquent and touching manner to the record of the gallant Custer. The lecture throughout its delivery was much applauded by the audience, who appeared greatly interested; and the proceeds reached a handsome sum.

The following entry occurs in the Journal under date, Chicago, September 12th, 1876:

"I shall now push on to Omaha and Cheyenne as rapidly as possible, in the hope of passing Sherman at the summit of the mountains before the snow is too deep to interrupt my progress. There are nine steps in my journey from Boston to San Francisco, namely, Albany, Buffalo, Toledo, Chicago, Omaha, Cheyenne, Salt Lake City, Sacramento, and San Francisco. I have now taken four of these nine steps, and shall undertake to pass the five remaining points by the first of December."

CHAPTER XXXIII.

FROM CHICAGO TO OMAHA.

Returns to Michigan City.—Joliet.—Thomas Babcock.—Herbert Glazier.—Ottawa.—La Salle.—Colonel Stevens.—Press Notice.—Taken for a highwayman.—Milan.—Davenport.—Press Notice. —Iowa City.—Des Moines.—Press Notice.—Attacked by prairie wolves.—Council Bluffs.—Omaha.

CAPTAIN GLAZIER having succeeded so far in his novel and adventurous undertaking, felt little concern as to his ability to accomplish the entire journey from ocean to ocean. He had ridden but one horse—his faithful "Paul," thus far, and having returned to Michigan City, found him quite recovered and ready to pursue the journey. On the sixteenth of September he took his departure from the latter city, and after riding a distance of twenty-eight miles, rested for the night at Hobart, Indiana.

On the seventeenth he crossed the boundary between Indiana and Illinois. On Grand Prairie, after dark, his ears were made familiar with the peculiar howl of the prairie wolf, numbers of which followed in his track for a distance of two or three miles. Not having seen any of these animals before, he supposed them at first to be dogs, until advised by "Paul's" manner and movements that they were animals less friendly to his equine companion.

At four o'clock in the afternoon, Glazier rode into Joliet, and met Mr. Thomas Babcock, his advance agent, on Jefferson Street. Preparations had been made here for the delivery of the lecture, and several prominent citizens called upon him, having heard of his projected visit to the place. His brother Herbert, who was also acting in the capacity of advance agent, had departed to Ottawa to prepare for a lecture there on the twentieth. While at Joliet, Captain Glazier stopped at the Robertson House, the proprietor of which, Mr. Conklin, sent word through the agent, that the captain was to consider himself his guest.

At the suggestion of Mr. Conklin, Captain Glazier on leaving Joliet, rode his horse along the tow-path of the Michigan Canal, and borrowing a hook and line from a gentleman who was fishing, caught twenty-three perch in less than half an hour, the canal being swarming with fish.

Leaving Morris, in Grundy County, Illinois, his journey lay along the north bank of the Illinois River, and after encountering a very severe rain storm, he reached Ottawa, September twentieth, stopping at the Clifton House. From the proprietors of this hotel he received many courtesies. The lecture, as arranged, was delivered in the evening with the usual satisfactory results.

On leaving Ottawa, the captain followed the telegraph poles along the Illinois River, passing a large number of very fine corn-fields, and overtaking an emigrant train on its journey from Ohio to Western Nebraska. La Salle was reached at six o'clock on the evening of the twenty-first. Here he enjoyed the society and hospitality of Colonel R. C. Stevens, and was introduced to a number of other prominent gentlemen, who were attracted to him by their interest in the projected monument to General Custer. The lecture was delivered at Opera Hall, Colonel Stevens making the introduction. The following letter may be presented here to show the estimation in which Captain Glazier continued to be held as he progressed in his journey westward:

LA SALLE, ILLINOIS,
September 25th, 1876.

TO CAPTAIN WILLARD GLAZIER: I take pleasure in expressing to you on behalf of many of our citizens, the gratification afforded our people who listened to your instructive and entertaining lecture given at Opera Hall on Saturday evening. While in conversation with several of our prominent citizens—among them, W. A. Work, superintendent of our public schools; A. J. O'Connor, clerk of the City Court; W. T. Mason, Esq., and others; all of whom were present and heard your lecture—I was requested to write you and tender their hearty thanks for the entertainment, and their good wishes for your success in your ride across the continent. Should you ever again visit our city, you can rest assured you will be most cordially received.

Very truly yours,
R. C. STEVENS,
Late Colonel U. S. Volunteers.

The La Salle *County Press* noticed the lecturer in the following terms:

"We have not often met with a more agreeable and pleasant gentleman than Captain Willard Glazier, who entertained a very respectable number of our citizens at Opera Hall on Saturday evening by delivering a lecture on 'Echoes from the Revolution.' The captain has a fine voice and his manner of delivery is decidedly interesting, while his language is eloquent and fascinating. His description of the battles of the Revolution, and the heroes who took part in them, from the engagement on the little green at Lexington down to the surrender of Cornwallis at Yorktown, was grand indeed, and was received with frequent and enthusiastic applause. In conclusion he referred in an eloquent and touching manner to the 'Boys in Blue' who took part in the late war for the Union, and all retired from the hall feeling that the evening had been spent in an agreeable and profitable manner.

"Captain Glazier served under Generals Kilpatrick and Custer during the late war, since which time he has devoted much labor to writing, and is now making the attempt to cross the continent from Boston to San Francisco on horseback, for the purpose of collecting material for another work. He left Boston in the early part of May, and will endeavor to reach the Sacramento Valley before the fall of the deep snow. His horse, 'Paul Revere,' is a magnificent animal, black as a raven, with the exception of four white feet. He was bred in Kentucky, of Black Hawk stock, has turned a mile in 2.33, but owing to his inclination to run away on certain occasions, was not considered a safe horse for the track. The captain, however, has broke him to the saddle, and also convinced him that running away is foolish business; consequently he and the captain have become fast friends, and with 'Paul' for his only companion, the gallant cavalryman proposes to cross the continent. Success attend him!"

Having heard at La Salle that he would find no difficulty in securing a night's lodging at a village named Hollowayville, Captain Glazier pushed on for that point, but on applying at the only place of accommodation for travellers, was looked upon suspiciously by the German host and his *frau*, who politely intimated their belief that he was either a highwayman or a horse-thief! These latter gentry had for some time infested that section of Illinois, and Glazier inferred from the manner of the people that they more than half suspected him to be one of the James or Younger brothers, whose exploits they had probably read of.

Turning his back on the "Grand Pacific Hotel," he at length succeeded by dint of much perseverance, in lodging himself and "Paul" at a farm-house for the night, but not before he had fully satisfied the worthy farmer and his wife that he had no evil designs in desiring to spend the night with them.

On the following day, September twenty-fifth, the captain rode through a rich farming country, replete with "corn-fields, fine stock and oceans of fruit."

Passed through Wyanet, Annawan, and across the

prairie—smiling corn-fields and ripe orchards occasionally relieving the seemingly interminable ocean of grass—and arrived at Milan, Illinois, on the evening of the twenty-seventh, remaining for the night.

Here he met a Mr. Pullman, an old and intelligent miner who had recently arrived from the Pacific coast, from whom he obtained valuable information concerning the country between Omaha and Sacramento. He also found a number of congenial spirits at Milan, chiefly New Yorkers, who had spent some years in the Far West, and their conversation partook of a practical nature bearing on his journey.

Leaving Milan on the following day, he crossed the Government Bridge, which unites Rock Island with the fine city of Davenport, Iowa, and registered at the Burtis House—the rider and his horse continuing in the best of health.

The lecture at Davenport was delivered at the usual hour at Moore's Hall to a very large and applauding audience, General Sanders presenting him. The brass band of the place volunteered their services, and appeared in full uniform. The Davenport *Gazette* of October fourth said:

"The lecture of Captain Willard Glazier at Moore's Hall last evening was attended by a large and appreciative audience. The captain was introduced by our worthy fellow-citizen, General Sanders, who spoke of the lecturer's career as a soldier and an author, and said he was *en route* for the Pacific coast on horseback, and lecturing for the benefit of the Custer Monument Fund. . . ."

The following notice is taken from the *Democrat* of the same city:

"We had the pleasure of meeting Captain Glazier this morning, who arrived here on horseback from La Salle on Saturday evening.

He is making the journey from Boston to San Francisco on horseback, and alone, for the purpose of seeing the country, studying the people, and gathering materials for a new work he is engaged upon. Captain Glazier is well known to fame as a writer, having published several valuable works, among them a war-record entitled, 'Capture, Prison-Pen and Escape.'

"At the breaking out of the war, Willard Glazier, then a mere youth, entered the Harris Light Cavalry, under Colonel Judson Kilpatrick, and remained in the service until the close of the rebellion, his career being marked by many adventures and hairbreadth escapes. His feat of riding on horseback across the continent, unattended, to gather materials for a book, is certainly without a precedent, and shows a brave and intrepid spirit. His horse 'Paul' was an object of great curiosity and interest."

Leaving Davenport, our traveller passed through Moscow and reached Iowa City October fifth. The weather was now becoming very cold, and he found it necessary to dismount occasionally and walk some warmth into his limbs.

Registering at the St. James Hotel, Iowa City, Captain Glazier lectured in the evening to a very full house, a profusion of cheers greeting him on his arrival upon the platform, whither he was escorted by George B. Edmunds, Esq.

Continuing his journey through Tiffin and Brooklyn to Kellogg, all in the State of Iowa, he witnessed, he says, some of the finest landscapes and grandest farms he had yet encountered during his journey. He rode into Colfax, October twelfth, and Des Moines on the following day.

"I have not seen a brighter or more stirring city in my line of march than Des Moines," writes Captain Glazier in his Journal. He wandered over the city in company with two or three of the leading citizens, admiring its numerous fine buildings and the evidences

A NIGHT AMONG WOLVES.

of its rapid progress; and the next day the *Des Moines Leader* came out with the following notice of his visit:

"Captain Willard Glazier, the horseback traveler across the continent, took in the Exposition on Saturday evening with intense gratification. He says he has seen no place, on his route from Boston, more promising than Des Moines. Among the calls he received at the Jones House was one from Captain Conrad, a prominent attorney from Missouri, and now settled in his profession in this city, who was a fellow-captive with Captain Glazier in Libby Prison during the rebellion. He continued his journey westward yesterday, with the best wishes of the friends he has made during his short stay here."

Captain Glazier speaks very highly of the extremely courteous treatment he received while at Des Moines.

Adel, and Dale City, and Minden were passed, and arriving at Neola, we find the following entry in the journal: "Weather most disagreeable. A drizzling rain made my ride to this place decidedly gloomy. My journey to-day, as usual, since entering Iowa, has been over the boundless, never-ending prairie. I have never in my life beheld a grander sight than this afternoon, when I reached the summit of an immense tableland between Avoca and Minden."

Wishing to reach Anita before halting for the night, he ventured to continue on the road after dark, although for some time before sunset he had been unable to see a farm-house or even a tree as far as the eye could reach. Giving "Paul" the rein, he followed a blind road, after crossing a sluice-way, which ultimately led them to a haystack on the prairie, where the captain decided to spend the night. A pack of prairie wolves, or coyotes, soon came upon the scene, several of which he shot, but he was shortly after reinforced by a friendly dog, who came to his rescue and kept the coyotes at bay for the remainder of the night. In the morning at daybreak he was glad enough to say adieu to the haystack where he had passed one of the most unpleasant nights of his journey.

It may here be mentioned that the *coyote* partakes of the natures of the dog and the wolf, and is less dangerous to encounter in the summer than in the winter, which is a characteristic of its wolfish nature. In the winter, when food is scarce, these animals will attack man, but if a bold resistance is offered, they speedily decamp.

Hastening forward on his journey through various small and more or less enterprising cities of the prairie, our traveler reached Council Bluffs at eight o'clock in the evening of October twentieth. This promising city is located three miles east from the Missouri River, and contains an enterprising population of some 20,000; its history dating from 1804. The locality is surrounded by high bluffs, and hence the name given to the city.

Striking the Missouri opposite Omaha, our horseman found he would be compelled to ride up the bank of the river and cross by ferry to the northern section of the city. On reaching the boat, "Paul" declined to embark, but with some encouragement and assistance he was at length made to understand that when rivers cannot be bridged or forded, they can sometimes be ferried, and so yielded to necessity.

Omaha is almost equidistant between the Atlantic and Pacific, and has sprung up, flourished and waxed great in the twinkling of an eye. It is now the grand gateway through which the western tide of travel and emigration is passing. The first house was erected here in 1853, and the population now numbers in the neighborhood of 30,000. Omaha can boast of as fine business blocks, hotels, school-buildings and churches as can be found in many older and more pretentious cities in the East. There are also numerous elegant private residences, with grounds beautifully ornamented with trees and shrubbery, which sufficiently attest the solid prosperity of Omaha's business men.

A story is told of the postmaster of Omaha which illustrates the changes made during the past few years. Mr. Jones, one of the first pioneers, was appointed to the office of postmaster in the autumn of 1854. At that time there was no office, while letters were rarities. The few letters that did come were kept by the postmaster in the crown of his hat till he met their owners. Only a few years have elapsed since this primitive state of things, and the post-office of Omaha has expanded from a hat into a handsome stone building, worth $350,000, in which some twenty clerks find full employment.

Hearing of the impossibility of riding his valuable horse across the Alkali Plains, he resolved to leave him at Omaha until his return from San Francisco, and to continue his journey on a mustang. In these plains the soil for two or three feet seems saturated with soda, and so poisons the water that if drunk by man or beast, after a fall of rain, is sure to be fatal. "Paul" was therefore turned over by his master to the care of G. W. Homan, proprietor of the Omaha Livery Stable; and a good serviceable mustang purchased of a Pawnee Indian, to replace him.

CHAPTER XXXIV.

CAPTURED BY INDIANS.

Captain Glazier as a horseman.—Cheyenne.—Two herders.—Captured by Indians.—Torture and death of a herder.—Escape.—Ogden.—Letter to Major Hessler.—Kelton.—Terrace.—Wells.—Halleck.—Elko.—Palisade.—Argenta.—Battle Mountain.—Golconda.—Humboldt.—"The majesty of the law."—Lovelock's.—White Plains.—Desert.—Wadsworth.—Truckee.—Summit.—Sacramento.—Brighton.—Stockton.—SAN FRANCISCO.

HAVING made several friends in Omaha, and obtained all the information within his reach concerning the remaining half of the journey, Captain Glazier mounted his mustang and proceeded on his route across the State of Nebraska. Over the great plains that lie between the Missouri River and the mountains, his nerve as a horseman was most thoroughly tested, and not less so, the mettle of his mustang, which carried him a distance of five hundred and twenty-two miles in six days. The approach of winter suggested the importance of reaching his destination at the earliest possible date; therefore on riding into Cheyenne October twenty-eighth, he lost no time in arranging to continue his journey.

The weather now became intensely cold, as he neared the highest point in his line of march. Since leaving Omaha, the ascent had been gradual but continuous, and the point now reached was eight thousand feet above the sea-level.

Cheyenne, the "Magic City of the Plains," about five hundred and twenty miles west of Omaha, stands at an elevation of six thousand feet above the level of the sea, and is perhaps the most progressive city west of Chicago. It is the capital of Wyoming Territory, the county-seat of Laramie County, and is the largest town between Omaha and Salt Lake City. The gold discoveries in the Black Hills of Dakota added greatly to its prosperity. In proportion to its population, Cheyenne has more elegant and substantial business houses than most any other western city. This is a wonderful change from a place known the world over by its fearful sobriquet of "Hell on Wheels." Churches have risen where gamblers once reigned, and many other edifices for religious and educational purposes have been erected. Cheyenne is the trading-post for the thousands of ranchemen and stock-raisers of the plains at the base of the Black Hills, and like all other frontier cities, has a history. It was once a very fast town, and it is not very slow now.

On leaving Cheyenne he was accompanied by two herders, who were on their way to Salt Lake City with a few mustangs and ponies. It was the custom of Captain Glazier to have company in his rides through this wild region whenever he could do so, and having made the acquaintance of these men in the city, it was arranged that they should journey together as far as their respective routes led them. The men were of the usual stamp of herders, rough in exterior and plain of speech, but apparently worthy of trust. The captain was not wanting in discernment, and his cordial manner won their confidence.

Sherman having afforded them a night's shelter and

refreshment, their course lay in the direction of the Skull Rocks, a huge mass of granite on the Great Laramie Plains, and so called from the resemblance of the rocks to human skulls.

The Skull Rocks being in front of them at no great distance, the conversation of the party turned upon their peculiar configuration, and opinions were advanced by each of a more or less intelligent character; the herders insisting on the probability of their having plenty of gold in them. Suddenly, over a slight elevation in the land, appeared a body of Indians, in number about thirteen or fourteen. Glazier and his companions were not at first surprised, as Indians are often found on these plains—some friendly and some hostile—but mostly those of the friendly tribes. The Indians now advancing upon them were clearly not on a friendly errand, and were pronounced by the herders to be a detachment of the Arrapahoes. They were decked in their war-paint, and on seeing the white men immediately raised their war-shout, which, as travellers on the plains are aware, always indicates an intention to attack.

The herders, knowing that they were in the presence of an enemy who would speedily relieve them of their merchandise, made conciliatory signs, by raising their hands, a signal which is equivalent to a flag of truce, and is so understood on the plains. The signal of truce was, however, ignored by the red-skins, who continued to advance at a rapid pace, gradually forming a circle around Glazier and his companions. This is the usual Indian form of attack. The circle is kept constantly in rapid motion, the Indians concentrating their fire upon a stationary object in the centre of the

CAPTURED BY INDIANS NEAR SKULL ROCK, WYOMING.

circle, while they render themselves a constantly shifting target, and are thus comparatively safe from the fire of the centre.

Riding around, and firing at intervals of a minute or two at Glazier and his companions, the latter did their best to defend themselves, and fired in return upon their cowardly assailants, who showed no desire for a parley. The firing from the centre was made over the backs of the ponies and mustangs, who in such emergencies are made to do duty as a breastwork. The circle of red-skins gradually lessened in diameter, as the firing on both sides continued, when a shot from the carbine of the Mexican herder killed one of the Indians.

The circle continued to grow less, until the Indians in a mass rushed on the three whites, disarmed them, secured them to each other with thongs at the wrists, and appropriated as their own the mustangs and ponies, which had been their primary object.

Before yielding, Captain Glazier and his little squad had nearly exhausted their ammunition, and felt that further resistance was not only useless, but would certainly cost them their lives. Without loss of time, the prisoners were compelled to mount, and the entire party—less one Indian killed—started off in a northerly direction.

Ignorant of their destination, the herders expressed their belief that they would in a few days find themselves in the presence of Sitting Bull, when their fate would be decided. They continued to ride at a full trot till about ten o'clock, when the whole party dismounted and camped for the night. A fire was speedily built, and some antelope beef partially roasted for their supper, of which the prisoners also partook.

The supper over, an animated conversation ensued among the Indians, while sundry furtive glances were cast in the direction of the Mexican who had killed one of their party during the attack in the morning. For a time they shouted and violently gesticulated, while one of them was observed driving a thick pole into the ground, at about fifty yards from the fire, around which the party and the prisoners squatted. Presently, at a sign from one of the Indians, supposed to be a chief named "Dull-Knife," four of the red-skins seized the Mexican and forced him towards the stake, where they stripped him to the skin, and then bound him to it with thick cords. The whole party then, without further ceremony, proceeded to torture the wretched man to death, as a punishment for his presumption in killing one of their party while defending himself from their murderous attack near the Skull Rocks. They heated their arrow-shafts in the fire, and held them in contact with his naked flesh, while others, at a distance of a few feet from their victim, cast at him their sharp-pointed knives, which, penetrating the body, remained embedded in the flesh, until he nearly died from the agony. One of the party now advanced with a revolver, and shot him in the head, thus ending his sufferings.

While the torture was proceeding, Captain Glazier and the remaining herder lay on the ground bound together by thick cords, and could offer no assistance to their tortured companion. The Mexican being dead, one of the party removed his scalp and fastened it to his waist, after which all sat down around the fire and seemed in high glee for the remainder of the evening, for the most part shouting and speech-making.

Willard Glazier had never before witnessed a case of torture by the Indians. It is true it was of a different character from that he and many of his old comrades had endured in Southern prisons; but in one respect was more merciful, as the sufferings of their victim were soon ended, while his own and his comrades extended over many months; in the one case the body was burnt and lacerated—in the other it was starved and emaciated.

The horses of the party having been tethered by long ropes to stakes, to enable them to graze during the night, a guard of two Indians was placed in charge of the prisoners, who, still bound together at the wrists, were made to lie down side by side, with an Indian on either hand. The remainder of the red-skins then disposed themselves around the fire for sleep.

Glazier and his companion slept but little, but pretended to do so. They were continually on the alert, and the guard, believing their prisoners to be asleep, dozed, and at length reclined their bodies in a restless sleep. About two o'clock in the morning, the two Indians were relieved by two others, and all remained quiet in the camp. At the first streak of dawn, the whole body leaped to their feet and were ready to resume their march northward. Glazier and the herder were assigned each a mustang, which they quietly mounted under the close scrutiny of their guards, and the entire party started off at a brisk trot.

No attempt at escape having yet been made by the captives, the surveillance became somewhat relaxed throughout the day, and the attention of the party was given to their own proper business of foraging. Wherever an opportunity offered, a momentary halt was called, and one of the party creeping cautiously up to a stray pony, would take possession by the simple process of mounting and riding him away. If more than one animal was to be appropriated, an equal number of Indians were detailed for the "duty," and each leaping on the mustang or pony he had selected, would ride off as only these freebooters of the plains can ride, with little prospect of being overtaken by the owners. Thus the day passed; as a rule, half the number of the Indians remaining as a guard to the prisoners, while the others foraged for food, and anything that could be conveniently carried off. They were now skirting the Black Hills, and Glazier had discovered by this time that they were making their way to their general rendezvous, about one hundred miles from Deadwood.

As the second night overtook the captives, the process of the previous night was repeated: they built their fire, cooked and eat their antelope steaks, and then prostrated themselves around the fire for the night. The captives were again bound together at the wrists, and lay between their two guards. Our friend was, however, on the alert and wide awake, though pretending to be asleep. Quietly he passed the fingers of one hand over the cords that bound his other to his companion, and concluded that with patience and vigilance the knot could be unfastened. While the guards dozed and slept as on the preceding night, the eyes of the prisoners stealthily sought the ponies and the arms.

The latter were always placed at the head of each sleeper, to be ready for immediate use in case of a surprise. Captain Glazier and his companion were fully convinced that any attempt to escape, if detected, would be followed by immediate torture and death; but were, nevertheless, resolved to make the effort. It was also known that if they quietly accompanied the Indians to their rendezvous or headquarters, they would be retained as hostages, probably for a long period, and be subject at any time to be tortured should a fit of vengeance seize their captors. They would not, however, make an attempt to escape unless there appeared a moral certainty of its successful accomplishment.

The third day arrived, and at dawn, after partaking of the usual breakfast of raw antelope or other game, they started again on their march. They rode all day, with the usual stoppages for forage, and about eight o'clock in the evening camped, supped, and lay down for the night, as before, after assigning the usual nightguards to the prisoners, who were again bound together.

Glazier, with the experience he had obtained in the South, and his companion, with his intimate knowledge of the plains, kept themselves constantly on the alert, prepared to take advantage of any opportunity that offered to escape from their captors. They had each fixed his eye on a pony in the herd. These animals were turned out to graze with their saddles on, in order that they might be ready for instant use, if required, in the night. The prisoners began snoring loudly under pretence of being asleep, and at the same time the guards dozed and slept at intervals, but were restless until about midnight, when they both succumbed and were fast asleep.

Glazier now worked at the cord on his wrist, and found he could unfasten it. While so doing, one of the Indians moved in his sleep, and immediately all was still as death with the captives. At length the time had arrived, the complicated knot was loosened, and the noose slipped over his hand, which at once gave him and his partner liberty of action. They knew where the arms lay, and each in the twinkling of an eye secured a large navy revolver without disturbing the Indians. They then simultaneously struck the two sleeping guards a powerful blow on the head with the butt of their revolvers. The Indian struck by the herder was nearly killed by the heavy blow, while Glazier's man was only stunned. They then made for the ponies, leaped into the saddles, and before any of the other Indians had shaken off their heavy slumber, had struck out with all their might in the direction from which they had come, and in the opposite one, therefore, to that in which the Indian party were proceeding.

In a minute, however, the pursuit commenced in earnest; vociferations implying vengeance of the direst character if they did not halt, were flung through the darkness, which only had the effect of spurring the fugitives to still greater speed. Glazier turned in his saddle and sent a bullet among his pursuers in reply to their peremptory invitation to him to halt. Another and another followed, and one Indian was dismounted, but the darkness prevented his seeing if his other shots had told. The Indians meanwhile, who had plenty of ammunition, were not slow in returning the fire, but luckily without any worse result than to increase the pace of the flying ponies.

Away they tore at the top of their speed, and soon entered a cañon in the mountain side. Only two or three of the Indians could now be seen in pursuit, and the herder, saying it would be better for both if they

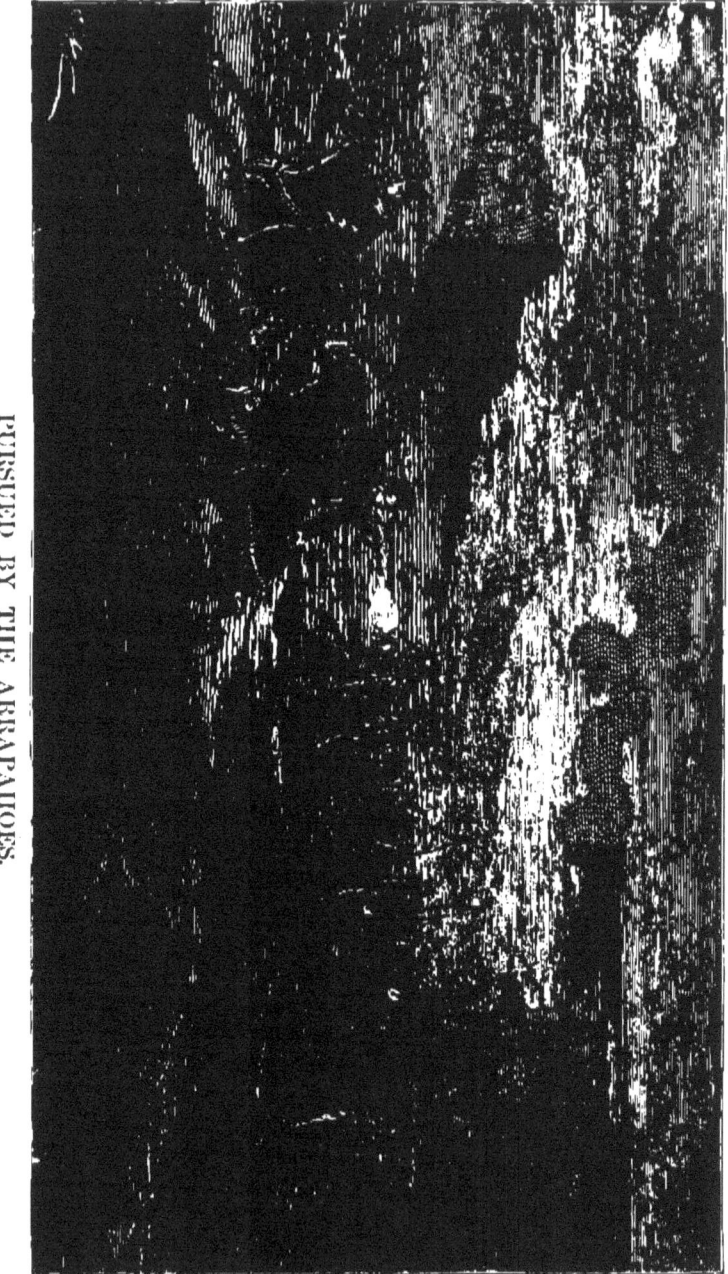

PURSUED BY THE ARRAPAHOES.

took different directions, at once struck off through a ravine to the right, and left Glazier alone. One Indian was observed to follow, but Glazier sent a bullet into the enemy's horse, and thus put a stop to further pursuit. The Indian now leveled his carbine at Glazier and dismounted him; and the latter's ammunition being exhausted, he ran off towards a gulch, and leaping in, remained hidden until daylight. Finding the coast clear in the morning, he emerged and at once set out walking in a southwesterly direction, which eventually brought him to a cattle-ranche, the owner of which supplied him with refreshment and a fresh mustang. Again turning his face to the west he pursued his way, covering the ground between himself and the Golden Gate at the rate of sixty miles per day.

Ogden, in the northern extremity of Utah, about forty miles from Salt Lake City, and five hundred and eleven from Cheyenne, was reached November thirteenth, after hard riding and sundry stoppages at ranches in quest of hospitality and information. No event occurred more exciting than the shooting of a buffalo that crossed his path—this being the third, beside sundry antelopes and several prairie wolves that had fallen to his revolver, in the course of his journey since leaving Omaha. On riding into Ogden, Captain Glazier was surprised to find it so important a city. It forms the western terminus of the Union Pacific, and the eastern terminus of the Central Pacific, railroads, and is the second city in size and population in the Territory of Utah. Besides the churches, a Mormon tabernacle was noticed, the population being largely of the polygamic persuasion and yielding their allegiance to the prophet of Salt Lake City.

One peculiarity of the towns in these western territories is the running streams of water on each side of nearly every street, which are fed by some mountain stream and from which water is taken to irrigate the gardens and orchards adjoining the dwellings. Ogden has a bright future before it. It is not only the terminus of the two great trans-continental lines before mentioned, but is also the starting-point of the Utah Central and Utah Northern railroads. Vast quantities of iron ore can be obtained within five miles of the city, and in Ogden cañon discoveries of silver have been made. Fruit-growing is very common in the vicinity, and a large quantity of the best varieties grown in the Territory are produced around Ogden. Utah apples, peaches and pears are finer in size, color and flavor than any grown in the Eastern or Middle States.

November eighteenth, Captain Glazier heard from his advance agent, Mr. Walter Montgomery, then in Sacramento, who was in ignorance of the captain's adventure among the Indians after leaving Cheyenne, except that certain startling rumors had reached him of the captain having been killed by the Sioux. Mr. Montgomery had accordingly written to various points for information of the missing horseman; and to allay the fears of his numerous well-wishers, who were in doubt as to his safety, Captain Glazier, after leaving Ogden, wrote the following summary of his adventure, addressed to his friend, Major E. M. Hessler, of Cleveland, Ohio:

WILD CAT RANCHE,
IN CLIPPER GAP RAVINE, NEVADA,
November 18th, 1876.

MAJOR E. M. HESSLER,
  Cleveland, Ohio.

DEAR SIR AND COMRADE: I learn through my advance agent, Mr. Montgomery, that a letter, manifesting some anxiety for my welfare, was recently addressed to you. I hasten to say that I am again in the saddle, and although for three days the guest of the Arrapahoes, I am still in the best of spirits, and with even more hair than when I left Cleveland. I should be pleased to give you a detailed account of my adventures among the red-skins, but have only time to tell you that I started from Cheyenne, October twenty-eighth, accompanying two herders who were on their way to Salt Lake City with a small drove of mustangs and Indian ponies. We were attacked on the thirty-first of the same month by a straggling band of Arrapahoes, near Skull Rocks, on the Laramie Plains. One Indian was killed, and my companions and myself were made prisoners after using up nearly all our ammunition in defending ourselves. The herder whose fire killed the Indian was afterwards tied to a stake and most cruelly tortured to death. I and my remaining companion were bound together, but further torture seemed to be reserved for us at the headquarters of Sitting Bull.

Breaking away from our captors on the night of November second, by killing two of our guards, we were followed some miles, firing and receiving the fire of the Indians as we galloped off on two of the ponies we had helped ourselves to. After being dismounted by a shot, and dismounting the Indian who had killed my horse, I finally eluded my pursuers by leaping into a gulch in the mountains, where I remained until daylight, when, finding no Indians in sight, I pursued my way on foot in a southwesterly direction, which brought me to a cattle-ranche late in the afternoon. Here I secured a fresh mustang, and once more turned my face toward the setting sun.

My money and personal effects were of course appropriated as "contraband" by the red devils. I am now moving westward at an average of over sixty miles per day, confidently expecting to reach San Francisco by the twenty-fourth instant. In our encounter on Laramie plains, five members of the "Lo!" family were sent to their Happy Hunting Ground, and in the matter of scalps you may score at least two for your humble servant.

With kind regards to friends in Cleveland, I close this letter to mount my horse,

And remain, ever truly yours,

WILLARD GLAZIER.

Captain Glazier's main object now was to push on to Sacramento as fast as his mustang would carry him.

Kelton (Utah), at the northwest corner of Salt Lake, was accordingly reached soon after leaving Ogden, where he halted a few hours. This station is seven hundred and ninety miles from San Francisco. Stock is extensively grazed in its vicinity, feeding on sage brush in the winter and such grass as they can get; but excellent grazing is found in the summer. The cattle are shipped to markets on the Pacific coast in large numbers. Terrace (Utah) was the next resting-place, seven hundred and fifty-seven miles from San Francisco, in the midst of a desert with all its dreary loneliness. Continuing his pace at an average of eight miles per hour—the temperature being very low at an elevation of nearly five thousand feet—Captain Glazier observed a few only of the salient features of the wild country he now passed through, his position on horseback being less favorable for topographical study than that of the tourist comfortably seated in a palace-car.

Wells (Nevada) was duly reached by the lonely rider, who found on inquiry that he was now only six hundred and sixty-one miles from his destination. This place stands at an elevation of five thousand six hundred and twenty-nine feet. Humboldt Wells, as they are designated, give celebrity to the place, which was a great watering-station in the days of the old emigrant travel. The emigrants always rejoiced when they had passed the perils of the Great American Desert and arrived at these springs, where there was always plenty of pure water and an abundance of grass for the weary animals. Hence it was a favorite camping-ground before the existence of the Pacific Railroad. The wells are very deep. A Government exploring party, under command of Lieutenant Cuppinger, visited the spot in

1870, and took soundings to a depth of seventeen hundred feet without finding bottom.

Halleck (Nevada) was the next resting station, at an elevation of five thousand two hundred and thirty feet. It is named from Camp Halleck, about thirteen miles from the station, where two or three companies of United States troops are usually kept. The land around is mostly occupied as stock-ranges.

Elko (Nevada), twenty-four miles nearer his destination, supplied his wants in the way of rest and food for the night. This is the county-seat of Elko County, the northeastern county of the State. The town has a population of 1500, and is destined to become an important city. The money paid for freights consigned to this place and the mining districts which are tributary to it, averages $1,000,000 per year. There are numerous retail stores, and a few wholesale establishments, with a bank, brewery, hotels, and three large freight depots for the accommodation of the railroad business. Indians, mostly the Shoshones, of both sexes, are frequently noticed about the town.

The valley of the Humboldt continued to widen after leaving Elko—the pastures and meadow lands, with occasional houses, were soon passed, and the rider pushed on to Palisade (Nevada), his next halting-place, thirty miles from Elko, and five hundred and seventy-six from San Francisco. For the last two hundred miles the road had been a gradual descent, and the change of temperature was very sensible. Palisade is a growing little place, with a population of about four hundred souls. The town is located about half way down a cañon, and the rocky, perpendicular walls give it a picturesque appearance.

Forty-one miles farther west Captain Glazier stopped again for refreshment and rest at Argenta (Nevada), in the midst of alkali flats. The road continued for a few miles along the base of the Reese River Mountain, when suddenly a broad valley opened out—the valley of the Reese River. Turning to the right he found himself at Battle Mountain (Nevada), at the junction of the Reese River and Humboldt Valleys. The town of Battle Mountain has several extensive stores, a public hall, an excellent school-house and a first-class hotel, with a large and rapidly increasing trade. Battle Mountain, about three miles south of the town, is reputed to have been the scene of a sanguinary conflict between a party of emigrants and a band of red-skins, who were defeated.

Golconda (Nevada) was reached, and is four hundred and seventy-eight miles from San Francisco. It is a small place, with three or four stores, a hotel, and several houses. Gold Run mining district, a little distance to the south, is tributary to the place. Having rested for the night, Glazier mounted at sunrise and directed his course to Winnemucca (Nevada), the county-seat of Humboldt county, with a population of fifteen hundred, among whom are some Indians and not a few Chinamen. The town has an elegant brick court-house, together with several stores, hotels, shops, and a school-house. *Winnemucca* was the name of a chief of the Piute Indians, who was favorable to the whites at the time of the laying out of the city.

Humboldt (Nevada) was reached in due time—an oasis in the desert. Here he was reminded that he was still in a land of cultivation and civilization. The first growing trees since leaving Ogden were seen here, with plenty of green grass and flowing fountains of pure water. Humboldt House offered its hospitality to our traveler, and the place and its surroundings reminded him of his home in the east. It was a great relief from the wearisome, dreary views which had everywhere met his gaze over the largest part of his journey since leaving Omaha. Humboldt is the business centre of several valuable mining districts, and has a bright prospect in the future.

The following incident is said to have occurred in one of the Nevada mining towns not many miles from Humboldt:

About the year 1852 or '53, on a still, hot summer afternoon, a certain man who shall be nameless, having tracked his two donkeys and one horse a half mile and discovering that a man's track with spur marks followed them, came back to town and told "the boys," who loitered about a popular saloon, that in his opinion some Mexican had stolen the animals. Such news as this demanded, naturally, drinks all around.

"Do you know, gentlemen," said one who assumed leadership, "that just naturally to shoot these greasers ain't the best way? Give 'em a fair jury trial, and rope 'em up with all the majesty of the law. That's the cure."

Such words of moderation were well received, and they drank again to "Here's hoping we may ketch that greaser!"

As they loafed back to the veranda, a Mexican walked over the hill-brow, jingling his spurs pleasantly in accord with a whistled waltz.

The advocate for the law said, in an undertone, "That's the cuss!"

A rush, a struggle, and the Mexican, bound hand and foot, lay on his back in the bar-room. The miners turned out to a man.

Happily, such cries as *"String him up!"* *"Burn the dog-goned lubricator!"* and other equally pleasant phrases fell unheeded upon his Spanish ear. A jury was quickly gathered in the street, and despite refusals to serve, the crowd hurried them in behind the bar.

A brief statement of the case was made by the advocate *pro tem.*, and they showed the jury into a commodious poker-room, where were seats grouped about neat green tables. The noise outside in the bar-room by-and-by died away into complete silence, but from afar down the cañon came confused sounds as of disorderly cheering. They came nearer, and again the light-hearted noise of human laughter mingled with clinking glasses around the bar.

A low knock at the jury door, the lock burst in, and a dozen smiling fellows asked the verdict. The foreman promptly answered, *"Not guilty."*

With volleys of oaths, and ominous laying of hands on pistol hilts, the "boys" slammed the door with— *"You'll have to do better than that!"*

In half an hour the advocate gently opened the door again.

"Your *opinion*, gentlemen?"

"Guilty!"

"Correct! you can come out. *We hung him an hour ago!*"

The jury took their drinks, and when, after a few minutes, the pleasant village returned to its former tranquility, it was *"allowed"* at more than one saloon that "Mexicans 'll know enough to let white men's stock alone after this." One and another exchanged the belief that this sort of thing was more sensible than "nipping 'em on sight."

When, before sunset, the bar-keeper concluded to sweep some dust out of his poker-room back-door, he felt a momentary surprise at finding the missing horse dozing under the shadow of an oak, and the two lost donkeys serenely masticating playing-cards, of which many bushels lay in a dirty pile. He was then reminded that the animals had been there all day!

Lovelocks (Nevada) is three hundred and eighty-nine miles from San Francisco, and its elevation above the sea-level three thousand nine hundred and seventy-seven feet. It is simply a station, with a few buildings connected with the Central Pacific Railroad; but is a fine grazing region, and large herds of cattle are fattened here upon the rich native grasses. There is quite a settlement of farmers near Lovelocks. Before the railroad came the pasture lands were renowned among the emigrants, who recruited their stock after the wearisome journey across the plains.

Leaving Lovelocks, Captain Glazier soon found himself again on the barren desert. A side track of the railroad, named White Plains, gave him rest for the night. The spot is surrounded by a white alkali desert, covered in places with salt and alkali deposits. Hot Springs is another station in the midst of the desert, and is so named from the hot springs whose rising steam can be seen about half a mile from the station.

Hastening forward he reached Desert (Nevada), which he found to be three hundred and thirty-five miles from San Francisco, and that the place is rightly named. The winds that sweep the barren plains here, heap the sand around the scattered sage brush till they resemble huge potato hills—a most dreary place.

The captain found it quite a relief on reaching Wadsworth (Nevada), a town of about five hundred souls, and three hundred and twenty-eight miles from the end of his journey. It has several large stores, Chinamen's houses, and hotels, in one of the latter of which he found refreshment and a bed. His route had been for several days across dreary, monotonous plains, with nothing but black desolation around him. Another world now opened to his view—a world of beauty, grandeur and sublimity. Reluctantly leaving this agreeable place, he crossed the Truckee River, and gazed with delightful sensations upon the trees, the green meadows, comfortable farm-houses and well-tilled fields of the ranches, as he rode forward.

He had now crossed the boundary line that divides Nevada from California, and Truckee was the first place he halted at. This is a flourishing little city of fifteen hundred inhabitants, one-third of whom are Chinese, and is two hundred and fifty-nine miles from San Francisco. A large number of good stores were seen here, and a considerable trade is carried on.

He next reached Summit (California). From this point the road descends rapidly to the Valley of the Sacramento.

Several intermediate places having been stopped at, in which our traveler obtained accommodation for a night, we hasten on with him to Sacramento, where, on November twenty-first, he found himself again surrounded with all the appliances of civilization. Sacramento has a population of twenty-five thousand. The broad streets are shaded by heavy foliage. It is a city

RIDING INTO THE PACIFIC—NEAR THE CLIFF-HOUSE, SAN FRANCISCO.

of beautiful homes. Lovely cottages are surrounded by flowers, fruits and vines; while some of the most elegant mansions in the State are in the midst of grassy lawns, or gardens filled with the rarest flowers. Here is the State capitol, a building that cost nearly $2,500,000 for its erection. Sacramento is an important railroad centre, second only to San Francisco.

Brighton was one hundred and thirty-four miles from the termination of his ride. At the farm-houses along the road numerous wind-mills were seen. These are used to fill reservoirs for household wants, and are common in all the valleys and plains of California.

A halt was made at Stockton, twenty-one miles from destination. This city has a population of about fifteen thousand, and is only twenty-three feet above the level of the sea. It was named to commemorate Commodore Stockton's part in the conquest of California.

Using all despatch, Captain Glazier pushed on to San Francisco, and entered the city November twenty-fourth, registering at the Palace Hotel. He immediately after rode, in company with Mr. Walter Montgomery, and a friend, to the Cliff House, reaching it by the toll-road. This beautiful seaside resort is built on a prominence overlooking the ocean. Captain Glazier walked his horse into the waters of the Pacific, and then felt that he had accomplished his task. He had ridden in the saddle from the Atlantic to the Pacific Ocean—from Boston to San Francisco—a distance of four thousand one hundred and thirty-three miles, in just two hundred days.

He was now no longer the slave of duty, and would rest for a few days and see the beautiful city before he returned to the east. He wandered about, mostly on foot, visited and inspected the numerous public buildings, the City Park, Woodward's Gardens, etc., and became convinced from personal observation of the greatness and magnificence of this city on the Pacific, with its three hundred thousand inhabitants, covering a territory of forty-two square miles, and the growth of less than thirty years. On its eastern front San Francisco extends along the bay, whose name it bears, bounded on the north by the Golden Gate, and on the west washed by the Pacific Ocean along a beach five or six miles in extent. It is not, however, a part of our plan to describe this wonderful city, which has been done most effectively by others.

CHAPTER XXXV.

RETURN FROM CALIFORNIA.

Returns to the East by the "Iron Horse."—Boston *Transcript* on the journey on horseback.—Resumes literary work.—"Peculiarities of American Cities."—Preface to book.—A domestic incident.—A worthy son.—Claims of parents.—Purchases the old Homestead, and presents it to his father and mother.—Letter to his parents.—The end.

WE now accompany our subject on his return journey to the east. His family and friends had naturally felt great concern for him during his long and perilous ride, and he was anxious therefore to allay their fears for his safety by presenting himself before them. He accordingly purchased a ticket and left San Francisco by rail on the twenty-eighth of November, and after a journey more rapid and comfortable than the one he had made on horseback, arrived in New York city on December sixth.

Several of the eastern papers, on hearing of the captain's safe return, furnished their readers with interesting, and, more or less, correct accounts of the journey. We can find room only for that of the Boston *Transcript:*

"It will be remembered that on the ninth of May, 1876, Captain Willard Glazier, the author of 'Battles for the Union,' and other works of a military character, rode out of Boston with the intention of crossing the continent on horseback. His object in undertaking this long and tedious journey was to study at comparative leisure the line of country which he traversed, and the habits and condition of the people he came in contact with, the industrious and peaceful white, and the 'noble' and belligerent red. According to the captain's note-book, he had a closer opportunity of studying the characteristics of the *terror* than the toiler of the plains.

"Accompanied by certain members of the 'Grand Army of the Republic,' on the morning of May ninth, as far as Brighton, he there took leave of them, and with one companion, rode as far as Albany, the captain lecturing by the way wherever inducement offered, and handing over the profits to the benefit of the Widows' and Orphans' Fund of the G. A. R. Many of these lectures were well attended, and the receipts large, as letters of thanks from the various 'Posts' testify.

" From Albany Captain Glazier pursued his journey alone, and rode the same horse through the States of New York, Pennsylvania, Ohio, Michigan, Indiana, Illinois, Iowa, and Nebraska, as far as Omaha. Thence he proceeded on whatever quadruped of the equine species he could obtain, which was capable of shaking the dust from its feet nimbly. That he was fortunate in this respect is proven by the fact that he rode from Omaha to San Francisco, a distance of nineteen hundred and eighty-eight miles in thirty days, making an average of about sixty-seven miles per diem. The distance from Omaha to Cheyenne, five hundred and twenty-two miles, he accomplished in six days; the greatest distance accomplished in one day of fourteen hours was one hundred and sixty-six miles, three mustangs being called into requisition for the purpose. The entire time occupied by the journey was two hundred days, the captain reaching the Golden Gate on the twenty-fourth day of November. The actual number of days in the saddle was one hundred and forty-four, which gives an average of twenty-eight miles and seven-tenths per day.

" During this strange journey of more than four thousand miles, Captain Glazier delivered one hundred and four lectures for the object before mentioned, and also for the benefit of the Custer Monument Fund, and visited six hundred and forty-eight cities, villages and stations. He tested the merits of three hundred and thirty-three hotels, farm-houses and ranches, and made special visits to over one hundred public institutions and places of resort. He killed three buffaloes, eight antelopes, and twenty-two prairie wolves, thus enjoying to the full all the pleasurable excitement of hunting on the plains.

" But on the thirty-first of October, while in the company of two herders, the tables were turned, and a band of hostile Arrapahoes suddenly disturbed the harmony of the occasion. After a lively encounter, in which one of the Indians was despatched to the Happy Hunting Grounds, Glazier and his companions were taken prisoners, and one of the herders was gradually tortured to death. All that now seemed to be required of the two survivors was patience —if they desired to share a similar fate. But in the early morning of the second of November, while their captors were asleep, they contrived not only to escape, but to secure the arms which had been taken from them; and, mounted on two mustangs belonging to the Indians, soon placed a considerable distance between themselves and their too confident guards. In the chase which ensued, Captain Glazier was separated from his fellow-fugitive, and made good his own escape by dismounting two of his pursuers, and eventually, after a lorg, hard gallop, dismounting and hiding in a gulch. What the fate of the herder was he had no means of discovering.

"Though a man of usually robust constitution, Captain Glazier felt the transitions of climate acutely, but he experiences no ill effects from the long journey now that it is over. The 'iron horse' brought him back to the East of this continent in a few days, and there are probably few men in the States who have formed a higher opinion of the blessings of steam, than Captain Willard Glazier."

Returned to Washington our soldier-author applied himself again to literature, his ever active brain having been sufficiently recruited by the comparative relaxation it had enjoyed during the long ride. One of the fruits of his pen at this time was a volume entitled "Peculiarities of American Cities," a subject upon which his flowing pen expatiates with great freedom and a nice discrimination. That the reader may perceive the bent of Glazier's mind at this period of his history, we here present the brief and succinct preface to that work:

"It has occurred to the author very often," he writes, "that a volume presenting the favorite resorts, peculiar features, and distinguishing characteristics of the leading cities of America, would prove of interest to thousands of persons who could, at best, see them only in imagination; and to others who, having visited them, would like to compare notes with one who has made their peculiarities a study for many years.

"A residence in more than a hundred cities, including all that are introduced in this work, leads me to feel that I shall succeed in my purpose of giving the public a book without the necessity of marching in slow and solemn procession before my readers, a monumental array of time-honored statistics; on the contrary it will be my aim in the following pages to talk of cities as I have found them in my walks from day to day, with but slight reference to their origin and history."

We will bring this volume to a close by recording one incident in the life of its hero, which, humble and common-place as it may be deemed by some, is one which, in the judgment of a majority of our readers we venture to think, reflects glory upon Willard Glazier as a son, and the nation may well feel proud that can rear many such sons.

A subject of great domestic interest which had occupied his thoughts for a considerable period, but to which he had, in his busy life, been unable hitherto to give the necessary time and attention, at this time again forcibly presented itself to his mind. Glazier's sense of a son's duty to his parents was not of the ordinary type. He was profoundly conscious of the moral obligation that devolved upon him, to render the declining years of his parents as free from discomfort and anxiety as it was within his power to do. They had nursed and trained him in infancy and boyhood; had set before him daily the example of an upright life, and had instilled in him a love of truth, honesty and every manly virtue. Their claim upon him, now that he had met with a measure of success in life, was not to be ignored, and to a good father and a good mother he would, so far as he was able, endeavor to prove himself a good son.

The Old Homestead near the banks of the Oswegatchie, in St. Lawrence County, New York, where his parents still resided; where all their children had been born, and where many happy years had been passed, was not the property of the Glazier family, and there was a possibility that the "dear old folks" might in time have to remove from it. The thought of such a contingency was painful to Willard Glazier. It was the spot of all others around which his affections clung, and he resolved to make a strenuous endeavor to possess himself of it, so that his father and mother might pass their remaining days under its shelter.

He accordingly opened negotiations with the owners of the property for the purchase of the Homestead, and was soon rejoiced to find himself the sole proprietor of a place endeared to him by so many associations.

The following letter to his parents will form a fitting conclusion to this volume:

102 WAVERLY PLACE,
NEW YORK, *May 1st*, 1878.

MY DEAR FATHER AND MOTHER:

I am just in receipt of the papers which place me in possession of the *Old Homestead*. This, I am sure, will be very pleasing news to you, since it is my intention to make it the home of your declining years: poor old grandmother, too, shall find it a welcome refuge while she lives. I have never felt that I could see the home of my birth pass to other hands; my heart still clings to it, and its hallowed associations, with all the tenacity of former days. The first of May will, in future, have special charms for me, for from this day, 1878, dates my claim to that spot of earth which to me is dearer than all others.

Imagination often takes me back to the Old House on the Hill, where your children spent many of the happiest hours of their childhood and youth. In fancy I again visit the scenes of my boyhood —again chase the butterfly, and pick the dandelion with Elvira and Marjorie in the shade of the wide-spreading elms.

* * * * * * * *

I have been working for you, dear parents, in the face of great obstacles since the close of the war. If you think I have neglected you—have not been home in ten long years, then I reply, I did not wish to see you again until I could place you beyond the reach of want. *One of the objects of my life is to-day accomplished:* and now, with love to all, and the fervent hope that prosperity and happiness may wait upon you for many, many years to come,

I remain, always,
Your most affectionate son,
WILLARD.

THE END.

www.ingramcontent.com/pod-product-compliance
Lightning Source LLC
Chambersburg PA
CBHW051200300426
44116CB00006B/387